KV-408-735

lonely planet

EPIC BIKE RIDES *of* EUROPE

Explore the continent's most thrilling cycling routes

OULANGER
PATISSIER

Easy Harder Epic

CONTENTS

Clockwise from top: © Cass Gilbert, Uroš Švigelj, Cass Gilbert, kovop58 / Shutterstock

INTRODUCTION

Since the modern 'safety bicycle' was first manufactured in England in 1885, this flowering of late Victorian ingenuity has found its way to most corners of the planet. Yet every cyclist knows that all roads lead back to the Old World, to Europe. To its fabled mountain ranges, rivers and coastlines, its historic cities and myriad cultures, and to the roads, byways and trails that on this compact continent are able to wind from alpine meadow to city cafe in a matter of hours.

It is the venue of the most famous bike races of them all, the Tour de France and the Giro d'Italia, as well as revered one-day 'classics' such as Paris-Roubaix. For those who want to toil up the alpine cols and rattle across the cobbles, recalling the exploits of Coppi and Merkcx, Sagan and Froome, Deignan and Vos, read on. But 'epic' is an adjective that ranges beyond emulating the sporting exploits of the professional peloton.

Once a niche pursuit, bikepacking – backpacking on a bike – is now a thriving international scene, with enthusiasts swapping routes, tips and inspiration online and on an ever-expanding circuit of races, rallies and events. We have commissioned some of its best-known names to recount their most exciting adventures. Lael Wilcox, the course women's record holder for North America's Tour Divide, writes about the Hope 1000, a dream of a bikepack across the Swiss Alps. Emily Chappell recalls the highs and lows of riding the Transcontinental, a self-supported race across the entirety of Europe (she was the first woman home in 2016). (As well as those truly epic efforts, we've made sure there are other routes for those considering their first bikepack.)

What else might epic mean in Europe? For Cass Gilbert and family, including his young son Sage, it meant a summer tour of the Netherlands. For the food writer Felicity Cloake, it was soaking up the great wines and cuisine of Burgundy, 'the stomach of France'. For Rob Penn, it was a race against time: would he complete a road traverse of the French Pyrenees in under 100 hours?

Time is probably on your mind as you plan your next big bike trip. We can't all take a sabbatical for cycling, so this book also reflects varying levels of commitment. Some of these rides take just a couple of hours, others a day or two, a week, or a month or more. We've given an indication of whether a ride is easy (in terms of terrain, distance, conditions or climate) or more challenging (steeper hills, longer distances, fewer snack stops). The goal is to inspire you to explore somewhere new with the wind in your hair.

Cycling is the perfect mode of transport for the travel-lover, allowing us to cover more ground than if we were on foot, but without the barriers that a car imposes. We are immersed in our surroundings, self-powered, independent, and forever pondering the question 'I wonder what's over there?'. Hopefully, this book will prove that there's no better way of simply experiencing a place, a culture and its people than by bicycle. And as some of these tales tell, arriving on a bicycle opens doors, literally and figuratively.

HOW TO USE THIS BOOK

The main stories in each regional chapter feature first-hand accounts of fantastic bike rides in that continent. Each includes a toolkit to enable the planning of a trip – when is the best time of year, how to get there, where to stay. But beyond that, these stories should spark other ideas. We've started that process with the 'more like this' section following each story, which offers other ideas along a similar theme or in the neighbourhood. Many of these ideas are well established routes or trails. The index collects different types of ride for a variety of interests.

© Tristan Cardew and The Service Course, kabVisio / Getty Images

NORTHERN EUROPE

On the road to Cape Wrath, northwest Scotland (see page 20)

IN PURSUIT OF SPRING

Max Leonard's ride in the century-old wheel tracks of the poet Edward Thomas reveals a vision of England from another era.

On Good Friday 1913, the poet and landscape writer Edward Thomas set off from London on a pilgrimage by bicycle. As he later wrote, in the opening lines of *In Pursuit of Spring*: 'This is the record of a journey from London to the Quantock Hills – to Nether Stowey, Kilve, Crowcombe and West Bagborough, to the high point where the Taunton-Bridgwater road tops the hills and shows all Exmoor behind, all the Mendips before, and upon the left the sea...'

The Quantocks were where his literary hero Samuel Taylor Coleridge wrote The Rime of the Ancient Mariner, but this was also a bike ride undertaken as an act of faith – faith that the long winter was ending and that resurgent spring would bring new life into the world.

Thomas' account is, in fact, so detailed that you can reconstruct his route from his front door in Clapham, southwest London, all the way to the top of Cothelstone Hill, where he stopped – and my friend Andy and I did just that, on Good Friday a hundred years later. Fairly quickly, around Morden, the suburban landscapes gave way to patchy fields and then proper countryside. In Thomas's day, these tarmacked roads might have been cart tracks, however, he would still have recognised the changing seasons in the hedgerows – the celandines, cowslips, blackthorn and

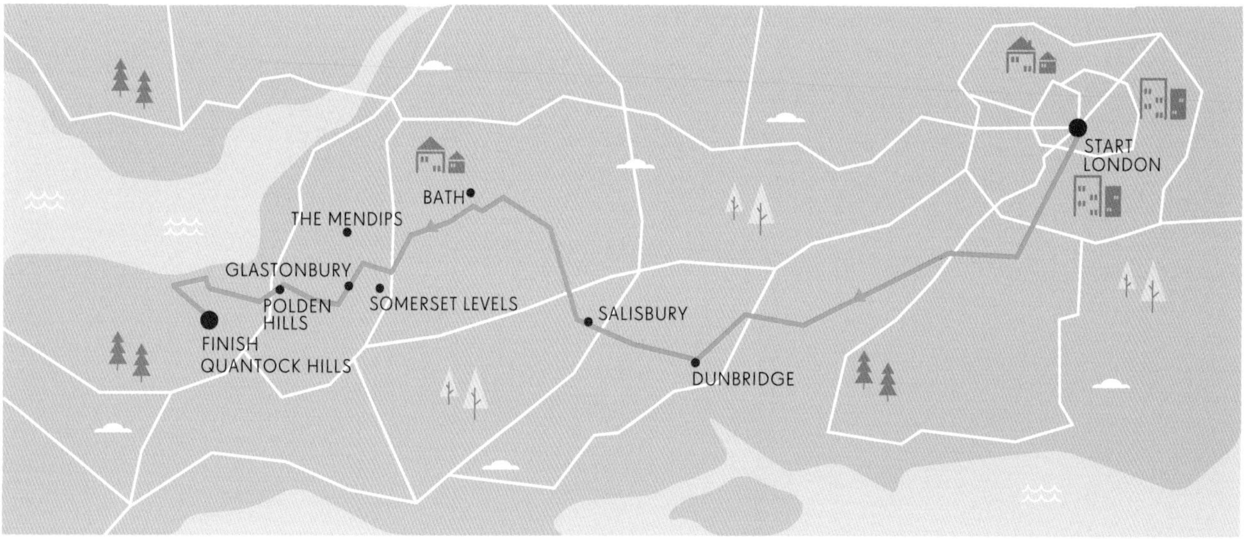

Previous page Jordan Gibbons, this page © Andy Waterman

bluebells that he describes so eloquently as battling against the receding chill.

Thomas took a week to make his journey, on a single-speed bicycle with bad brakes. We had multiple gears, panniers and disc brake-equipped touring bikes and so decided to do it in three days. After taking main roads out of London, we sought out the byways of Surrey – the hidden lanes, bridleways and muddy tracks that run parallel to the main concrete arteries, which felt closer to what we believed Thomas himself would have experienced.

On the first night, we planned to stay at the Mill Arms, in Dunbridge in the Test Valley in Hampshire, an inn that had turned Thomas away when he'd been looking for a bed for the night. Luckily we had reserved a room on the internet, and so, with red sun setting behind bare trees and evening mist descending on fields of sheep, we dismounted from our bikes for well-earned showers, dinner and pints of local ale.

We awoke the next morning for another 100-mile day. It started under the ridge of Dean Hill in Hampshire and took us through Salisbury, past the military on manoeuvre on the chalky plateau of Salisbury Plain (which necessitates a detour if the red flags are flying over the drovers' roads Thomas took), and looping around Trowbridge. Through picturesque villages and past venerable stately homes and castle ruins we rode, before conquering one more range of hills, riding steeply up the easterly ridge of the

"Thomas would still have recognised the changing seasons in the hedgerows – the celandines, cowslips and bluebells"

Mendips. There on the deserted uplands we had the hedge-lined lanes entirely to ourselves, save for a friendly local cyclist and a man walking his dog. With most of the day's climbing coming in the last 20 miles, it felt good to speed down in the gathering dusk to Shepton Mallet, and another inn that would be our resting place for the night.

Our final day would be the shortest, but also the wettest: overnight, the departing winter had sent cold winds and clouds to Somerset. We set off to the sound of soft raindrops and the swish of tyres on wet tarmac. From Wells to Glastonbury the rain worsened and became torrential as we climbed up to the ridge of the Polden Hills, where the views of the Somerset Levels were obscured by mist. But with each pedal stroke into the westerly wind we left the bad weather behind, and soon the sun was cautiously peeking out again.

At Bridgwater we refuelled and contemplated the challenge ahead: the Quantock Hills sitting darkly on the horizon. Thomas' route skirts their northern edge, almost to the sea, taking in

© Andy Waterman

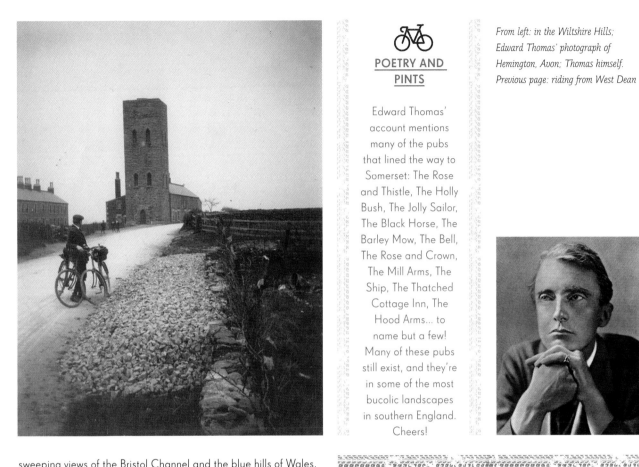

POETRY AND PINTS

Edward Thomas' account mentions many of the pubs that lined the way to Somerset: The Rose and Thistle, The Holly Bush, The Jolly Sailor, The Black Horse, The Barley Mow, The Bell, The Rose and Crown, The Mill Arms, The Ship, The Thatched Cottage Inn, The Hood Arms... to name but a few! Many of these pubs still exist, and they're in some of the most bucolic landscapes in southern England. Cheers!

From left: in the Wiltshire Hills; Edward Thomas' photograph of Hemington, Avon; Thomas himself. Previous page: riding from West Dean

sweeping views of the Bristol Channel and the blue hills of Wales, before passing through the village of Nether Stowey where Coleridge lived. And then up, on steep lanes in dappled shade and sun, to Cothelstone Hill – where Thomas proclaimed that he had found 'Winter's Grave', and where he ended his journey. After a steep slog to the high point of the Taunton-Bridgwater road we stopped, took some pictures and read the final lines of his book. Satisfied, we descended to Taunton to take the train back home, where 21st-century civilisation awaited. How did Thomas return? In the book he says only: 'I was confident I could ride home again and find Spring all along the road.'

One of the pleasures of reading Thomas is his description of a lost world – one almost without motorcars, in which country life had little changed since the Domesday Book. At points in our ride – on forest bridleways or in the Quantocks themselves, where some of the muddy red lanes seemed more marked by horse hooves than car tyres – it was almost possible to believe that his world still existed. But in reality it disappeared not long after Thomas captured it on the page: in 1914, the Great War descended on Europe and swept everything ancient away.

Thomas did not survive either. He enlisted in 1915 and in 1917 was killed in action, hit by a blast wave from a shell that stopped his heart as he stood from the trenches to light his pipe. Always a pacifist, he nevertheless gave his life for the land he loved. **ML**

TOOLKIT

Start // Edward Thomas' house, number 61 Shelgate Road, Clapham, London
Finish // Cothelstone Hill, the Quantocks
Distance // 248 miles (400km). (NB: the Mendips and the Quantocks can be steep.)
How to get there (and back) // Clapham Junction is the closest station to the start, Taunton to the ride's end.
When to ride // In spring, for the full experience, having read In Pursuit of Spring, of course.
What to take // This is a multi-day ride, so some extra clothes and light shoes (or flip-flops) for the evenings are advisable. Also, a good rain jacket for the April showers.
Map // www.strava.com/routes/281632

© Special Collections and Archives, Cardiff University, Ken Welsh / Getty Images

Opposite: approaching Wasdale, Cumbria; the Transfagarasan highway, Romania

MORE LIKE THIS
LITERARY PILGRIMAGES

CYCLING THE LAKE DISTRICT, ENGLAND

Wander lonely as a cloud through the Lake District in Cumbria, Northwest England, and enjoy the landscapes that inspired Romantic poets such as William Wordsworth, Robert Southey and Samuel Taylor Coleridge. Although there is some great road riding in the Lakes, why not take a mountain bike from Dove Cottage, William and Dorothy Wordsworth's house in Grasmere, to Ullswater, where Wordsworth reputedly saw his daffodils waving in the breeze. Or, for a challenging mixed terrain 'rough stuff' loop, start at Wasdale Head and climb over the 1600ft (488m) Sty Head. The trail down towards Borrowdale is fun, but once you hit the road, turn left to climb Honister Pass. Follow that with Scarth Gap and Black Sail Pass before descending to Wasdale Head again for a well deserved pint. Think that was tough? In 1893 a man called Amos Sugden crossed Sty Head with a solid-tyred bicycle weighing 50lbs (23kg)!
Start/Finish // Wasdale Head
Distance // 16 miles (25km)

BIKING WITH A DONKEY IN THE CÉVENNES, FRANCE

In 1878 Robert Louis Stevenson was in his late 20s, in fragile health and recovering from a love affair that his parents did not approve. So he headed to the south of France, to the rugged Cévennes region and began a tour, taking 10 days to walk 120 miles (193km) from Le Monastier-sur-Gazeille to Saint-Jean-du-Gard.
It took him through some of the most remote countryside in France – this was wolf and brigand territory – with only an obstinate donkey called Modestine as his companion, and the resulting book, *Travels with a Donkey in the Cévennes* (1879), is considered one of the pioneering works of travel literature. The route he took is now the GR70, a long-distance hiking trail, and it's permitted to cycle it all. Much of the route is above 1000m (3300ft) in altitude, but it's probably best done in the mellow early autumn, when the weather is settled and the leaves are changing colour.
Start // Le Monastier-sur-Gazeille
Finish // Saint-Jean-du-Gard
Distance //120 miles (193km)

THE TRANSFAGARASAN, ROMANIA

Built by Romania's communist dictator, Nicolae Ceaucescu, the Transfagarasan is a military route dynamited slap bang through the middle of the Carpathian Mountains, connecting Transylvania to Wallachia through a series of five tunnels, 27 viaducts and over 800 bridges – as well as countless switchback bends looping like wet spaghetti up the mountainside. Built between 1970 and 1974 in anticipation of a Soviet invasion, the road is 71 miles (114km) in total, but the gradients are never steep. Top Gear dubbed it 'the best driving road in the world', though it is also called the 'Road to the Clouds' and – because of the major losses of life during its construction – 'Ceaucescu's Folly'. It climbs to 6699ft (2042m), and passes the scenic Balea Lake and Waterfall, as well as, on its south side, Poenari Castle, home of Vlad the Impaler, who was Bram Stoker's inspiration for Dracula.
Start // Cartisoara
End // Curtea de Arges
Distance // 71 miles (114km)

© Peter Lane / Alamy Stock Photo, Horia Bogdan / Alamy Stock Photo

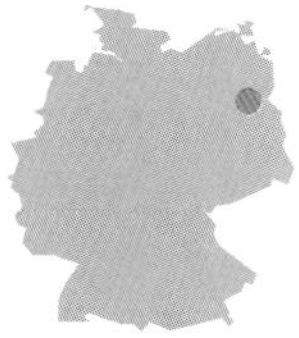

THE BERLIN WALL

Where the Cold War was once waged, there are now parks, galleries and funky neighbourhoods. But the city cannot forget its grim partition.

It wasn't quite 6am, but thanks to the long summer days of northern Europe the sky was already brightening when I arrived at the aptly-named Mauerpark, or Wall Park, in central Berlin. It was 13 August – not coincidentally the 58th anniversary of the day the Berlin Wall went up – and I planned to ride the entire 96-mile (155km) length of the infamous barrier in a day with friends.

More than any city I know, Berlin has made its past a prominent part of its built environment. There are dozens of memorials scattered around the city, from the grim concrete columns of the Monument to the Murdered Jews of Europe to thousands of brass plaques in sidewalks, dedicated to victims of the Nazi regime.

Ironically, for many years the Berlin Wall – the barrier that made the city synonymous with the Iron Curtain and the Cold War -- was an exception. Shortly after East Germans were granted the right to cross it freely in November 1989, the vast majority of its barbed wire, concrete barriers, land mines and watchtowers were torn down, ripped up, and removed. In the 1990s, thousands of pieces of the Wall were given to museums abroad or snapped up by collectors. Prime real estate in the middle of the city was sold off to developers, who rushed to build apartments and office buildings on the former 'death strip'.

Over the past decade, that's changed. Most Germans under 40 barely remember the Wall, and as of November 2019 no German under 30 was even alive when it split the city in two. For most residents and tourists alike, the Wall can feel like ancient history. That's made preserving what's left an urgent task.

In 2001, the city decided to preserve what was left in the form of a bike path. Completed in 2006, it follows the course of the Wall: In central Berlin, it twists and turns past, through and around some of the city's most prominent landmarks and popular neighbourhoods. As we set off, the bike path follows a double line of stones inlaid in the pavement, occasionally punctuated with bronze plaques marked 'Berlin Wall 1961-1989'. All day long, the stones will reappear in unlikely spots – outside a gas station on the outskirts of the city, curving around the Brandenburg Gate, disappearing under an office tower.

The sun hadn't even peeked above the horizon when we passed one of the best-preserved bits, a 300ft (100m) stretch of the original fortifications, including a tall watchtower and groomed-sand death strip. It's part of the Berlin Wall Memorial, an outdoor

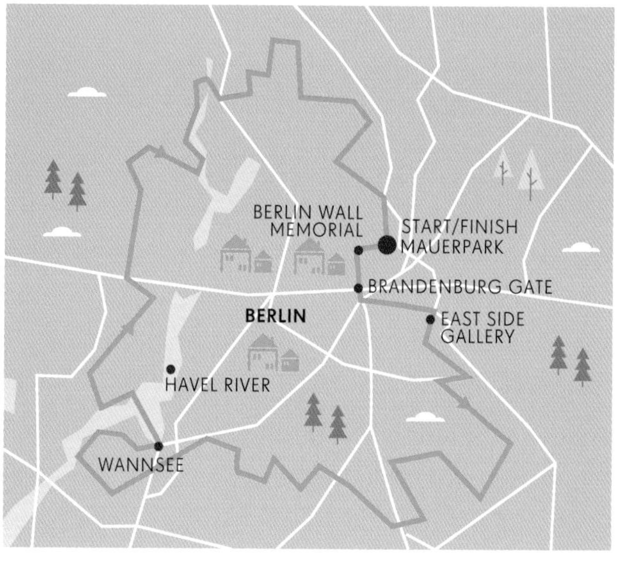

© Steffen Weigold

SLAG
CITY

museum dedicated to the wall and its history.

Within just a few miles of Mauerpark, we cycled slowly past some of the city's most recognisable landmarks, new and old: the glass-and-steel main train station, built in 2006, and the Brandenburg Gate, built in 1791. Then came the German parliament building, known before the war as the Reichstag. Potsdamer Platz, a few hundred feet further on, was a thriving commercial centre reduced to a wasteland to put up the Wall. Now it's glass skyscrapers and high-end hotels. Bike bells chiming, we merged with early-morning commuters and pedalled on, winding through residential neighbourhoods just waking up.

Soon we passed the East Side Gallery, a kilometre-long stretch of concrete along the Spree River that's the best-preserved part of the Wall. Across the street, cranes rise into the sky: what was once a wasteland near the Wall is now being transformed into offices for internet start-ups and international media companies.

I've lived in Berlin since 2005, and many of the streets and neighbourhoods the path sliced through are familiar. But stringing them together gave me a new perspective on just how omnipresent the Wall was. The broad, straight canal-side path that each Wednesday-morning group ride turns into a hammer-fest? This time I slowed to take in the stone memorial to Chris Gueffroy, a young man shot trying to cross to the West in 1989, just months before the fall of the Wall. It was barely 8am, but already someone had laid fresh flowers.

It was the first of many such reminders that day of just how deadly and oppressive the Wall was. At least 136 people were killed trying

"Along the way, orange pillars tell the stories of some of the 136 men and women who died trying to cross the barrier"

BERLIN'S EXCLAVES

The Berlin Wall's path was anything but logical. In some spots, it created 'exclaves' of West German territory completely surrounded by East Germany. Communist authorities respected the law: in one case, a cut-off cluster of 10 houses was supplied by helicopter until a half mile-long road could be built to connect it to the rest of West Berlin. And at Erlengrund, owners of plots in a 4-hectare garden colony were supplied with their own door in the Wall, complete with buzzer.

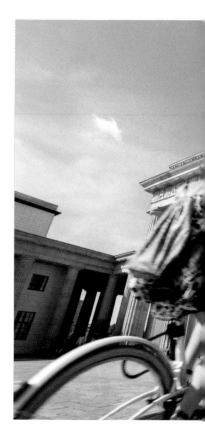

Clockwise from above: Brandenburg Gate; Wannsee; a section of the Berlin Wall Memorial. Previous page: riding along a remnant of the Wall

© struvictory / Shutterstock

to flee the German Democratic Republic, and hundreds more were wounded in the attempt. As a result, the loop also serves as an open-air museum and memorial: At 29 spots along the way, orange pillars tell the stories of some of the men and women who were killed trying to cross the heavily-guarded barrier. For a long while after I stopped to read them, I found myself reflecting on a system that would execute people trying to flee it.

There are a few spots along the wall bikes can't go. Where the border crossed the Havel river south and west of the city, the river itself – heavily mined and patrolled, of course – was the 'Wall'. We wheeled our bikes on to a ferry in Wannsee for a short ride, picking the path up in leafy Kladow on the other side.

Wheeling north and east again, we passed through sandy pine forests and fields of ripening corn, a bucolic landscape that hasn't changed much in the decades since East Germany vanished. If it weren't for the occasional trail markers and road signs, it would have been easy to forget we were still in Berlin.

As afternoon shadows grew longer, we turned south again. The terrain had turned ever-so-slightly hilly. We emerged from a wild moor, part of a nature preserve on the city's northern edge, to see the lonely spike of Berlin's 1207ft (368m) television transmitter tower far off in the distance. For the rest of the ride I was back on familiar ground, passing through ever-denser Berlin neighbourhoods. For the first time all day I feel a chill. Evening shadows, or the shadow of the past? I can't quite decide. **AC**

© Iain Masterton / Alamy Stock Photo, LaMiaFotografia / Shutterstock

TOOLKIT

Start / Finish // Berlin, Mauerpark

Distance // 100 miles (160km)

Crossing the river // Ferries are part of the excellent Berlin public transit network, but they run infrequently – research in advance. Bike capacity on them is limited – be early on peak summer days.

Where to eat // On the edges of Berlin restaurant options are few. Get a beer and bratwurst at Loretta am Wannsee, a Bavarian-style beer garden across from the Wannsee ferry.

To make it a two-day ride // Ride from the city centre south and west along the Wall to Wannsee, then catch an S-Bahn back to the centre. The next day, head north and east to Kladow, then return via the ferry and S-Bahn from Wannsee. Pressed for time? Ride the Wall's eastern length: start near the Schoenefeld Airport S-Bahn station, take in the city centre's landmarks, end near Hermsdorf station – about 30 miles (50km).

MORE LIKE THIS
GERMAN ADVENTURES

MECKLENBURG LAKES

Situated 100 miles (160km) north of Berlin, the Mecklenburg Lake Plateau (*Mecklenburgische Seenplatte*) was shaped 12,000 years ago, when the last glaciers retreated from Europe. Today it's known as 'the land of 1000 lakes' – there may not be quite that many, but it can feel like it as you spend days pedaling from one placid lake to another across the pancake-flat plateau. One popular route circles the Mueritz, Germany's second-largest lake, and passes through the country's largest national park. Used as a private hunting preserve by Prussian kings and Nazi bigwigs until 1945, the Mueritz National Park is now a Unesco-recognised wildlife preserve. In recent years, some of the first wild wolf packs spotted in Germany in more than a century have made a home among its primeval beech groves.

Start/Finish // Waren

Distance // 112 miles (180km)

THE GREEN BELT

When Germany was divided after WWII, the border between East and West ran through the divided country like a scar. Over time the heavily militarised border was fortified with steel-mesh fences, concrete watchtowers, and 1.3 million mines. After German reunification in 1990 environmental groups pushed to turn the former 'death strip' into an unusual nature preserve. Their efforts created a protected path 870 miles (1400km) long and between 150ft and 650ft wide, running essentially unbroken from the Baltic Sea to the Czech border. Today it's home to more than 1200 threatened species and served by a well-developed cycle path. Most of the fortifications have long since been removed, but at a few memorials – such as Grenzhus Schlagsdorf, not far from Lübeck – the border fortifications are uncannily, unsettlingly preserved, down to replica SM-70 land mines.

Start // Lübeck

Finish // Hof

Distance // 870 miles (1400km)

THE ODER AND NEISSE RIVERS

A well-developed bike path traces the Polish-German border, following the Oder and Neisse rivers. It lies mostly on the German side but offers ample opportunities to cross over into Poland. The carefully restored streets of Görlitz, in the south, are a favourite for cinematographers hoping to capture the look and feel of 1930s Germany (Wes Anderson's *Grand Budapest Hotel* was shot in an abandoned department store in the city centre). Further north, there's Eisenhuettenstadt, a former steel-mill town founded in 1951 that was originally called Stalinstadt. Its carefully planned architecture and the Documentation Centre of Everyday Life in the GDR capture the realities of communist-era East Germany like nowhere else in the country. Finish in Szczecin, a port active since the Viking era that passed from German to Polish control when the border was re-drawn in the wake of WWII.

Start // Forst, Germany

Finish // Szczecin, Poland

Distance // 290 miles (465km)

© imageBROKER / Alamy Stock Photo, Westend61 / Getty Images

Above: the Mecklenburg Plateau, 'land of a thousand lakes'. Left: the picturesque town of Görlitz, eastern Germany

CAPE WRATH & THE WILD NORTHWEST

Escape to the most forsaken corner of the British mainland via its remotest road and join the Cape Wrath Fellowship for your efforts.

Chugging across the Kyle of Durness in a dinky ferryboat, it would be easy to assume the approaching jetty was the gateway to a wild island. In fact, this landing is where the 11-mile (18km) track to Cape Wrath begins; a road to the end of the world. As we lugged loaded bikes over the rocking gunwale and set rubber on land again, skipper John pointed to the bow: 'The very first boat I ever had, a wee lobster boat, was called the *Beulah*, so I decided to call this one *Beulah* too. It means "mystical place, religious paradise, land of paradise". Youse are off there now...'

The slither of broken tarmac and gravel ahead of us cuts across 25,000 acres of wilderness and desolate moorland – known hereabouts as the Parph – to the Cape Wrath lighthouse, the northwesterly point of the British Mainland. The track is arguably Britain's 'loneliest' road, as described over 70 years ago by Rex Coley, the man who founded the Cape Wrath Fellowship.

We four had set off in May 2016 with the aim of joining the

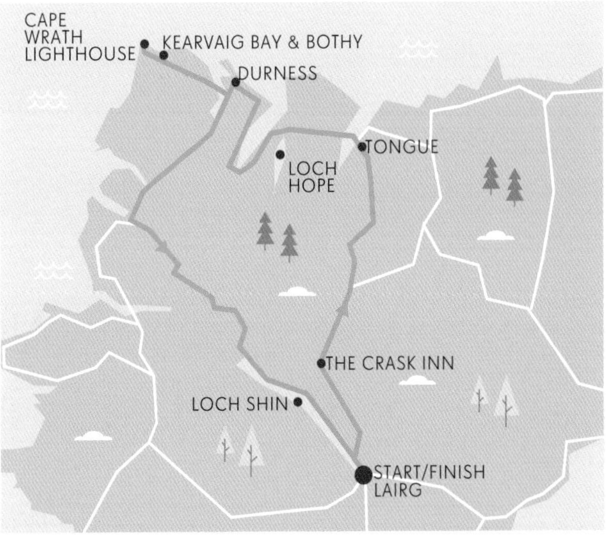

© Jordan Gibbons

© Jordan Gibbons

Fellowship, as part of a three-day bikepacking tour. Our own journey into the wilds of Scotland was inspired by a 1971-75 Ordnance Survey Second Series Map: in particular, Cape Wrath and its jagged coastline jutting into the blue of the Atlantic. Once I found that old map of the track, I decided to plot a bike tour across the far north of Scotland to include it. The village of Lairg – 'the crossroads of the North' – was the farthest we could get on the train up from Inverness, making the station the gateway for a 155-mile (250km) journey. From Lairg, we could head north on single-track logging lanes, via the characterful Crask Inn to Tongue, before joining the picturesque coast road around to Keoldale on the Kyle of Durness. Which is where John ferried us across on the *Beulah* to begin the trail to Cape Wrath.

The road to nowhere was built in the early 19th century to provide access to the 1828 lighthouse and subsequent coastguard station at Cape Wrath, perched a couple of miles west of the Clo Mor cliffs – the highest sea cliffs (921ft, 281m) on the British mainland. The cape is a site of special scientific interest and protection area for birds, and against the whipping wind, the cacophony of 50,000 nesting puffins, razor bills, fulmars, kittiwakes and guillemots makes for quite an arrival. The name 'Wrath' has its roots in the Old Norse word 'Hvarf', or 'turning point' – the headland was where Viking visitors turned their ships east towards home. Riding the rugged coastline, the ocean crashing hundreds of feet beneath, it's clear to see why a lighthouse is needed, though it's been over 20 years since it was manned.

> *"Skipper John had named his ferry Beulah. 'It means mystical place, land of paradise. Youse are off there now.'"*

Coley set up the Cape Wrath Fellowship in 1949. Known by his pen name Ragged Staff, he was at the time a well-known cycling journalist, and an advocate for adventure by bike. To be admitted to the Fellowship you were required to submit a photo of yourself (with your bike) at the lighthouse, and obtain the signature of the lighthouse keeper. Until his death in 1985, Coley issued a certificate and badge, and Cycling UK now run the Fellowship, which celebrated its 70th Anniversary in 2019 (Cycling UK are looking for more riders to join the Fellowship: go online for details – a photo of yourself and your bike at the lighthouse will do).

To join the Fellowship is to partake of a long chapter in Scottish cycling. And it's obvious what inspired Coley. Look north and west and there's nothing but ocean and the sense of the Faroe Islands, Iceland, Greenland and Newfoundland somewhere over the horizon. To the south and east lies desolate moorland.

KEARVAIG BAY

This a detour from the Cape Wrath track that more than repays the effort. Down a steep, rocky, river valley lies paradise: Kearvaig Bay. Chill and swim on the wide, sandy beach amongst sea stacks, crashing waves and roaming sheep, cook and stay at the ace Mountain Bothy Association bothy – be considerate, tidy, and prepared to replace anything you use for the next travellers – and daydream about the simple but harsh life as a crofter on the bay in bygone years.

From left: John, skipper of the Kyle of Durness ferry; puffins nest on the local cliffs; the Cape Wrath lighthouse. Previous page: to the lighthouse across the Parph

That track is the only route to the lighthouse. The only viable route by land, that is. Supplies are now brought in by boat, apparently, leaving the track to intrepid cyclists – though not entirely: a minibus trip shuttles tourists from the jetty to the lighthouse and back. (There is another overland route, up from Sandwood Bay to the south, on the last section of the Cape Wrath Trail, across vast boggy grasslands). So remote is the headland that swathes of its moorland are a designated Ministry of Defence (MOD) training area and live fire zone for British and international troops. The only features not marked on my old map were the striking, chequered MOD sentry points dotted at key points along the track's 11 miles (18km). During military exercises, access is restricted at these sentry points. The barriers were up. We were safe, and free to pedal onwards to the relative comfort of Kearvaig Bay, our stop for the night on the way to the lighthouse. There a bothy, beach, sunset, campfire meal and a wee dram awaited us.

Plenty more sticks in the memory from our arrival at the lighthouse cafe: canteen-style cheese and pickle sandwiches, instant coffee, Wagon Wheels, and interesting conversations with Cape Wrath Trail walkers. Like the Norse sailors of old, this was our Hvarf, too; time for us to follow our tyre tracks back along the road, to honour our promise to John the ferryman that we'd be back for a lift back across the Kyle of Durness at 2pm. **SA**

TOOLKIT

Start/Finish // Lairg, Scotland
Distance // 155 miles (250km)
How to get there // By train from Inverness to Lairg
When to ride // The ferry runs seven days a week May to September (https://capewrathferry.wordpress.com). That's also midge season, so come prepared. For Cape Wrath Firing Range notices: www.gov.uk/government/publications/scotland-firing-times or call 01971 511242.
What to take // A bike with good trail tyres. Binoculars. Food and water (or filtration supplies), and appropriate clothing (the route is remote). Tongue, Durness and Lairg are the towns for resupply and accommodation. You can wild camp in Scotland (follow 'leave no trace' guidelines).
More info // pannier.cc/beulah-bikepacking-cape-wrath/. Search 'Beulah Cape Wrath' online for Pannier's short film.

© northlightimages / Getty Images, Stefan Amato

Opposite: forging ahead on the North Coast 500

MORE LIKE THIS
GREAT SCOTTISH RIDES

THE LONG ROAD, JURA

In close competition for Britain's 'remotest, loneliest road' has to be the Isle of Jura's lone road running for 32 miles (51km) from the main Feolin ferry slipway, along her east coast to the very north of the island, and what feels like the end of the world. In 1724, it was described 'rough, ragged and impassable for the most part, that not above ten-miles can be ridden without hazard'. Starting as single-track tarmac and passing through the island's only town – Craighouse (home to the Jura Distillery and Hotel) – the road skirts around bays and across grassy moorland, before turning into a wild gravel track and ending at the estate, Barnhill, where George Orwell wrote 1984 (he described it as an 'extremely un-get-atable place'). More info: pannier.cc/journal/the-long-road-bikepacking/.

Start/Finish // Feolin Ferry Terminal, via Kennacraig Ferry Terminal (Mainland) and Port Askaig (Islay)
Distance // 64 miles (102km)

WEST HIGHLAND WAY

One of Scotland's original 'Great Trails', the West Highland Way was established as a long-distance hiking journey from the Lowlands, just north of Glasgow, to the Highlands, via Glen Coe. The route is more than suitable for cycling, if you have the right bike for heading off the beaten track. The stunning route follows a mixture of ancient roads – droving and military roads – through several places for re-supply, such as Tyndrum, and passes near some establishments that can offer rather more than mere resupply, such as Glengoyne Distillery at Dumgoyne and the Clachaig Inn in Glencoe. Parts of the route are challenging – Devil's Staircase and Rannoch Moor spring to mind – but with a short time spent over a map you can detour around certain sections if you wish. We'd suggest avoiding long stretches of the main A82 road. Otherwise, a fantastic two or three days on the bike. More info: westhighlandway.org/.

Start // Milngavie
Finish // Fort William
Distance // 96 miles (153km)

NORTH COAST 500 (NC500)

A much longer road tour, encompassing the entire Scottish coastline north of Inverness, and recognised as one of the world's great coastal routes. The 516-mile (830km) route is largely on single-track tarmac roads and passes through beautiful places such as Tongue and Ullapool, peaking at Bealach na Ba – a winding climb up though the mountains of the Applecross Peninsula. Keoldale (the start of the Cape Wrath track I featured in the main story) is on the NC500 route so joining the Cape Wrath Fellowship could be a small detour as part of of a bigger trip in Scotland. Keen endurance cyclist? At the time of going to press, the record for the NC500 stands at 31 hours 23 minutes, set by the former professional cyclist James McCallum in 2016. Good luck breaking that! More info: northcoast500.com.

Start/Finish // Inverness
Distance // 516 miles (830km)

© Jordan-Gibbons

THE SOUTH DOWNS WAY

Bucolic views over England's south coast, Iron Age settlements, country pubs, history and lots of hills: this is the South Downs Way, the easy way.

'Did you call them?'

'No,' I admitted. And now my phone had no signal. Mike was normally the most mild-mannered of men, so it was a shock to sense his exasperation. I began to panic.

We continued, Mike riding ahead of me as usual. After a few more minutes, I noticed the signal-strength bars on my phone increase again; I stopped and dialled.

'Hello, can I help you?'

I explained our desperate predicament. There was a pause, then a reply:

'So, that's one roast beef with potatoes and veg and one roast lamb with potatoes and veg?'

'Yes, that's right,' I replied, with relief. 'We'll be there just after nine o'clock. Thank you.'

I relayed the news to Mike, that the kitchen at the Fox Goes Free pub in Charlton, our overnight stop on the South Downs Way, would start cooking our supper before they closed for the evening. The tension dissipated immediately.

It was now around 8pm on a balmy summer's evening and we were cycling on a narrow chalk path through the middle of a field of barley, the bristles swaying in a light breeze. A skylark sang high

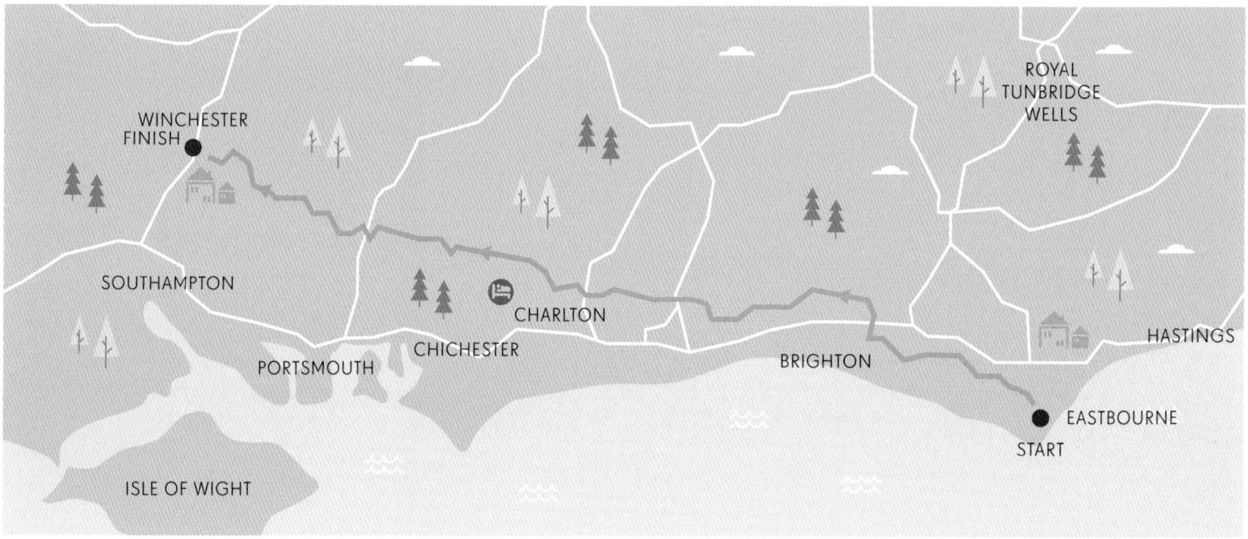

© BANANA PANCAKE / Alamy Stock Photo

above us. Golden light from the setting sun suffused the scene.

The South Downs Way runs diagonally across England's southern counties of Hampshire and Sussex, from Winchester in the northwest to the coastal town of Eastbourne in the southeast. It's an ancient, and still unpaved, right of way, running up and down the spine of low hills that make up England's newest national park, the South Downs. The route is popular with hikers, horse riders and mountain bikers – and one Easter I even encountered a man dragging an enormous wooden cross over his shoulder along it.

Central to the appeal of the South Downs Way is that both ends (and several towns along the route) are served by railways with fast connections to London, with journeys of around an hour. Most cyclists spend at least a couple of days riding the route, or part of it, but there is a big South-Downs-Way-in-a-Day scene: 100 miles (161km) starting at dawn on the longer summer days, finishing around 13 hours later. There are also people who take on the Double – there and back, nonstop. Mike and I preferred the South Downs Way the easy way: 60 miles (97km), a pub dinner and a comfortable bed, then another 40 miles (64km) to finish.

Cyclists typically ride from Winchester towards Eastbourne, in the direction of the prevailing wind. To be contrary, we started from Eastbourne train station and we started late, after midday, hence the rush to beat the setting sun and last orders at the pub's kitchen. In hindsight, the Eastbourne start was a good decision. It

"As dusk fell, we rolled into the pub to find our meals ready, pints pulled, and a starlit garden beckoning"

meant that we got the only section that was difficult navigate – the confusing network of route options and roads behind Brighton – out of the way early on. And we also dispatched the bigger hills of the Eastbourne end of the Way first, with fresh legs, starting with the pearly white cliffs of Beachy Head (the trail veers behind them but it's easy to detour up to the cliff edge). These crumbly cliffs are the exposed edge of a chalk layer that extends across the Channel and resumes in France. It was pushed up, ruptured, to form this undulating ridge more than 70 million years ago. England's early settlers, from Iron Age people (500BC) to the Romans, found the hilltops made perfect vantage points.

Riding from Eastbourne, we had already conquered our first Iron Age hill fort at Chanctonbury Ring. The place has a long history of pagan worship, including sacrifices. Our only sacrifice was not stopping to explore. We also whizzed past the chalk outline of the Long Man of Wilmington, which is now thought to be not quite as old as believed, dating from the 16th or 17th century.

As the sun inched down the sky, we left the sea to our left and angled inland towards our overnight pit-stop. The Fox Goes Free sits at the foot of the Downs. It's just a couple of miles from the

© Justin Foulkes / Lonely Planet; Lesley Pardoe / Alamy Stock Photo

RIDGEWAYS

In prehistoric times, travelling by foot along ridgeways was often preferable to hiking along the valley floor. Ridgeways, such as the SDW, were well-drained and offered great visibility – the penalty being that they were also exposed to the weather and were rarely flat. For these reasons, ridgeways often became ancient roads, used by drovers to drive livestock to market (and soldiers attacking settlements). Today, the traffic is of bikers and hikers but evidence of the importance of these ridgeways remains all around.

From left: near Firle Beacon at the east end of the South Downs Way; the Fox Goes Free pub, midway; the Seven Sisters chalk cliffs . Previous page: near Bignor Hill, midway

Weald and Downland Open-Air Museum at Singleton, where buildings from the 13th century and onwards are restored. As dusk fell, we rolled into the pub to find our meals ready, pints pulled, and a silent, starlit garden backing onto the hills.

Rejoining the South Downs Way the next morning, we had perhaps the prettiest section of the route ahead. This central part of the route passes through east Hampshire on chalk-white tracks, with views over green fields and flint-built villages. The trail, as well signposted as ever, darted through woodland, including the beech forest of the Queen Elizabeth Country Park where we tackled the mountain bike trails, before climbing the highest point of the South Downs Way, Butser Hill. Here too there is an Iron Age (300BC) farm and fort.

But for fort aficionados, the best was yet to come: the Iron Age fort of Old Winchester Hill. This would have been the guardian of the fertile Meon valley. It remains unexcavated but you can easily see the earthworks – ditches and ramparts – that would have protected the site. There's also a Bronze Age cemetery here (look out for tumuli the whole length of the South Downs).

From Old Winchester Hill, we were on the home stretch, heading towards Winchester, an ancient capital of England. We passed the statue of Alfred the Great in the city, then one of Europe's largest Gothic cathedrals, before arriving at the railway station for our afternoon train to London. But we would have happily turned the clock back one day to that hour of magical light and the fields of gold. **RB**

TOOLKIT

Start // Eastbourne (though Winchester-Eastbourne, with the prevailing wind at your back, is more common)
Finish // Winchester
Distance // 100 miles (161km)
Where to stay // The Fox Goes Free (www.thefoxgoesfree.com) in Charlton offers bed and breakfast (and dinner). There are other halfway options, including youth hostels.
What to take // A mountain bike is best. Use a saddle bag to carry overnight gear. Stay hydrated by filling up water bottles or hydration packs at the public taps along the route, detailed on the National Trails website (www.nationaltrail.co.uk/south-downs-way).
When to ride // Weather is an important factor. Check the wind direction before deciding where to start. Summer days are best; in the wet the chalk becomes treacherously slippery.

© Justin Foulkes / Lonely Planet

MORE LIKE THIS ANCIENT WAYS

THE RIDGEWAY, ENGLAND

Running through the Chilterns and along the Wessex Downs in central southern England, the Ridgeway links several important prehistoric sites, including Avebury stone circle and Silbury Hill, a manmade mound dating from 2300BC. All are part of Wiltshire's Neolithic collection of sites around Stonehenge. Originally, the 5000-year-old route, used by travellers, soldiers and merchants, extended between the coasts of Dorset and Norfolk but now it meets the Icknield Way in the Home Counties (where it also becomes a footpath towards its eastern end). The whole route, like the South Downs Way, is thoroughly signposted and treacherous to ride in winter. In summer, however, such sights as the Bronze Age White Horse of Uffington in Oxfordshire are marvellous. Look up to spot resurgent red kites, England's once-almost-extinct graceful birds of prey.
Start // Ivinghoe Beacon, Buckinghamshire
Finish // West Kennett, Wiltshire
Distance // 87 miles (140km)

ICKNIELD WAY TRAIL, ENGLAND

Arguably the oldest long-distance path in England, the Icknield Way begins in South Norfolk, at the foot of the Peddars Way (also bikeable) and follows veins of chalk to Ivinghoe Beacon in Buckinghamshire, where it meets the Ridgeway. English poet Edward Thomas walked the Icknield Way in 1911 and his journal still inspires hikers to travel the 150 miles (241km) along it. Thomas describes the Icknield Way as a 'white snake on a green hillside'; while it's true that rural sections remain unspoiled, other parts of the route now pass through industrial areas and towns. But that's part of the experience, with layers of history overlapping each other. Cyclists have to take the Icknield Way Trail, following the Neolithic axe emblem; the multi-user trail follows most but not all of the route of the ancient footpath, starting and ending in different locations.
Start // Ashridge Estate, Hertfordshire
Finish // Knettishall Heath Country Park, Suffolk
Distance // 170 miles (274km)

RENNSTEIG CYCLE PATH, GERMANY

Germany's oldest ridgeway trail is the Rennsteig, which traverses the deep, dark Thuringian Forest in central Germany's green heart. Much of the route lies along a ridge, above the treeline, affording outstanding views across the countryside. The Rennsteig was first used by messengers in the Middle Ages but it's now Germany's most popular hiking trail. There's a parallel shared-use track for cyclists (mostly mountain bikers). It passes the spa town of Masserberg, the winter sports resort of Oberhof, and the birthplace of Johann Sebastian Bach in Eisenach, also home to Wartburg Castle. At Blankenstein the trail ends at the Saale River. There are plenty of places to stay along the Rennsteig; refuel on sausages and beer. Mind the wild boar.
Start // Horschel
Finish // Blankenstein
Distance // 120 miles (193km)

© David Noton / Lonely Planet

Scenes from the Icknield Way Trail as it passes from Norfolk to Buckinghamshire

THE STYRKEPRØVEN

The Styrkeprøven is one of the oldest and most challenging cyclosportives in the world: a 337-mile 'trial of great strength' through the forests and over the mountains of Norway.

When a couple of buddies asked if I wanted to go to Norway to do this sportive called the Styrkeprøven, I said yes straight away. I tapped open the link on my phone and saw it would take place over a June weekend. Trondheim to Oslo, 337 miles (543km) – a fun two- or three-day event, I thought.

About a month later, we were out on our bikes together. One of the guys asked me what I had been doing to get ready for the Styrkeprøven.

'Nothing', I said.

He'd done a 185-mile (300km) loop the previous weekend that had gone okay, but he was still worried. That's when it dawned on me. We had to ride 337 miles (543km) in under 24 hours. I whipped out my phone and took another look at the website. Styrkeprøven, I learned, translates as 'trial of great strength'. My friends laughed so hard they were falling over.

Only once we had flown over the North Sea and were looking down at mists swirling over lakes and around snowy peaks, brushing rocky hills and huge pine forests, did the scale of the Styrkeprøven hit me. On the back-of-seat screen I noticed the little icon of our plane flickering over Oslo. There was still an hour to go until Trondheim – at the speed of a jet. That we had to ride the whole way back the next day on our bicycles was absurd. I ordered another mini-bottle of wine.

Briny fog blew over the tarmac at Trondheim. At the race headquarters, I realised just how big an event the Styrkeprøven is. Over 6000 people were set to take on the challenge from six different starting points, though the original 337-mile event is the most prestigious. When it was first organised by Norwegian war

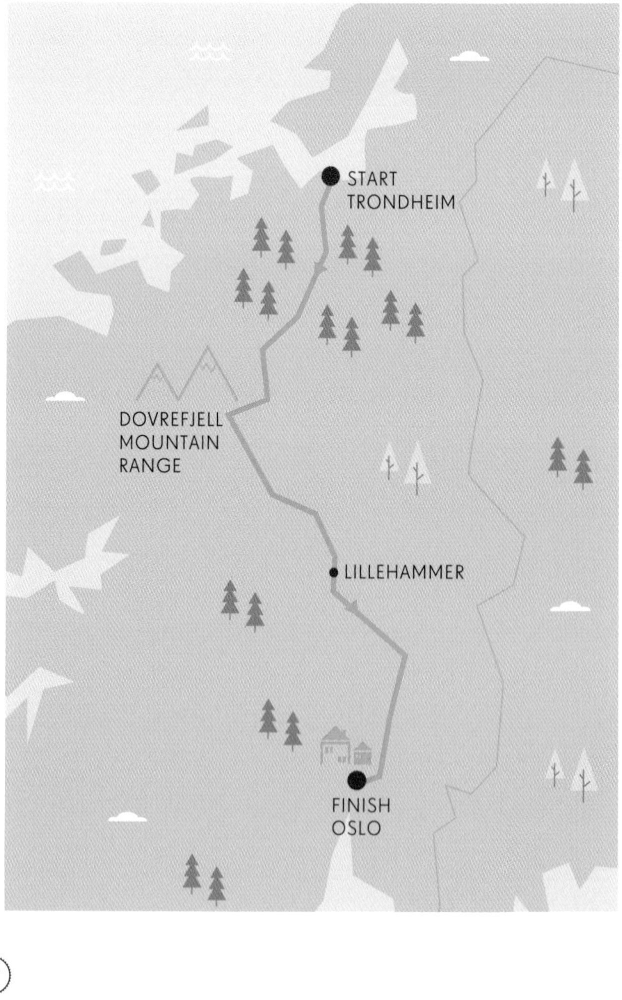

© Styrkeprøven AS

hero Erik Gjems-Onstad in 1967, 100 took part. Now, roughly 1500 ride the full distance every year in what the organisers claim is the world's oldest and longest sportive. Most set off in the evening and aim to finish within 24 hours. Our race was scheduled to start at six the next morning, but at these northerly latitudes in June, it was still too bright to sleep, so we checked in to the hotel and went out for beers.

The next morning, I was still rubbing my eyes and waiting for the instant coffee I'd choked down to wake me up. Spicy-sweet embrocation wafted through the air, and riders buzzed around in pristine kit. The PA crackled and we all lined up. The starter's shot echoed thought the city's quiet, cobblestone streets.

We rolled past farms and lumber yards and dark, wet fir forests. After 60 miles (100km), we arrived at the first feed station. I had just enough time to piss, pull off my leg warmers, and stuff a couple of sandwiches into my pockets. The peloton was already 300ft up the road when I saw my two friends huddled under the tent with hot cups of coffee.

'Good luck,' they shouted.

And then it was a bike race.

Many hours later, I found myself lying on the Astroturf floor of the Oslo arena. Someone fed me salty soup. At some point, they

"Three riders finally caught up with me at the front of the race. I knew I had one 10-second effort left"

got me up and gave me flowers and a medal. The next day, at noon, I woke to something worse than a hangover. My friends had arrived in the middle of the night and were still fast asleep. Over lunch in Oslo on a sunny patio, as we swapped stories, memories flitted back to me.

The road rose upwards, first through the trees and then out on to a boulder-strewn slope. Mountains towered over us. Rapids crashed beside us. Blasts of cold air blew out on to the road whenever we passed a waterfall.

By the 150-mile (250km) mark, there were only a dozen of us in the lead group. My arms had gone numb, and I was drifting into a daze. I pulled up to the table at a feed zone and shovelled four slabs of chocolate cake into my mouth, while a volunteer stuffed bottles into my pockets. A few kilometres down the road I came alive again. I started to think like a bike racer. By 220 miles (350km), I had attacked with another rider; he fell back and suddenly I was alone, in front.

© Styrkeprøven AS

GETTING OVER THE DOVREFJELL

Home to one of Europe's last herds of wild reindeer, the Dovrefjell mountain range divides eastern Norway from Trøndelag, the region around Trondheim. The Styrkeprøven passes over a high plateau surrounded by the range's greatest peaks, including the 7500ft (2286m) Snøhetta. Exposed to the wind, it can be one of the most challenging parts of the course. Don't despair. Once you've crossed the upland, there's a beautiful descent.

From left: dusk on the road to Oslo; reindeer en route; a team about to depart. Previous page: a group pushes across the Dovrefjell mountains

From then on, all I can remember is elation. The sun was out, and the road rolled through leafy forests, past lakes and rivers. On every roundabout, people cheered and waved their red-and-blue flags. I tucked into the wind and rode fast.

A hundred miles later, my throat was dry, and it hurt to swallow. My vision had gone blurry. An old man who had started the night before gave me some water, which revived me. Three riders finally caught up. I knew I had one 10-second effort left. I stayed on a big Norwegian guy's wheel, but when the sprint came, he beat me cleanly. After just over 14 hours of racing, I had finished second.

My friends had ridden with big groups and small groups, fought the wind together and alone, made new friends, and faced moments of great joy and utter desperation. After midnight in the outskirts of Oslo, one of the guys had stopped at a gas station to buy cigarettes. The other cried when he realised he was going to make it.

We saw so many people in the city that day who had ridden the Styrkeprøven. We could pick them out by their hobbled walks and hollowed cheeks, the smiles on their faces. Each had her or his own story.

Mine was of a bike race. Without it, I'm not sure I would have made it. **KP**

TOOLKIT

Start // Trondheim
Finish // Oslo
Distance // 337 miles (543km)
Getting there // There are regular flights to Trondheim from Oslo, as well as direct flights from several European cities. The Styrkeprøven's organisation offers a shuttle service to get your baggage from Trondheim to Oslo during the event.
What to take // If you expect to be riding through the night, bring lights; also an extra battery pack to power your cycling computer and phone. Norway's weather can be very turbulent, so pack a good waterproof jacket and arm and leg warmers.
More info // https://styrkeproven.no

© Jiri Hrebicek / Shutterstock, Styrkeprøven AS

Opposite: crossing the Scottish borders near Moffat on the London-Edinburgh-London challenge

MORE LIKE THIS
LONG-DISTANCE SPORTIVES

PARIS-BREST-PARIS, FRANCE

Paris-Brest-Paris was first organised in 1891. Originally a race for professionals, which was held every 10 years to show off the reliability of French manufacturers' bicycles, it evolved into a randonneuring event for *touristes routiers*. By the 1950s, too few pros were willing to take on the 750-mile (1200-km) challenge, though it was more popular than ever with amateurs. It has since been held, first every five years and now every four, as a brevet (a cycle event in which riders pass through a series of checkpoints). In order to qualify, riders need to complete a series of sanctioned rides of 200km, 300km, 400km, and 600km within a year of the event. Several thousand riders take part. They are welcomed in villages all along the rural route. The organisers insist that Paris-Brest-Paris isn't a race, though a first-placed finisher is crowned.
Start/Finish // Paris
Distance // 750 miles (1200km)

MILANO-SAN REMO GRAN FONDO, ITALY

Milano-San Remo is one of cycling's great classics and the longest race on the professional calendar. Its 185-mile (298km) course heads south through the Italian countryside from Milan before crossing the Passo del Turchino and descending down to the Ligurian coast, which it follows over flowery hills to the Cipressa and the Poggio, the two iconic climbs that determine who gets to sprint for victory on the Via Roma. It is often said that Milano-San Remo is the hardest of the Monuments to win, but the easiest to finish. Sprinters, climbers, and rouleurs all have a shot in the finale. In June, amateurs have the chance to complete the course during the Gran Fondo Milano-San Remo. The inclement weather that often batters the racers in March is less of a threat, though the locals can be just as competitive.
Start // Milan
Finish // San Remo
Distance // 185 miles (298km)

LONDON-EDINBURGH-LONDON

Like the Paris-Brest-Paris, this ride runs every four years (the next event is August 2021, ballot entries open 7 January 2021) and gives you 125 hours to complete one of Britain's toughest cycling challenges at around 930 miles (1500km). You set off from The Mall in central London and head north across the flats of Cambridge and Lincolnshire, over the Humber Bridge, before tackling the Pennines, and skirting the Yorkshire Moors. The route then takes you through countless small villages and into the Scottish Lowlands. From Edinburgh your return journey provides a bit of variety, but exhaustion and fatigue will be keeping your mind firmly fixed on getting back to London. There are no qualification requirements and the entry fee (£350) covers all your sleep stops, bike repair support and bag drops, so you can be assured of a fresh pair of bike shorts somewhere along the route. More info: www.londonedinburghlondon.com.
Start/Finish // London
Distance // 930 miles (1500km)

© Oliver Malms / Getty Images

A SNOWDON DOUBLE

A sunny day in Snowdonia? Make the most of it by getting up and down the tallest mountain in Wales as many times as the weather and the walkers permit

Mount Snowdon is irresistible. Though not quite as elevated as Ben Nevis in Scotland, the 3560ft (1085m) Snowdon massif in North Wales is more accessible. This easy proximity has long drawn visitors, in ever greater numbers. Each year more than half-a-million flock to it, from hikers to day trippers who either tramp up its paths or take the railway to crowd around the summit pillar for a selfie and then wander into the visitor centre for an oggie (meat-filled pastry). So popular are the trails over the massif that in 2003 the Snowdon Voluntary Cycle Agreement was drawn up, by which cyclists agree to stay off the mountain's trails from 1 May to 30 September between 10am and 5pm. All of which rather suggests that riders shouldn't bother with Snowdon. But we should. Because there is perhaps no more grand day out on a mountain bike in the British Isles than a double ascent and descent of its second-highest mountain.

Timing is all. We plumped for a late April weekend, just ahead of the cut-off, giving us nearly 15 hours of daylight. Daylight can be a theoretical term in North Wales: Snowdonia receives 120 inches of rainfall a year, so do whatever you can to sort the weather. The instigator of our trip, Ed, had evidently pulled in a few favours: from the moment the five of us crawled from our tents at 6am until we rolled back 9 hours later, we toiled happily beneath a cloudless blue sky.

Our departure point was the edge of Llanberis, to the north of Snowdon. A vast disused slate works, once the largest in the world, looms over the small town. But we didn't linger; we were intent on making good time away from the campsite on the lanes to the south and east that quickly gave way to moorland trail, and joined the Llanberis Path, a wide and mostly rideable mixture of slab paving, hard pack and looser sections. This path is the longest and least demanding approach to the summit (the Snowdon Mountain Railway track runs alongside it). Up we span in the shade as the rising sun lit the greens and dun browns of the far side of the valley. At its head, high in the distance, was the junction with one of the other popular summit paths, the Ranger – which we'd be riding both up and down in a few hours.

Pleasingly, it was still early enough that the only other travellers we met were summit bivouackers, ambling down after a starry night, and a few local dog walkers – runners, actually – bagging

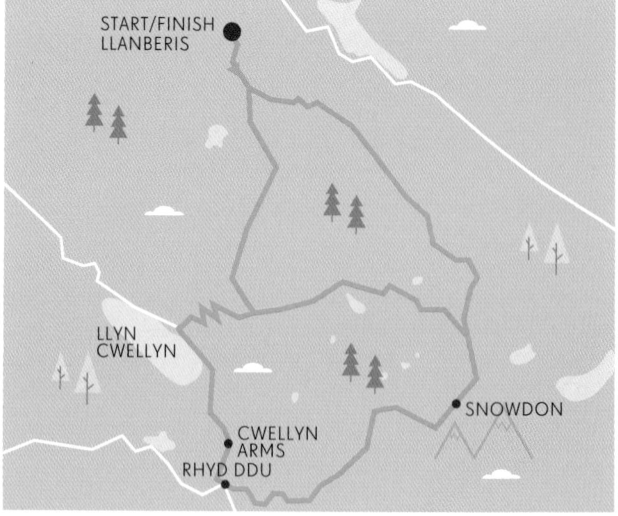

© Gavin Higgins

an impressive up-and-down before breakfast. We levelled out on the saddle beneath the summit and took in the narrow ridge of Crib Goch just to the east, and the horse-shoe leading round to it. By now we were in the company of a few dozen walkers, and a small queue was already forming at the foot of the steps up to the summit cairn. But instead of impatience, there was palpable excitement – we and everyone around us knew what a rare sight the day was giving us, with the Marches to our east, the Irish Sea and Ireland itself way out west and, to the south, the hills of Wales retreating into the haze.

Then the riding proper began. Even on a dry, clear morning such as this, the Rhyd Ddu path, the southwesterly trail off the summit, is to be taken very carefully. We freewheeled gently past the summit Visitor Centre then on to the path itself which takes you first to the left of the jaggedly rocky ridge line, and then, steeply down, to its right – a drop of over 300m lies on either side of the ridge. We walked the first section, and gingerly rode the second until, with a sickening crunch and howl, Bernie went over his bars and landed chest first on a sharp rock. In the event, he was winded rather than seriously injured. But it was a reminder that the consequences of a fall here are potentially serious.

From here the vertiginous ridge line softened into a gentle flank to our left, but a plummet down to Cwm Clogwyn remained, metres to our right. Nevertheless, It's a joyous descent, swooping down loose, rocky terrain (we were always careful to give way to

"We tried – and failed – not to look too exhausted before the walkers on the hike-a-bike up the Ranger Path"

THE WELSH RIVIERA

An earlier Snowdon summit building was built by the eccentric architect Clough Williams-Ellis, who is better known for his fantasy community an hour away at Portmeirion. Referencing Italian architecture, Williams-Ellis began constructing the village around a vision of a Mediterranean piazza on a private peninsula in the 1920s, importing artefacts and entire buildings until the 1970s. The cult TV series *The Prisoner* was shot there in the 1960s, and it's still a popular attraction.

Clockwise from above: hike-a-biking the Ranger Path; the summit cairn; the Snowdon Mountain Railway. Previous page: on the Rhyd Ddu knife-edge

© stockerr970 / Shutterstock, Gavin Higgins

the few walkers we came across). Just when you think the fun's over, a challenging rock garden pops up in the final section of the mountain proper. Buzzing, we rolled into the hamlet of Rhyd Ddu itself and the Cwellyn Arms for a brunch of lemonade and crisps. Out came the factor 30 – on a Welsh April day! – and out came the smartphones to size up the run-in to ascent number two: the Ranger Path.

After a short northerly spin up the valley road on the eastern shore of Lyn Cwellyn, we turned right after the youth hostel and began the climb – at first gentle, soon anything but – of the Ranger. Bikes were shouldered as the path steepened rapidly in a series of boulder-strewn switchbacks (make sure your riding shoes can take the punishment of a two-hour hike-a-bike). We tried (and failed) not to look too exhausted in front of the incredulous walkers we passed, but took consolation that every rock we were labouring over, we'd be flying over soon enough.

And so it went. By early afternoon, the summit was thronged and not a place to stick around, so we ate what was left of our food and saddled up for the descent of the Ranger Path – which delivered on all its alpine promise: steep in places, fast, rocky. On it flowed, easing, until a gated ford marking the turn north on a bridleway over an easy pass and back down to Llanberis. The other tourists, the often-appalling weather, the restrictions – there are any number of reasons to balk at riding Snowdon. But on a day like this, it's irresistible. **MH**

© john finney photography / Getty Images

TOOLKIT

Start/Finish // Llanberis
Distance // 21 miles (34km)
How to get there // A four-hour train ride from London to Bangor – from there, a 20-minute cab or an hour's ride.
What to take // A full-suspension mountain bike and spares (ensure your bike is in good condition). The OS Snowdon Explorer map (don't rely on GPS apps). Food and water; a thermal layer, gloves and waterproof. First-aid kit.
When to ride // Spring to autumn; check the Met Office Snowdon area report for summit conditions. NB: for details of the Voluntary Cycle Agreement in place from 1 May to 30 September: www.mbwales.com/listings/snowdon/
Where to stay // Camping in Llanberis campsite is cheap and convenient. The Cwellyn Arms, Rhyd Ddu, offers rooms, a bunkhouse and camping at the southern end of Lyn Cwellyn, where there is a nearby YHA hostel too.
More info // www.mbwales.com/listings/snowdon/

Opposite: on Drochaid Coire Lair, Torridon – northwest Scotland is home to some of the best natural descents in the British Isles

MORE LIKE THIS
NATURAL TRAILS IN BRITAIN

JACOB'S LADDER, ENGLAND

That the Peak District, between Manchester and Sheffield, is one of Britain's busiest national parks is not surprising. It's home to some the country's most inspiring landscapes, and the mountain-biking there is no less enthralling. The riding is often steep and rocky, demanding technical ability and fitness. If you're curious but nervous, search for a short loop that takes in Ladybower Reservoir and The Beast, a favourite local descent – its chunky boulders will test your suspension and your nerve. Appetite whetted? Then consider the Dark Peak route, a loop starting from Hayfield. Its signature is Jacob's Ladder, a teeth-chattering, rock-strewn gulley descent, and it includes descents off Rushup Edge and Roych Clough, much of which requires skill and commitment. The climbing is tricky, too, so make sure you're in good condition. Master this classic route and a world of other riding in the Peaks opens up to you.

Start/Finish // Hayfield
Distance // 18 miles (29km)

ELAN VALLEY, WALES

Wales is spoilt for choice when it comes to natural trails: the Brecon Beacons, the Gower Peninsula, Snowdonia... The Elan Valley lies between them all, in mid-Wales, and offers up its wide range of riding against a historical backdrop of Victorian dams, old railways, reservoirs and woodlands. Base yourself at the Visitor Centre (which also has bike hire, cafe and a ranger service) or the nearby town of Rhayader (Clive Powell Mountain Bikes has been there over 25 years, bike hire available) and choose from trails for all abilities – from easy blues all the way up to the 37-mile (60km) all-dayer, Elan Epic. As ever with Wales, consider the weather and take the appropriate clothing: even if it's shaping up dry the day you plan to ride, check that it hasn't been pouring down for three weeks, as the ground will be considerably softer and slower. More information: www.elanvalley.org.uk/explore/cycling/mountain-biking.

Start/Finish // Rhayader
Distance // 37 miles (60km)

TORRIDON, SCOTLAND

Away up in the northwest Highlands, around some of the oldest and most spectacular geology in the British Isles, you'll find true wilderness riding. The backdrop alone is worth the considerable effort to get there (1.5-2hrs by train or car from Inverness): titanic glacial valleys on either side of which tower imposing peaks. And it's the rocks that make up the landscape that in part give the riding its character: the sandstone will give your tyres plenty of grip (but look out for tyre-shredding shards of quartzite, too). Between the A890 road to the south and A896 are more than half-a-dozen trails bookended by the peaks of Beinn Damh in the west and Carn Breac in the east. There is plenty of single track, and some memorably great descending, though all the trails require good fitness and ability – and this being remote Scotland come well prepared for the worst in the event of finding yourself stranded.

© Jon Sparks / Alamy Stock Photo

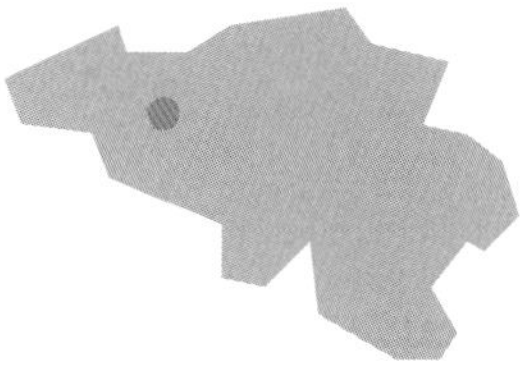

THE BEERS OF FLANDERS

You want a tour of the breweries of Belgium that includes a guaranteed bottle of the rare Trappist Westvleteren 12, 'the best beer in the world'? Pedal this way...

Belgium is a small country with lots of breweries: more than 200 and counting, many run by families for generations. So where to start on a beer tour by bike? With the help of a tour operator's self-guided itinerary (see Toolkit), my wife, Selina, and I headed to the Flemish area of Westhoek, west Belgium, aiming to make the most of the province's appealingly high concentration of hops and breweries over six days and 200 miles of riding.

We headed out on a Friday afternoon in late July just south of Bruges, where we'd left our car (we had driven from the Netherlands, where we live). This was to be our longest day in the saddle, 52 miles, mostly through small villages and farms, along quiet country roads flanked by fields of flax and Brussels sprouts. We kept on course to arrive in Ypres for an event that marked a sobering start to the trip: the Last Post, with buglers, a reading and the laying of a wreath. This public commemoration for soldiers killed in WWI has been held every evening since 1928.

Ready for a bit of levity (and a beer), we visited The Times, a bar popular with locals off the gorgeous historic market square. We started with the locally brewed Wipers Times, a blond ale ('Wipers' was the British soldiers' pronunciation of Ypres), followed by hoppy, bold beers brewed in the next day's destination of Watou – a St Bernardus Tripel and a Poperings Hommelbier (*hommel* is the local dialect for humulus, the botanical name for hops).

Any questions I had about hops were answered the next day at the fascinating Hop Museum Poperinge, housed in a beautiful and aromatic 19th-century building that once held the municipal hops weighing and storage facility. Don't miss the museum's 'wall of beer', which contains hundreds of bottles from every Belgian province, many for sale in the gift shop.

From there, we dropped in on nearby De Plukker, a brewery run by organic hop farmer Joris Cambie (tastings on Saturday afternoons only). We sampled a Keikoppenbier, a fresh blond, top-fermented ale, and chatted with Cambie. At his invitation, we departed through his 35-acre farm, passing tall rows of hops. At this point, our self-guide notes posed a challenge: 'Like the idea of more mileage and hills? Consider cycling over the border into France to visit the Mont des Cats Trappist Monastery.' Mais oui!

On the 15-mile detour, we passed several war graveyards, by now a familiar sight, including the 9901 graves of mostly

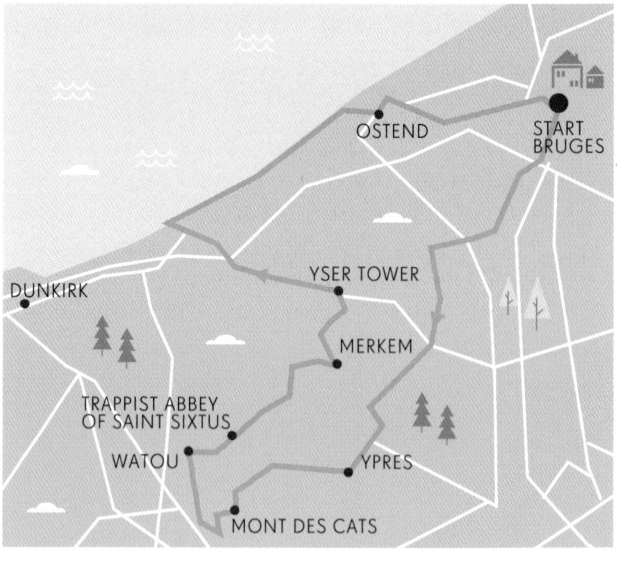

© Jennika Argent / Alamy Stock Photo, Be Good / Shutterstock

HENRI MAES
HENRI MAES
HENRI MAES

unidentified British Commonwealth soldiers in Lijssenthoek Military Cemetery. We worked up a thirst climbing the steep hill to the monastery, which has a gift shop and cafe. The abbey, known mostly for making cheese, in 2011 revived its amber-beer recipe after a 163-year hiatus, although it's brewed by another abbey.

We spent the night in Watou, a small, sweet Belgian town with a historic square. Dinner at our hotel on the square, Het Wethuys, included a crêpe-like 'pancake' made of beer batter and stuffed with meat and vegetables, and two pints of their house beer, a sweet, earthy concoction brewed with local hops.

Sunday started with a pilgrimage to the Holy Grail of Trappist beer: Westvleteren, made at Trappist abbey of Saint Sixtus in Vleteren. The modest-looking abbey, founded in 1831 by a monk from Mont des Cats, is private, but across the street is the modern cafe In de Vrede, said to be the only place in the world guaranteed to stock Trappist Westvleteren 12 (10.2% by volume). How do you follow a brew some have called the best in the world for its complex flavours? By speeding off, a little tipsy, to a family-run brewery, De Dolle Brouwers ('the crazy brewers'), 17 miles (27km) away in the small town of Esen. There we refreshed our palates in the brewery's cafe with fresh, hoppy ales.

The next day was more about battlefields than beer as we visited two fascinating spots in Diksmuide. First, the Museum on the Yser. It is housed in a 275-foot-high tower that reigns as Flanders' nationalistic symbol in its struggle against the country's French-speaking Walloon region. Visitors start at the top for an amazing

"I couldn't resist the 2015 Aestatis, a strong, musty saison, while Selina had a dark beer from Malheur, in East Flanders"

THE MONKS WHO BREW

Trappist beer is brewed by Trappist monks, who live a simple and silent life in the abbey. There are 14 Trappist beers, but only 12 carry the Authentic Trappist Product label, meaning they were brewed at the abbeys themselves. There are six Trappist breweries in Belgium, two in the Netherlands, and one each in Austria, Italy, England and the United States. (The abbeys in France and Spain do not brew their own.) Trappist beer is recognised and authenticated by the International Trappist Association (www.trappist.be).

Clockwise from above: beer-hunting in Bruges; the Holy Grail of Trappist beers, Westvleteren; hops; the Half Moon Brewery. Previous page: bottling at the Half Moon; historic Bruges

© Nigel Jarvis / Shutterstock, Selina Kok

360-degree view, all the way to the North Sea, then descend its 22 floors, where exhibits detail the fallout from the war and also the Flemish Movement. Next, we rode a mile north to the trenches (now re-created), along the Yser River, used by the Allied forces for more than four years of fighting German forces. The perfect antidote to the grim reminders of death and destruction was a spin west to the sunny seaside, where we shared miles of paved walkways and cycle paths with beachgoers and pop-up markets.

The last day of our tour started with a serene ride along a canal leading directly to the bustle of Bruges. Consider a tour at the Brouwerij de Halve Maan (Half Moon Brewery) if you appreciate state-of-the-art facilities and don't mind big tour groups (it does have a lovely cafe). From there we hopped over to the cozy Cafe Rose Red, and its long beer list. I couldn't resist the 2015 Aestatis, a strong, musty saison (fizzy, fruity pale ale), while Selina had a dark beer from Malheur, a family brewery in East Flanders.

After some famous Belgian fries and a must-do canal tour we were ready for our final hop stop, at Staminee De Garre. This low-key, old-world tavern off the market square maintains its local cred despite an ever-growing fame among hopheads. Stealing the show among De Garre's 100-plus beers is its exclusive house beer Tripel de Garre, a hearty abbey blond served in a goblet set atop a paper lace doily, a nod to traditional Belgian lace. The nose was sweet and hoppy, a fitting farewell to Flanders. **DD**

TOOLKIT

Start/Finish // Bruges
Distance // 127 miles (205 km)
Getting there // Bruges can be reached by train or bus from Brussels.
Guided and self-guided tours // Beercycling's 'West Flanders Self-Guided Information Packet' details routes, services and breweries. The tour company also leads guided trips in Belgium, France, Italy and Germany (www.beercycling.com).
Where to stay // The guesthouse at St Bernardus Brewery in Watou is next to fields of hops (www.brouwershuis.com). Also look for lodging above village taverns.
When to ride // Spring to autumn, with hops visible late summer. Poperinge stages a hops festival in September every three years, with 2020 next (www.hoppefeesten.be).
What to ride // Touring or hybrid bikes are best.

© Fabio Nodari / Alamy Stock Photo, Arterra / Getty Images

Clockwise from top: the Spezial-Keller beer garden, Bamberg; a pint at the Hawkley Inn, Hampshire; the Paname brewpub on the Quai de la Loire, Paris

MORE LIKE THIS
EUROPEAN BEER RIDES

A HAMPSHIRE PUB CRAWL

The English county of Hampshire is blessed with several world-class pubs, beautiful countryside and sufficient quiet lanes that a route can be plotted from one good pub to another. Start from the town of Petersfield (an hour by train from London's Waterloo station). From here, cycle to Steep and up to Hawkley for the village's heavenly inn. Return past Priors Dean (and the patchy Pub With No Name) southwards then west to cross the A32 at West Tisted and follow lanes to Alresford before turning south again for Cheriton and the Flower Pots brewery. From this pub, cross the A272 to Kilmeston and a climb up to Beacon Hill. Freewheel down to Exton and follow the Meon Valley Cycle Trail to the Thomas Lord pub. Then follow lanes back via East Meon, Bordean and Froxfield to Steep's cosy Harrow Inn for a final pitstop. Note that this is a very hilly ride and beer may not enhance performance.

Start/Finish // Petersfield
Distance // 37 miles (60km)

THE PARIS BREWPUB SCENE

Thanks to France's growing craft beer scene, there are alternatives to the bland, gassy *pression* – and you needn't travel far from the centre of Paris to enjoy the results. Head out to Jacques Bonsergent on the Metro, pick up a Vélib' bike, then cycle north along Quai de Jemmapes for a mile and a half (2.5km) to Quai de la Loire where you'll find the Paname Brewing Company brewpub in a striking waterside warehouse space – try the Casque d'Or, a floral saison, brewed with 100% French hops, orange rind and candied ginger. Next, spin over to 'Little Africa', home to Brasserie La Goutte d'Or (on the street of the same name), Paris' first micro-brewery. Wheat beers, porters, IPAs, lagers... they're all brewed winningly here. Still thirsty? Cross the Quai de la Loire (to the east) for the Paname Brewing Company, which serves five flavour-packed beers and street food snacks.

Start/Finish // Paris
Distance // 6 miles (10km)

BAMBERG AND BEYOND, GERMANY

Bamberg, in the Franconia region of Bavaria, is renowned for its special Rauchbier, or smoked beer, and there's nowhere better to try it than in Schlenkerla, a timbered pub and brewery in the Unesco Word Heritage-listed city centre. A 10-minute ride from the centre, at the top of a hill, you'll find Spezial-Keller, which also serves a lighter Rauchbier and much else besides. Tuck into a pork knuckle and sauerkraut and enjoy the views back to Bamberg. Also be sure to pop into Mahrs Bräu, a small, family-run brewpub, near the river – its smooth, malty U-beer is a must. Need more miles in your legs and beers in your belly? There's a 137-mile (220km) Brewery and Beer Cellar Tour taking in many of the county's 70 breweries; a full tour would take 3-4 days, but it's a figure of eight, around and east of the city so it can be shorteneed easily. More information: https://en.bamberg.info/

Start/Finish // Bamberg

© David Davies / Alamy Stock Photo, Adrienne Pitts / Lonely Planet, Myles New / Lonely Planet

The Beers of Flanders

FROM SEA TO SEA

A rite of passage for active Brits (and inquisitive foreign riders) through the dramatic landscape and history of the north of England.

Great Britain's best-known challenge ride is attempted by thousands of people every year but it still has plenty of bite. Some come away scarred by the steep gradient of some climbs, especially on the Pennine sections, or vow never again to tackle the longer ascents. Others mutter curses about the northern English weather, which can throw tempests at you any time of year. Known also as the Coast to Coast (C2C on signage along the route) by many who ride it, this is a journey undertaken by all kinds of cyclists, from touring couples to older families to groups raising money for charity.

This is a fabulously open ride: anyone with a bike in decent condition with a long weekend to spare can dip their back wheel in the Irish Sea and a few days later victoriously place the front wheel in the North Sea. Some riders take longer, while others manage the whole thing in one (very) long day.

The route can be travelled in either direction. We headed west to east, getting the major climbs out of the way earlier and – in theory at least – leaving the rainier side of Britain behind. Our party of three mustered at various points on the train ride north, then swung south from Carlisle to Whitehaven, overnighting in the first of three B&Bs en route.

Whitehaven's rich history and lovely marina made for a

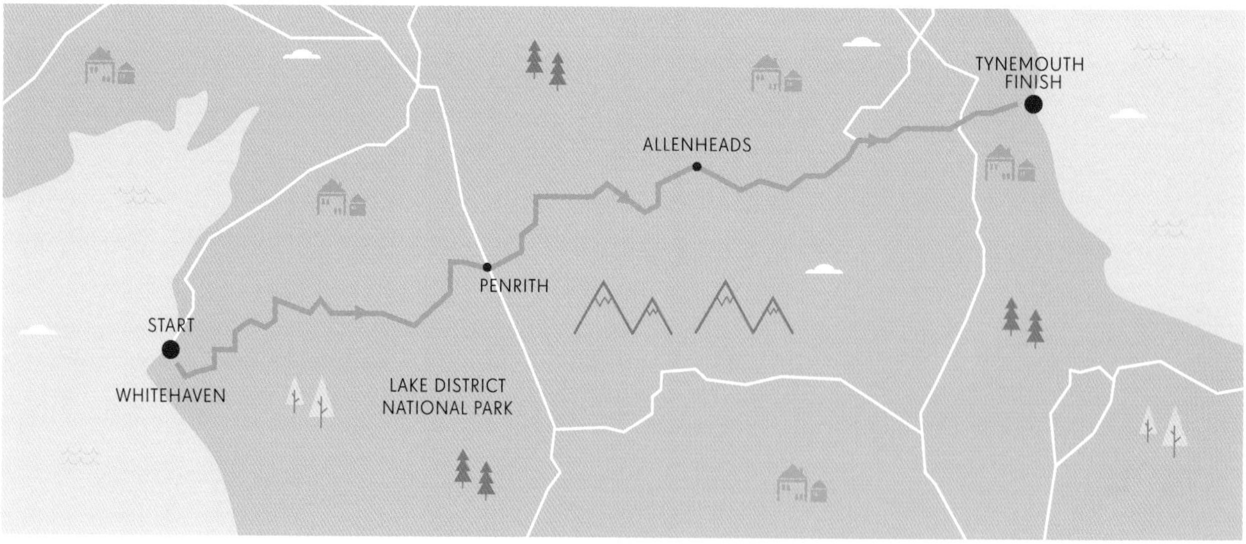

© Douglas Pearson / Getty Images

surprising start to the journey. Once we'd left the town behind – you can also start the signed route from nearby Workington – the path passed sculptures and quickly entered classic Lakeland scenery. On one hand this meant we were riding through deep beauty. On the other, the road was certain to soon go up. A lot. The first major landmark is the long haul over the Whinlatter Pass followed by the off-road descent into Keswick. Whinlatter is, happily, not as severe as most other Lake District passes, and ascending riders are kept on a quiet road away from the main road. Care must be taken on the descent. The tight curves are easy to skid over, and new Lycra shorts are not cheap.

Beyond Keswick, the mountains begin to peter out and, once past the looming summit of Blencathra, the scenery becomes more rolling and less rocky. If it felt odd to be effectively leaving the Lakes so soon, it was also heartening that we were making real progress. Castlerigg Stone Circle is a must-stop, with stellar 360-degree views that suggest a pre-bicycle civilisation that knew a thing about the value of round things. From here the path twisted and turned alongside and away from the busy A66 to Penrith. This underrated market town offered a welcoming place to pause and, like many other places en route, had excellent facilities for cyclists, which was just as well, as my front wheel wasn't happy at being asked to work hard and needed replacing at short notice. A bike service before setting out is essential.

The most memorable challenge of the route for me was the ascent of Hartside, the dramatic behemoth emerging from the Eden Valley a few miles after leaving Penrith. On busy summer weekends there's a steady stream of cyclists on the C2C – and Pennine Cycleway that also uses the route – puffing up the switchback climb to the 1912ft summit. It's a steady not steep climb, but feels like the defining moment of the journey, possibly because you get to look at dozens of other riders making their way to the

WIGGO'S WAY

The popularity of the C2C has led to the establishment of several alternative sections, including the unofficial Wiggo's Way, a route dedicated to British cycling legend Bradley Wiggins, and various off-road sections that can be tackled by those with fatter, knobblier tyres. You may not feel like Wiggo when riding some of the more challenging sections, but you will have taken on an iconic British ride that's been often imitated but never bettered.

Clockwise from above: crossing Hownsgill Viaduct in County Durham; dip a toe in at Tynemouth; Penrith; setting off from Whitehaven. Previous page: Castlerigg Stone Circle near Keswick

© Pascal Mauger / Alamy Stock Photo, John Morrison / Alamy Stock Photo

top from the cafe once you're at the summit.

The middle section of the ride is the toughest, and includes a beast of an incline out of Garrigill, steep climbs out of former lead-mining villages, such as Allenheads and Rookhope, and the highest point on the entire ride at Black Hill, where Cumbria and Northumberland meet. Take a breather, and a photo opportunity. Yes, parts of this route hurt a lot, but it felt like honest toil, with the reward of one incredible view after another, and a sense of achievement at the end of each day.

The C2C shows off northern England at its most green and pleasant, with a landscape that varies from mighty mountains to rolling hills descending to the sea. This being England, many villages and towns have a fine selection of local shops and pubs. In fact, cyclists make a significant contribution to the regional economy: for bonus points, go for local produce where you can. Given that each night will see you collapse into a B&B in need of extra-large refuelling for the coming days' efforts, this probably won't be a problem.

The final stretch, with no significant climbs and few sights after the dramatic crossing of the Hownsgill Viaduct outside Consett, inevitably became focused on the finish. After several days aiming at Tynemouth, getting here was always going to be sweet, with front wheels duly dunked, and ice cream beside salty sea air as a reward. We knew we had to ride back to Newcastle, but those final miles flew by, or at least seemed to in the fog of the celebratory beers that followed. The alternative finish at Sunderland, with a lovely beachside setting, competes with Tynemouth for the best possible ending, and both have merits.

The C2C isn't an exclusive club for elite cyclists, more a ticket to smile more times than you may expect and say 'I did that', all for the price of one long weekend of unbeatable riding. **TH**

"The C2C isn't an exclusive club for elite cyclists, more a ticket to smile more times than you may expect"

TOOLKIT

Start // Whitehaven

Finish // Sunderland/Tynemouth

Distance // 140 miles (230km), Whitehaven to Sunderland

Getting there // Trains can get you to the start of the ride then home again, but bike space should be reserved (via railway booking office or phoning the relevant train company). There's no charge but space is limited. Failing that, a (moral) support car can help with transport.

What to take // You don't need a full-spec mountain bike to cover the route, but a road bike won't be up to off-road sections. A gravel or cyclo-cross bike offers the right compromise (or follow signs to avoid unpaved sections).

More info // See www.c2c-guide.co.uk. The printed Sustrans route map (www.sustrans.org.uk) is an essential companion.

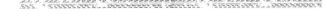

© Clearview / Alamy Stock Photo, Jason Friend / Alamy Stock Photo

Opposite: setting off from the Hoe, Plymouth, with two moors ahead

MORE LIKE THIS
BRITISH C2C RIDES

LÔN LAS CYMRU, WALES

The Lôn Las Cymru (Welsh Green Lane) is the perfect way to discover Wales' wonderfully hilly hinterland. This 253-mile (407km) route runs from Cardiff in the south to Holyhead in the north. The route follows the Taff Trail railway path, then crosses the Brecon Beacons, the Wye Valley and over to the sea at Machynlleth. From here, Snowdonia offers tough climbs and wonderful seaside views before crossing onto Anglesey via the magnificent Menai Bridge. This is one of the toughest routes on the National Cycle Network, even if you start in Chepstow rather than the Welsh capital and stay on tarmac for most of the ride. The reward for traversing hundreds of miles of mountains is a special insight into the great beauty of Wales, and a sense of satisfaction for having travelled across it from one wonderful corner to another.

Start // Cardiff/Chepstow
Finish // Holyhead
Distance // 253 miles (407km)

SCOTTISH C2C, SCOTLAND

Completing Britain's coast-to-coast quartet is the Scottish C2C, running from Annan to the Forth Bridge across the Southern Uplands of Scotland. Given Scotland's rightly rugged reputation, this is a surprisingly easier and marginally shorter ride than the English C2C, but that doesn't mean it should be taken lightly. There are some testing sections and the odd lengthy climb as the route winds through the borders on a mix of lightly trafficked country lanes and railway paths. The C2C reaches its climax passing through Edinburgh before reaching the Firth of Forth.

Start // Annan
Finish // Forth Bridge, Firth of Forth
Distance // 122 miles (196km)

TWO MOORS, ENGLAND

Dartmoor, dominating the southwest county of Devon, is one of the few places you can still wild camp (with due care and sensitivity) in England. This rolling and scenic route links it to Exmoor in the north of the county and makes for an appealing long-weekend adventure. Staying off-road to start, the route gains height as it pushes on to the moor. Here, old mining works and wind-blasted tors dot the landscape. Continuing as far as you see fit (or your legs allow), a campout towards the park's northern edge will set you up nicely to take on the tarmac-covered middle section the following day. Hitting the edge of Exmoor at the end of the second day means you can avail yourself of one of the area's many excellent pubs, and still leave a full day to navigate the final off-road section to the finish in Minehead. Both the start and end are well served by rail, making this an accessible slice of the wild Southwest.

Start // Plymouth
Finish // Minehead
Distance // 116 miles (186km)

© Dave Henrys / Alamy Stock Photo

A DUTCH SUMMER HOLIDAY

The flat Netherlands may not be typically 'epic', but Cass Gilbert says that there's no better destination for your family's first big tour in Europe.

To some, the term 'epic' embodies a grand, arduous or heroic deed, perhaps, or even a poetic story, if we're to take its Greek roots, *epikos*, more literally.

But it is a relative term, too. For my sister, who has lived with mobility issues and partial sight throughout her life, a ride across Holland might be considered epic. And, for my six-year-old son Sage, covering over 125 miles (200km) under your own steam is epic, no matter how pancake flat the destination.

Similarly, cycling into the bowels of an international ferry, for the overnight crossing to the Hook of Holland, can be epic in its own way, as I could see from Sage's look of wonder. As soon as we – my partner, my sister, Sage and I – passed through its open jaws and were swallowed into its belly, we tied up our bikes and excitedly grabbed what we needed for this first, seafaring leg of the journey.

Heading north, we followed EuroVelo route LF1 along the coast, wending its way independently of main roads. This signposted route is marked by a string of dunes, cafes, and seaside towns. It's almost completely traffic free, with beachside parking that heaves with bicycles and cargo machines. LF1 is an alternate biking universe where cars soon become a distant memory; road markings, speed bumps, and crossings are all shrunk down to

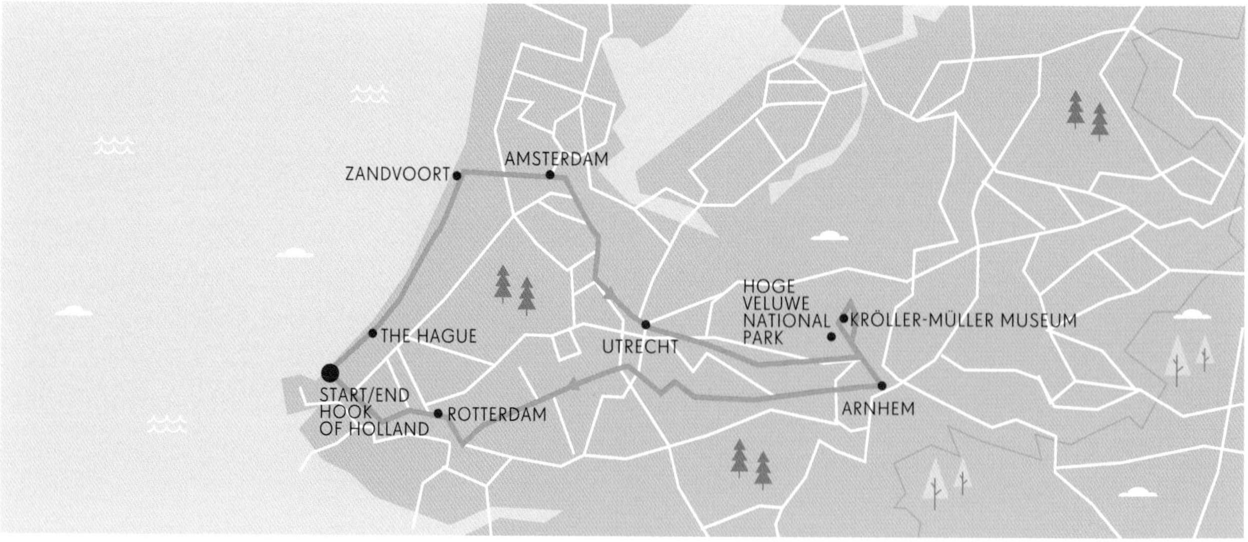

© Cass Gilbert

TOLIARI 12

biking proportions. All without fuss and fanfare. I saw a mum with two children and a sun parasol in a cargo bike. A man with a surfboard attached to the side of a cruiser. An elderly lady's city commuter replete with a dachshund in a wicker basket. Throw in sunshine and a light tailwind, and you have a nigh-on perfect debut to a family trip.

From the coast town of Zandvoort, we headed inland to Haarlem and Amsterdam. Whilst the scenery isn't quite as impressive, it was still an appealing route for our group, given that we barely touched a main road. Onwards, a train whisked us to Arnhem, where the second part of our journey began: a ride to the Kröller-Müller Museum, located somewhat unexpectedly for a museum of such international repute, in the heart of the Hoge Veluwe National Park. The museum dates back to 1938 and houses a vast Van Gogh collection. But for families, it's probably the sprawling sculpture garden outside that's of most intrigue. The surrounding forest is the setting for works of art that either blend seamlessly with their surroundings or magnificently do not. Benches and chairs offer perfect spots to contemplate each in the changing light of the day. The park offers a fleet of free bikes, parked on the edge of the forest, that can be used to reach the museum for visitors who arrive by car; cue groups of white bicycles gliding this way and that across the rolling heathland and beguiling dunescapes. The

"Sage darted boldly past me whenever there was a break in the cycling traffic, delightedly independent"

Hoge Veluwe National Park is a wonderful, whimsical place that completely enchanted all of us.

Meanwhile, my son's cycling was improving. He suffered just one crash that resulted in grazes – a culmination of his increasingly brash riding, too many miles in the saddle that day, and a late bedtime the night before. But after the inevitable tears, he bounced back and seemed to genuinely love almost every minute of our holiday. He darted boldly past me whenever there was a break in the cycling traffic, with the heady delight of a child experiencing independence for the first time. In a week, he'd transformed from one who understood the basics of riding but lacked road awareness and confidence – wobbling from one side of the path to the other – to a cyclist who could now pedal safely on a public road and cover distances of up to 20 miles a day.

Likewise, I was delighted that my sister was getting into the swing of things too. I'd borrowed an unusual-looking tandem that would allow me to ride behind with her in a recumbent position up front. It positioned us perfectly to chat, whilst sharing the joys of

BIKE AND BED AND BREAKFAST

Affordable summer accommodation can be tricky to find in the Netherlands. We signed up with Vrienden op de Fiets, which offers B&B-style accommodation to cyclists. Derek The Lifelong Smoker made room for us in his tiny terraced house, nipping out to smoke rollies between making us comfortable. Otherwise, carry a tent – despite the extra weight, it affords more options and removes the pressure from distances you'll need to cover each day.

From left: catching the ferry; the author's son Sage enjoying his first 'epic'; passing through Amsterdam. Previous page: Sage rode as many as 20 miles a day

the pedalling and the propulsive nature of bike touring. Together with my partner, who carried a pannier full of food, the four of us stopped for lunchtime picnics, always a personal highlight of any bike tour. 'This is exactly how I'd imagined a bike trip would be,' my sister said. She read stories to my son when we paused in the shade, and in turn, he helped her with the clasp of her bike helmet. Watching them together made all the effort of organising the ride, and seeing it through, so very worthwhile.

Calling upon the train system again, we finished our trip with two days riding along the Linge River, for the typical Dutch experience of windmills, canals, barges, and flowers, before heading back to the Hook.

Holland's incredible cycling infrastructure is a game changer for family tours. Distances are manageable and the country's bike-friendly public transport system opens up a variety of scenery in a short space of time. No wonder so many Dutch see riding bikes as an unremarkable activity; their approach is inspiring.

In fact, I'd recommend a tour of the Netherlands to any family looking for an active holiday that has the transformative power to both improve a child's cycle sense, and transform perceptions of what we should all should be striving for in our society.

Glorious Holland: it may not be epic by Greek standards, but it offered just the right challenge for us. **CG**

TOOLKIT

Start/Finish // Hook of Holland
Distance // 280 miles (451km), but there are options. Riding LF1, crossing the Hoge Veluwe National Park, and following the Linge River, boarding trains where noted, amounts to around 130 miles (210km), or a week's mellow family riding.
Dutch railways // Bike friendly, and lifts in Dutch train stations are big enough for family setups too – details like this make a big difference.
How to get there // Stena Lines sails to the Hook of Holland from the UK twice a day; one is an overnight service. Rotterdam, Amsterdam and Arnhem are all major rail hubs – check ahead for bike-carrying capacity.
When to ride // As ever, long summer days are best.
More info // www.hollandcyclingroutes.com/ is the official Dutch website for recreational cycling.

All photos © Cass Gilbert

Opposite: the author's son Sage makes easy work of the Sierra de Aralar, Spain

MORE LIKE THIS
FAMILY-FRIENDLY ADVENTURES

MAAS CYCLE ROUTE, NETHERLANDS

If you're after more traffic-free riding, then the Dutch section of the International Meuse Cycle Route – aka EuroVelo 19 – is sure to provide a mellow but worthy family-friendly adventure. Maas Cycle Route (Maasfietsroute) follows the Maas River over 298 convoluted miles (480km), arcing in a northeastern direction from Maastricht to the Hook of Holland. Along the way, it flits from one side of the river to the other, thanks to 12 ferry rides. The grades are gentle and most of the route is either free of cars or along very quiet backroads, peppered with occasional gravel paths. Think typical Holland: windmills to dykes to ancient fortified towns to fruit orchards, in the company of lumbering river barges. The route has recently seen a big update with new signposts along the way, making navigation simple. There's a great website too: https://www.lfmaasroute.nl/en

Start // Maastricht
Finish // Hook of Holland
Distance // 298 miles (480km)

ÎLE DE RÉ AND ÎLE D'OLERON, FRANCE

These twin islands off the southern side of the Pertuis d'Antioche strait on France's Atlantic coast, promise family-friendly nirvana come summer. The cycling infrastructure on both islands is excellent, dotted with picture-perfect market villages, and wild and windswept beaches aplenty. Expect fine dining too: adults can enjoy fresh oysters and mussels, washed down with excellent wine. The islands offer all manner of loops, on both paved bike paths and forest tracks. Although the distances are short, give yourself up to five days to cross both islands at a family-friendly pace. The best access point is La Rochelle (reached by TGV from Paris), an appealing city to spend a day exploring, the outskirts of which are connected with the Île de Ré via a 2-mile (3km) bridge. Note that in July and August you'll be sharing the islands with many, many French families on school holiday. And don't forget to bring your kite, as it can get windy!

BASQUE COUNTRY, SPAIN

The lush and rugged Basque Country is nigh on perfect for families, thanks to its many bike paths and largely bike-tolerant drivers. Consider spending a couple of days in San Sebastián – both the beach and the bike paths are excellent – before striking south into the Sierra de Aralar, via a network of Vías Verdes (converted rail trails) that come replete with regular access to water. There are tunnels too, the longest almost 2 miles (3km) in length – sure to add to the fun. Expect to climb a steady 5000ft (1500m) to reach the higher spots within the Aralar Natural Park and bring your knobbly tyres as the terrain can be rugged in places. Five days should be enough time to create a circular loop into the mountains and back, though you can always hop on a train (children under five and bikes travel free of charge) if you need to shorten the trip. More info: www.viasverdes.com/.

Start/Finish // San Sebastián

© Cass Gilbert

RIDING INTO HISTORY ON WAYFARER PASS

Jack Thurston commemorates a pioneer of off-road cycling with a pass-storming day out on the Welsh 'rough stuff' where 'Wayfarer' first left the asphalt behind.

'We're not riding over that, are we?', asks Matt, looking up at the dark mass of the Berwyn range. 'But there's no road.' A glance at the map confirms this to be the case. We have just ridden up the Ceiriog Valley on a gently rolling minor road and are standing beneath a black-and-white painted fingerpost in the last village before the Berwyns. A pair of old drovers inns face each other across the road and a stream chuckles behind a low stone wall.

'This had better not be one of your roads to nowhere,' warns Matt, with an air of bitter experience of a long-suffering riding companion. It is true that I have a habit of spotting a promising-looking track that is good to begin with but ends up, miles further on, with the pair of us ankle deep in a muddy quagmire, shouldering our bikes across a vast field of tussocks or pushing through a thicket of brambles. On the map the paved road ends a mile beyond where we are standing and continues across the moor as a faint and uncertain-looking dotted red line. But on this occasion I know I'm on safe ground. The mountain track that awaits us has been a favourite among adventure-loving cyclists for more than a century.

'It'll be fine,' I assure him. 'At least it's not snowing.' Of course it's not snowing. It's midsummer. Matt shoots me a look, says nothing, and we get back to readying ourselves to go over the top.

Back in 1919, just months since the end of WWI, 'going over the top' had an altogether different, darker meaning. But this was also the title of a magazine article published that year describing a crossing of Berwyns by three intrepid cyclists from the Anfield Bicycle Club. The author was Walter MacGregor Robinson, a leading cycling journalist of the day who wrote under the pen-name of Wayfarer and had himself fought in the trenches of the Western Front. It was the last weekend in March and Wayfarer and his friends were riding the long way home after a Saturday club run. They stopped at an inn for the night with a plan to cross the Berwyns the next morning. During the night it snowed heavily. The locals warned them not to continue, but they decided to have a go. Clad in tweed jackets and plus fours the trio pushed, carried and very occasionally rode their fixed-wheel bicycles through the snowdrifts and over the mountain.

Their journey of 10 miles (16km) took four hours and Wayfarer's account of the ride inspired the interwar generation of British

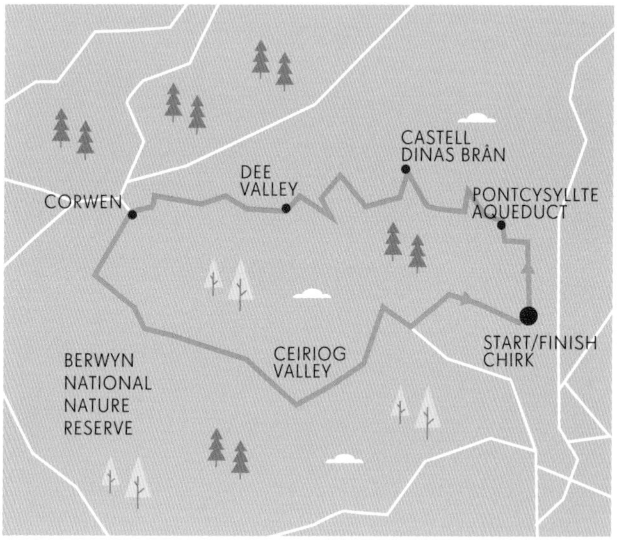

© Jack Thurston

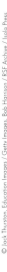

Clockwise from top: the author (left) at the Wayfarer Memorial; a Rough Stuff Fellowship archive shot; the Grouse Inn on the Dee river. Previous page: a spot of pass-storming

© Jack Thurston, Education Images / Getty Images, Bob Harrison / RSF Archive / Isola Press

cyclists to seek out the rougher, wilder ways. In 1955 a group of like-minded cyclists founded the Rough Stuff Fellowship as the world's first club devoted to off-road cycling. Wayfarer was one of their heroes, and when he died the following year they built a small memorial at the pass.

Matt and I pause at the memorial to take in the view of the long, winding track we've followed across the moor. It's an old drove road, and though its official name is Nant Rhyd Wilym, generations of British cyclists know it as 'the Wayfarer'. Even in midsummer it was rough going in places: loose stones, deep ruts, puddles the length of swimming pools and a treacherous section of wobbly railway sleepers.

"Clad in tweed, the trio pushed, carried and occasionally rode their fixed-wheel bicycles through the snowdrifts"

As we rode we heard nothing but the sounds of the hills – skylarks above, the wind through the moorland reeds and grasses, the trickle of a stream and the crunch of gravel under wheel. We had the mountain entirely to ourselves.

Though its heartlands are northern England, Wales and Scotland, members of the Rough Stuff Fellowship have explored the high mountain tracks of the Alps and were the first cyclists to cross Iceland and to reach Everest base camp. Rough stuff cycling – taking a bicycle on terrain beyond what it was designed for – has its absurd side but it's a kind of cycling that has adventure and camaraderie built in and there is no room for inflated egos.

Beside Wayfarer's memorial is a small metal box containing the Rough Stuff Fellowship visitors' book. Matt and I add our names to the thousands of others who have followed in Wayfarer's tyre tracks. The descent to the Dee Valley is on firm gravel and we drop like stones, reaching the road in no time. Matt stops, dismounts his bike and kneels down to kiss the tarmac. It feels good to be back on terra firma, but as Wayfarer reminded his readers, 'some of the best of cycling would be missed if one always had to be in the saddle or on a hard road'.

We ride on to Corwen and pick up the old stagecoach road that's now a quiet lane on the far side of the River Dee. We stop for lunch at the Grouse Inn, and bask in the sunshine on its terrace overlooking the river. A few miles later we're climbing again – up to the Panorama, a cracking road cut into the limestone crags above Llangollen. We pass close to the ruins of Castell Dinas Brân, a medieval castle built by Welsh princes on a narrow spur above the valley.

It's then another fast descent to the Pontcysyllte Aqueduct, a masterpiece in iron and stone designed by Thomas Telford that's the longest canal aqueduct in Britain and highest in the world. The canal towpath leads us all the way back to Chirk, a gentle way to round off a day out on the rough stuff. **JT**

PASS STORMING

Riding from one valley to another on rough, unsurfaced tracks was a popular pastime among cyclists of the 1930s and 1940s who challenged each other to seek out out ever wilder routes. Some of the classics have since been tarmacked, but there are still plenty of passes waiting to be stormed. Just get a map at a scale of 1:25,000 and find a pair of dead-end mountain roads linked by a track over the top.

TOOLKIT

Start/Finish // Chirk, Wales
Distance // 47 miles (75km)
How to get there // Chirk is 2 hours by train from Manchester, 3 hours from London.
When to ride // Easiest when dry in summer.
What to take // 35mm+ tyres; SPD or flat shoes.
Where to stay // Wayfarer and his friends stayed at the West Arms Hotel in Llanarmon Dyffryn Ceiriog, which is still a comfortable country inn.
What to read // The author's *Lost Lanes* series of cycling guide books. Also *The Rough-Stuff Fellowship Archive* (Isola Press).
More info // The Rough Stuff Fellowship https://rsf.org.uk; the Anfield Bicycle Club www.anfieldbc.co.uk; Club des Cent Cols www.centcols.org.

Opposite: Members of the Rough Stuff Fellowship on the Col du Bonhomme, in the French Alps, 1961

MORE LIKE THIS
ROUGH STUFF ROUTES

NORTHERN PENNINES, ENGLAND

The tarmac road up to the radar station on Great Dun Fell is the highest road in Britain and an epic climb in its own right. But it's just the beginning of a rough stuff odyssey over the roof of England. This is the Northern Pennines at its wildest and not for the faint-hearted. The tracks are rough, the wind can be terrifying, the peat moorland is as soggy as a wet sponge and there may be fords to wade across. But that just adds to the fun, right? Start from Knock and a mile short of the radar station, turn right on to the bridleway heading east along Troutbeck and an old mining track to the village of Garrigill where there's a great pub. For the return take the old corpse road over Cross Fell, past Greg's Hut mountain bothy and down to Kirkland.
Start/Finish // Knock
Distance // 29 miles (46km)

MASTILES LANE, YORKSHIRE

There's no landscape quite like the Yorkshire Dales, with its rare limestone geology and pretty farmland defined by neat dry stone walls and sturdy stone barns. It's a joy to explore by bike, and both on road and off there are plenty of tracks. The porous limestone helps keep them relatively dry and rideable, even after heavy rain. Mastiles Lane, on the uplands between Ribblesdale and Wharfedale, is a perfect introduction to rough stuff. It's steeped in history. In medieval times it was part of an important long-distance route used by the monks of Fountains Abbey to travel to their estates in the Lake District, while the remnants of a Roman marching camp suggest much older origins. The track runs for 5 miles (8km) between Malham Tarn and the village of Kilnsey and is easiest ridden west to east; it can be incorporated into a longer ride, which could be almost anywhere in the Dales.
Start // Malham Tarn
Finish // Kilnsey
Distance // 5 miles (8km)

COL DU PARPAILLON, FRANCE

Members of the Rough Stuff Fellowship toured extensively in the Alps and the Col du Parpaillon in the southern French Alps is rideable rough stuff that's a firm favourite among adventurous cyclists. For many years it was the highest road in France and somehow it escaped the asphalt. It's a harsh mountain environment and there can still be snow in June so late summer is the safest time to ride. From Embrun the climb is 17 miles (28 km) long with 6200ft (1900m) of ascent. The final third is unpaved and at the limit of what you can ride on a road bike. At the top an unlit 1600ft (500m) long tunnel makes for an eerie climax to the ascent – so pack a torch. Either return the way you came, or for a big loop descend the eastern side and return via the paved Col de Vars.
Start/Finish // Embrun
Distance // 34 miles (56km) there and back; big loop 63 miles (102km)

© Bob Harrison / RSF Archive / Isola Press

A BALTIC ODYSSEY

Between Berlin and Copenhagen lies a journey past lakes and through ancient forests, across the sea to the rugged islands of Denmark.

Turning down a forest path, I see something large start to move, a bird spreading giant wings and fanning the ground. As it gains height and flies off into the nearby pine foliage, I realise I have just seen my first-ever wild eagle. It wasn't going to be the only one I saw on my journey.

The coniferous woodlands in which I had the good fortune of spotting this great raptor run the length of the German leg of the epic journey between Berlin and Copenhagen. Once you leave the concrete metropolis of Berlin, and pass the surrounding towns, this inter-capital, cultural highway leads you through protected nature reserves and rich woodlands, down by sprawling lakesides, across the sea, through age-old Norse villages, and along stunning coastal routes. You mount your bike by Berlin's central and most critical landmark, Brandenburg Gate, and finally dismount in the modern, bustling centre of Denmark's capital.

The route itself is just a small part of the much larger, transcontinental bike superhighway, the EuroVelo 7 'Sun Route', and is, for the most part, an off-road, dedicated bike path. On the German leg, the route veers off on to woodland paths, through canopies of pine and birch, and flowing fields threaded with rows of wind turbines, apparently sprouting through the earth.

I'd lived in Berlin for over 10 years before deciding to follow my heart, and the signs pointing the way to Denmark. At a leisurely pace, I recommend taking around 15 days to enjoy the trip. But knowing myself, my biking speed, and the absence of inclines on the route, I decided to make it in a week.

Along the Havel river I rode, towards the Baltic Sea, and after my first sighting of one of Germany's most majestic of birds (along with assorted woodpeckers, hawks, and plenty of long-legged

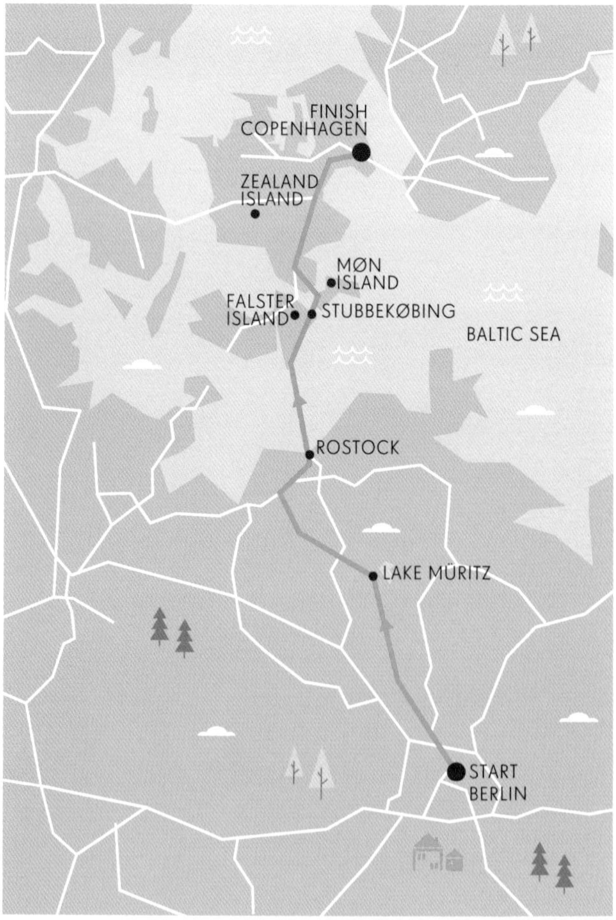

© thesouthcoastofdenmark.com

storks coming home to roost), I arrive at Waren on the picturesque Lake Müritz, and one of the most modern campsites I've ever visited. With sockets at every pitch, WiFi throughout, and of course hot showers, it's the perfect place to recharge. Waren sits in the heart of the area's veritable lake district, which spreads out across 2300 square miles (6000 sq km). Here fresh-water fish abound, smoked, baked, or grilled, with a variety of potato salads, and German pickled vegetables. I grab a baked zander with potato salad, along with a beer from the tap, as appetising as they come.

Reaching the port of Rostock, I line my bike up next to the freight and traffic to board the ferry to Denmark. The crossing takes just two hours, but in that small amount of time the world around you transforms. Emerging from the ferry into the tiny port of Gedser, the immediate contrasts in character and landscape are apparent. Here the ever-present forest is gone, replaced with a salt-stained Baltic air, flat landscapes, and small farmhouses with thatched roofs and horses with manes that droop down in front of their eyes.

The Nordic landscape is a serene green beneath a steel sky. Snapping across the horizon are triangular, red and white Danish flags proudly waving from the top of anything that's standing. The Scandinavian weather becomes a new character to accompany you along your ride, changing moods depending on which way the wind decides to blow.

Journeying around the wooded coastline of the island of Falster I pass cottages and stark beaches. Here I camped at the old industrial port town of Stubbekøbing, and wondered where everybody was, while I enjoyed a picnic, attempted to coax a wild hedgehog to join my party of one and watched the late sunset across the water. The distances between major towns on the Berlin to Copenhagen bike route leads to many such moments, when

"Fresh-water fish abound in Lake Müritz. I grab a baked zander with potato salad, and a beer from the tap"

PRUSSIAN PALATIAL DETOUR

The German state of Brandenburg is littered with picturesque royal relics from the 18th century, of which Prussian King Frederick the Great was particularly fond. Rheinsberg Palace is one of Frederick's most beautiful getaways, and is a brief 12-mile detour from Wentow. Bask in the regal gardens, walk around the moat and soak up the architecture from this prime period of Renaissance-imperialism, and explore its treasured artworks.

Clockwise from above: Copenhagen waterfront; Klink castle near Waren, northern Germany; the Danish coastline; baked zander. Previous page: a detour to Dybsø fjord, Denmark

© Food Centrale Hamburg GmbH / Alamy Stock Photo, RicoK / Alamy Stock Photo

© Atlantide Phototravel / Getty Images, ALLTRAVEL / Alamy Stock Photo

the beauty of the natural surroundings are most apparent. On average, 7000 bikers make this pilgrimage every year, according to the owner of a cafe and hostel in the Danish village of Praestø, which specifically caters to riders on this route. In late May, however, I only meet a handful.

With the solitude comes history, ancient and slightly more recent. The near-Tolkienesque Danish islands of Falster, Møn, and Zealand offer some striking juxtapositions: Bronze Age burial sites face across the water from the chalky white facade of the Kalvehave church, built in the 13th century. Fishing harbours line the coastline, and shingle beaches lie beneath the cliffs that dominate the coastline.

On day seven, after camping just outside the Danish capital, I embark on my final stretch, cruising by the beach and past the modern harbours, galleries, and suburban estates that lie on the city's outer edge. A sense of accomplishment sweeps over me, as a week-long cross-country exodus comes to an end. Almost 430 miles (690km) north of where I started, I cycle in over one of Copenhagen's many bridges, past the Royal Library to City Hall Square, falling in with the many bikers that make up the city's commuters. Copenhagen is just the place to finish a long bike ride, emerging from a period of contented solitude to one of blissful joy, in a cultured city that loves cycling as much as I do. **DC**

TOOLKIT

Start // Brandenburg Gate, Berlin
Finish // City Hall, Copenhagen
Distance // 404 miles (630km)
Where to stay // There are plenty of campsites en route. Bespoke biking accommodation available with Bett+Bike (www.bettundbike.de).
When to ride // Between June and September, although it's feasible year round as long as it isn't snowing.
What to take // With no hills to tackle, an ample touring bike will suffice, along with waterproofs and sunscreen. It can be many miles between stops and villages, so always stock up on water and food, especially if you're camping.
More info // www.bike-berlin-copenhagen.com/

Opposite: island hopping along the coast of Norway

MORE LIKE THIS NORTHERN EPICS

BALTIC SEA ROUTE, DENMARK

If Berlin to Copenhagen has whetted your appetite, here's another Baltic adventure. It's a breathtaking round-trip that spreads out from Jutland across all the islands of Funen, Zealand, Møn, Lolland, Falster, Fyn, Lillebælt and back again. Hugging the coastline all the way, this escapade brings you face-to-face with the Baltic at every turn, providing epic views, lush forest paths, yet more history, brisk salt air, and a sailor's selection of fresh fish at every stop off. Regarded as one of the most spectacular bike journeys, the Sea Route is a vibrant mix of natural wonder and heritage, accessible to pretty much every ability of cycling enthusiasts – as long as you don't mind a strong head wind along your way.

Start/Finish // Padborg
Distance // 510 miles (820 km)

ATLANTIC COAST ROUTE, NORWAY

Not only epic, but also immensely challenging and time consuming, the Atlantic Coast Route hugs almost the entirety of the Norwegian coast from Bergen to the very tip of the Arctic Circle. This stunning ride along the EuroVelo1 bike route will challenge your soul and enrich your life, with plentiful views of fjords and dramatic coastline scenery. For those who don't have an entire month or more to commit to such a challenge, then, about 300 miles (480km) north of Bergen, there's the Atlantic Road, a smaller 50-mile (80km) stretch between Kristiansund and Bud, that takes you through a tunnel literally under the ocean, across some outstandingly designed bridges, and Norway's most striking islands and nature points.

Start // Bergen
Finish // The North Cape
Distance // 1555 miles (2500 km)

THE ROMANTIC ROAD, GERMANY

A journey through the very heart of Germany, from the centre of Bavaria down to the foot of the Alps, where you can almost touch the Austrian border. As the name suggests, the route has an obvious appeal, full of Bavarian character. The beginning is easily in reach of Frankfurt, and the route follows the Tauber River before crossing the Danube, leading up to the Alps. An easy-going ride along which you can sample some of the best, local wines, meats and see some of the country's more legendary castles – including the notorious, fairytale-esque Neuschwanstein Schloss – before arriving at Füssen, which lies at just under 1000m (3280ft) above sea level. From here you can journey on across the border and challenge yourself to Alpine rides, or just relax with a finely brewed German beer.

Start // Würzburg
Finish // Füssen
Distance // 274 miles (440 km)

© Per Kvalvik

A CULTURED CRUISE FROM COPENHAGEN

Be a Dane for a day on this leisurely coastal spin out of one of the world's most bike-friendly cities to Denmark's must-see Louisiana Museum of Modern Art.

Riding over Knippelsbro Bridge, with views of copper-roofed Christiansborg Palace, the Danish parliament, from the island of Christianshavn in central Copenhagen, it seemed as if I had slipped into a parallel universe; a City of the Cyclists, in which bicycles ruled the roads and unhurried riders glided like shoals of fish through the city. And this little fish, relishing the freedom, couldn't wipe the grin from his face.

Laid out over a series of islands, Denmark's capital is the most bike-friendly place I have pedalled. Some streets see 30,000 cyclists per day; and dedicated traffic signals and junctions, cycle lanes separated by kerbs from cars, and supersized bikeways all help to keep them moving safely. Indeed, in 2015 the city opened an aerial bikeway, the *cykelslangen*, swooping above the harbour and a shopping mall.

Here, a bicycle is the best way to encounter the fun-loving side of Copenhagen, from the cafe-backed beach park at Amager to the parks and gardens of Frederiksberg. Architecture fans can pedal down Ørestads Blvd for Jean Nouvel's blue-clad concert hall, food-lovers can tootle along the canals of Christianshavn, home to numerous cafes and restaurants (and Noma's newest little sister, 108). Danes cycle to work, they cycle to school and they cycle to bars and parties.

But, irresistible though the city is on two wheels, I have an out-of-town trip in mind: a 25-mile (40km) or two-hour jaunt north along the Danish Riviera to the Louisiana Museum of Modern Art, near Helsingør (Elsinore), where castle Kronborg was the setting for Shakespeare's *Hamlet*.

Before I plan my route, though, I have a coffee with photographer-turned-bicycle-ambassador Mikael Colville-

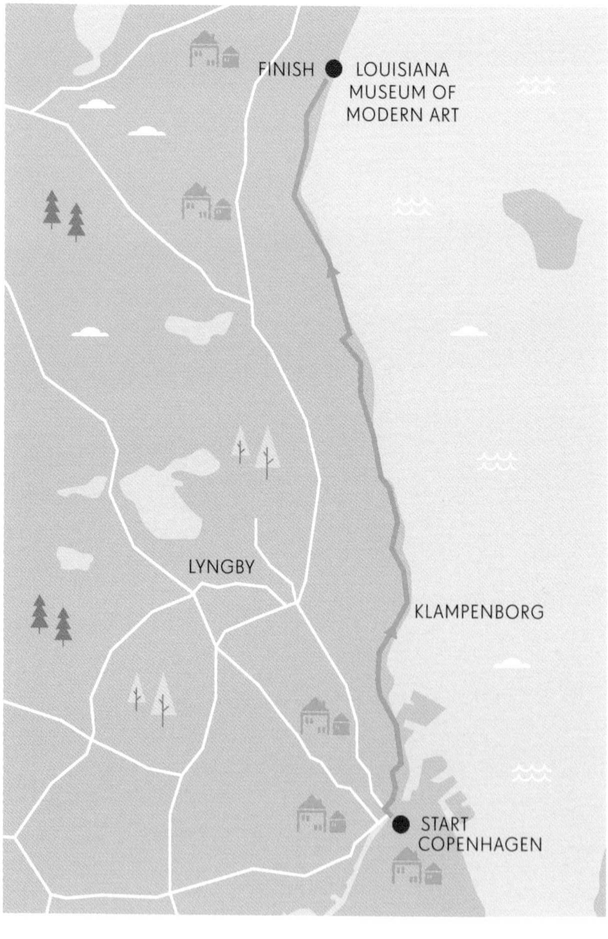

© Sarah Coghill / Lonely Planet

S.A.98

Andersen, who agrees cycling is a quick entry point into a country's culture. 'If you're standing shoulder to shoulder with 100 cyclists at a red light, smelling the perfume of the person next to you, that contributes to a sense of community.'

Danes pedal with panache: women wear heels and skirts, men sport suits. 'Anything you can walk in, you can cycle in,' says Mikael. Few wear helmets, feeling as safe on their bikes as they do on foot or in a car, and none break the rules – I spy not a single red-light jumper. Danes ride all year round ('Viking biking' Mikael calls it), easily navigating the city, in wind, rain or sun, on robust town bikes.

'Bicycles are like vacuum cleaners in Denmark', Mikael tells me, 'we all have one and we all use them every day but we don't think about them all day, we don't have ten of them, and we don't polish them; it's a tool.'

The next day I borrow one of these tools from a friend in Frederiksberg and set off on my Danish Riviera trip, starting with a big breakfast. Lying at the end of a cobbled lane next to a canal and embodying the Danish concept of *hygge* (warmth and wellbeing), Parterre satiates with avocado on rye toast, skyr with muesli, and fresh-baked pastries.

At the far end of Christianshavn and its colourful canal-side buildings is Copenhagen's landmark opera house. Once you've taken a spin around the island and some photos, head back

"It was no longer unusual to see somebody pedalling a cargo bike with their dog in the front"

onto Torvegade, Christianshavn's main road, and over the Knippelsbro Bridge.

From here, I jump onto Bredgade and turn north through the city, cruising past the star-shaped Kastellet fort.

The roads are busy but cyclists have a segregated path to themselves. I remember Mikael's most important point of etiquette and keep to the right side of the lane so faster cyclists, or at least those who know where they are going, pass me to the left. Young or old, male or female, it seemed that everybody was on a bicycle and moving along with an elegant efficiency. It was no longer unusual to see somebody pedalling a cargo bike with their dog in the front, or breeze around a corner, head up, skirt billowing.

Eventually the city's industrial zone peters out, to be replaced by a marina. This is where navigation becomes a cinch: just keep the sea to your right. Soon, the bike path runs alongside the waterfront: on the other side of the stretch of sea lies Sweden.

This is the start of the Danish Riviera. When the sun is out, the

© Michal Krakowiak / Getty Images, Visions Of Our Land / Getty Images

CHRISTIANIA

Christianshavn is also home to Christiania, the alternative enclave and self-proclaimed 'free state', known over the years as a marketplace for cannabis (and police raids). Epic Rides readers will, naturally, be more interested to learn the place has lent its name to a range of practical cargo bikes, in which Danes ferry their groceries and families. Christiania is also the only place where unusual upright Pedersen bicycles are made (and can be bought at www.pedersen-bike.dk).

From left: cycling Danish-style; Copenhagen's Opera House; graffiti explodes across a wall in Christiania; Superkilen public park in Copenhagen. Previous page: Nyhavn waterfront in Copenhagen

clear blue water is speckled with white sails and slowly turning wind turbines. But in overcast weather, the view can be as gloomy as a Scandinavian detective drama. I pedal on, my heavy town bike dictating the sedate pace, though unimpeded by any hills. I roll through Klampenborg, a low-rise village with yachts moored just beyond the sea wall, then through Taarbæk and Skodsborg, the sea always just a few metres off my right shoulder. Bike Route 9 seeks out more traffic-free paths and lanes.

The signposts suggest that I'm nearing my destination, the Louisiana Museum of Modern Art, a long and low white building best known for its collection of works by Alberto Giacometti. Louisiana was founded by Knud Jensen in 1958 – his original intention was to display Danish art, but he soon changed direction and decided to promote international art in Denmark.

I park my bike outside – I'm not the only person to have cycled here – and go exploring. Louisiana's best feature is a seafront sculpture garden, featuring works by Henry Moore and Joan Miró. It's a sunny day and families picnic on the lawns, dabbling in the sea and running around the sculptures.

As the afternoon passes, I begin to think about getting back to Copenhagen. I cycle to the local railway station and jump on a S-Train from Humlebæk to Nørreport station in central Copenhagen with my bicycle – simple, sensible, practical. So very Danish. **RB**

TOOLKIT

Start // Copenhagen
Finish // Louisiana Museum of Modern Art, Humlebæk
Distance // About 25 miles (40km) one-way
Getting there // Fly to Copenhagen international airport; there are easy-to-navigate rail services into the city centre.
Where to stay // City-centre hotels, hostels and B&Bs.
Bike share // From 125 bike-sharing stations and also rail stations, such as Osterport (www.rentabike.dk). Bycyklen bikes (www.bycyklen.dk/en; from 36kr per hour) with GPS screens are available. For cargo bikes (and normal bikes) try www.christianiacykler.dk in Christiania.
What to take // Wet weather gear.
More info // Maps of cycle routes from tourist information offices: www.visitcopenhagen.com. Louisiana (www.louisiana.dk) is open 11am-10pm Tue-Fri, to 6pm Sat and Sun.

© Pierre Aden / Getty Images, Terry Mclaughlin @asteryx / copenhagenmediacenter.com

Opposite: Vélib' riders plot a route in Paris

MORE LIKE THIS
CITY SPINS

PARIS, FRANCE

The Vélib' Métropole (*vélo liberté*, bicycle freedom) bike-share scheme was one of the first and it recently introduced an electric bike into its range. But serious disruption to the service following a change of operator a few years ago dismayed locals and tourists alike, and allowed private bike-hire competitors to challenge its preeminence. Yet Paris is still trying hard to make cyclists welcome: the Champs Élysées and roads in arrondissements 1-4 of the city centre, including those along the Seine, are closed to motor vehicles one Sunday each month; yes, that includes the Louvre and Jardin des Tuileries. One great route is to follow the 3-mile (4.8km) Canal St-Martin from République to Quai de Valmy pausing at cafes for *ravitaillement* (refreshment) as required. You can continue to follow canals, such as Canal de l'Ourcq, for as far as you want.
Start // République
Finish // Quai de Valmy
Distance // 3 miles (4.8km)

BARCELONA, SPAIN

By fringing its medieval streets with a modern maze of bike lanes (130 miles/209km of them), Barcelona has evolved into a cycling city in the last decade. Its 'Bicing' scheme is for local inhabitants (there are over 100,000 subscribers and last year the city successfully introduced a new generation of bikes) – but bike-hire facilities and cycle-tour experiences are ubiquitous. Take a spin to Montjuïc Castle, a 17th-century hilltop fortress and former prison with spectacular city and sea views, or do an urban loop from Plaça Catalunya, through the Barri Gòtic, past Santa Maria del Mar to Ciutadella Park. Ride up passeigs de Lluís Companys and de Sant Joan, under the Arc de Triomf and swing a right to the Sagrada Família at Gran Via, before returning via La Casa Batlló and La Rambla.
Start/Finish // Plaça Catalunya
Distance // 5 miles (9km)

AMSTERDAM, THE NETHERLANDS

Bikes form part of the fabric of Amsterdam, possibly the planet's most cycle-friendly capital. Each day, 400,000 riders trundle along 319 miles (513km) of dedicated cycle paths, which wend around every corner and canal in this 17th-century city. Unsurprisingly, the city and its surrounds are as flat as a Dutch pancake, so cycling is easy. Bikes in the Dam are typically low-slung cruising machines, ridden with a jaunty upright gait. Pedal around the city centre, taking in the main sights, or loop out along the banks of the River Amstel to Ouderkerk aan de Amstel, before riding to Abcoude and the fortress town of Weesp, via the Bullewijk, Waver, Winkel and Gein rivers. Then trace the River Vecht to Castle Muiderslot, passing through Diemerpark, back to the centre.
Start/Finish // Amsterdam Centraal train station
Distance // 28 miles (46km)

© Fabrice LEROUGE / Getty Images

LIGNE
N°4
CITÉ
LIGNE
N°4

GOD'S OWN RIDE

This 110-mile loop around Yorkshire is beautiful, but a bit of a bugger, says Helen Pidd – just ask the professionals, who tackled the same climbs in the 2014 Tour de France

Alpe d'Huez, Mont Ventoux… le Côte de Buttertubs? Le Côte de Blubberhouses? The riders in the 2014 Tour de France must have thought the organisers were having a laugh when they saw the names of the climbs in the opening chapters of that year's edition. Most had probably not even heard of Yorkshire, and yet, after a spectacular lobbying effort from the local tourist board, stages 1 and 2 of the world's biggest cycle race came to the self-styled God's Own County for 'the grandest Grand Départ in Tour history.'

I was on top of Buttertubs Pass, fortified with Wensleydale cheese and Black Sheep beer, when Jens Voigt crested first in what was to become the German's final Tour de France. We'd made a proper effort to welcome him, writing 'Ey-up!' and 'Chuffing 'eck' on the road in chalk, wearing flat caps and waving walking sticks as he passed.

A few years later it is me crossing the cattlegrid at the top of Buttertubs, heart pounding, eyes stinging from sweat trickling down my forehead. There is no one to cheer me on, just a few bored-looking sheep and the voice in my head wondering if I'd bitten off more than I could chew when I signed up for the Etape du Dales a few months previously.

The 110-mile (177km) sportive was established on Britain's cycling calendar long before the French were seduced by Yorkshire's lumps and bumps. A beautiful if brutal tour of the toughest climbs in the Yorkshire Dales, it uses roads so quiet that there's not a single traffic light en route. (You can ride the route any time free of charge; the sportive raises money for the Dave Rayner Fund, which supports young cyclists at the start of their professional careers.)

I'd been pressured into it by some of the more relentless

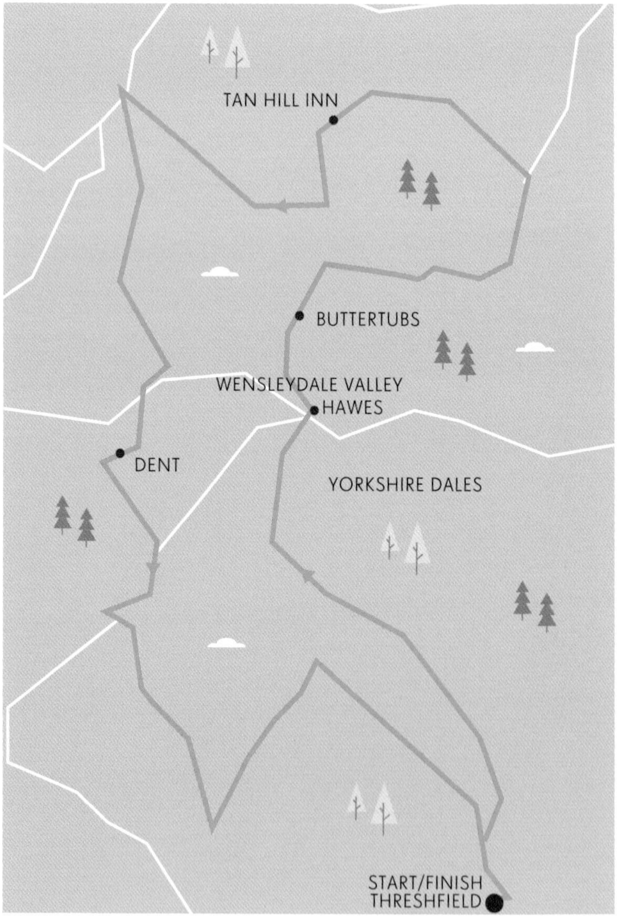

Plus Sports Images / Alamy Stock Photo

MOBBERLEY

members of my ladies-only cycling club, who were fed up entering events and being the only women on the road.

The adventure begins in Threshfield, nine miles north of Skipton. It follows the Tour de France route – and indeed sections of the path of 2019's rain-lashed UCI World Championship men's road race – until Buckden, where the organisers clearly decided the professionals had it far too easy and send us left towards Fleet Moss instead. More seasoned cyclists in my group insist we are going up Yorkshire's highest road the 'easy way', south to north, but my thighs are still screaming when we finally reach the top, the agony numbed by the sight of the glorious Wensleydale valley and the town of Hawes.

There is no time, alas, to sample the famous cheese, nor to visit one of Yorkshire's best chip shops, the majestic Hawes Chippie, and certainly not to pop into the town's bookshop, once notorious for having the grumpiest owner in Britain. We have to digest Buttertubs next, the name a pleasing reminder of bygone days, when farmers stored butter in cool craters on the moors while resting on their way to Wensleydale market.

The pain is all worth it for the view of the next valley: Swaledale, the most rugged in all the Yorkshire Dales. We pass stone barns

"Buttertubs may only have a fifth of the altitude of the Col de la Bonette – but it goes straight up and down dale"

and tinkling brooks, inhaling the perfume of wild flowers, then head for the highest pub in England, the Tan Hill Inn. Never before have I worked so hard to get a cup of Yorkshire Tea, after a sudden 50mph (80kmh) headwind turns the seven-mile (11km) climb into an hour-long ordeal. At the pub feed station, riders look shell-shocked, cheeks burnt by the gale, already planning how to excuse their slow time on Strava.

I just want to avoid being forced into the broom wagon, rationalising the torture by remembering the shock of some of the best climbers in the pro peloton who came to Yorkshire with their biggest chainrings, thinking England was flat. Yes, Buttertubs (1726ft, 526m) has a fifth of the altitude of the Col de la Bonette (9193ft, 2802m). But Yorkshire folk are famously tight with their wallets – and their tarmac. Why build a set of switchbacks when you can save money building a road straight up and down dale?

© RacingSnakes.com

YORKSHIRE DELICACIES

Hawes is the home of Yorkshire Wensleydale Cheese, a crumbly, creamy delicacy made famous by the Wallace and Gromit animated films. The Wensleydale Creamery has an interactive museum and a shop selling 20 varieties, with free samples. Before you fill your boots, remember that in a few miles you will be faced with an appropriately named climb that could make all that dairy come back to haunt you: Buttertubs Pass.

From left: the first climb of the Etape du Dales, Halton Gill; the highest pub in England, Tan Hill Inn, Swaledale. Previous page: the 2014 Tour de France peloton is welcomed on 'le Côte de Buttertubs'

A case in point: the Coal Road, from Garsdale Head over to lovely little Dent. Sounds innocuous enough, but it is, to use the local parlance, a bit of a bugger, soaring straight up 219m in just 2.3km. Soon the same blokes who had patronised me earlier for my triple chainset are walking, ruining their cleats on the vertiginous asphalt. Thanks to my lovely low gears I stay on the bike and am rewarded at the summit with my favourite view of the day, across to the higher Lake District hills, before passing England's highest railway station at Dent.

Almost ten hours after I left Threshfield, I am finally done – literally and metaphorically, after more than 10000ft (3048m) of climbing. I foolishly rehydrate on Black Sheep ale and am drunk after two pints, cheering like a loon when my friend Carol staggers in to the race HQ with her arms aloft. She has finished 36 seconds inside the 12-hour time limit, and proceeds to down a pint of ale with her helmet on.

A few months later she leads 20 women from our club on the same route, but over two days, stopping over at the back-to-basics youth hostel in Hawes. They have time for a chippie tea and an argument with the angry bookseller and can still boast that they rode some of the Tour de France – in Yorkshire. **HP**

TOOLKIT

Start/Finish // Threshfield, near Grassington
Distance // 110 miles (177km)
Getting there // Skipton railway station is 8.7 miles (14km) from Threshington.
When to ride // May to October. Some of the climbs are prone to ice and snow in the winter months.
What to take // Layers, water and plenty of snacks: there are long sections nowhere near a shop.
Where to stay // Rent a stone cottage or stay in a B&B – book well in advance if you are doing the sportive.
More info // www.etapedudales.org

© Justin Foulkes / Lonely Planet

Opposite: changing down a gear for the horribly steep Hardknott Pass on the Fred Whitton Challenge

MORE LIKE THIS
SADISTIC BRITISH SPORTIVES

FRED WHITTON CHALLENGE

Probably the most notorious of the UK's sportives, the 'Fred' takes riders on a very painful but very beautiful 112-mile (180km) tour of the Lake District. It starts and finishes in the village of Grasmere and includes all of the Lakeland passes: Kirkstone, Honister, Newlands, Whinlatter, Hardknott and Wrynose. Hardknott is as tough as its name suggests, with even hard nuts being forced to push on the steepest sections. Keep an ear out for bell ringers at the top of Whinlatter: if you can hear them clang, the top is not too far away. The ride commemorates a popular member of the Lakes Road Club, which organises the ride each May. The fastest riders complete the Fred in under six hours but times of 11 hours and over are not uncommon for the average sportive rider.
Start/Finish // Grasmere, the Lake District
Distance // 112 miles (180km)

CHESHIRE COBBLED CLASSIC

Nicknamed 'The Bastard' by many who have attempted it, the Cheshire Cobbled Classic is a dastardly 67-mile (107km) sportive in the Peak District. It features 12 cobbled sectors, including five cobbled climbs that exceed 20% in gradient. Most fearsome is the dreaded Corkscrew, which includes a near-impossible section at 45%. The path, inaccessible by cars, is what's left of an ancient cart track once used by donkeys transporting salt from nearby mines to the docks at Manchester. Among those who have been forced to get off and push is Olympic champion Owain Doull, who won gold for Great Britain in the velodrome in Rio. Do not attempt this unless you have very low gearing and can unclip from your pedals in a split second, and do accept that you will have to leave your dignity at the start-line. More info: https://cycleclassics.co.uk.
Start/Finish // Lyme Park, Cheshire
Distance // 67 miles (107km)

WELSH DRAGON RIDE

Claiming to be the UK's toughest sportive, the Welsh Dragon Ride offers four different distances, the hardest being the 186-mile (300km) Devil, which can take participants over 15 hours to complete. Satan makes a number of appearances, mocking you up the 10.3% Devil's Elbow and the even harder Devil's Staircase, which rises up from the gorgeous Abergwesyn Pass in Powys and includes a section at 25%. Despite 16,400ft (5000m) of climbing, you will need to maintain an average speed of 20kmh/13mph to avoid the broom wagon. The Dragon Ride was started in 2004 by an Italian, Lou Lusardi, who wanted to introduce the Gran Fondo concept to the UK. Only 280 riders took part in the first edition in 2004; now over 5000 cyclists ride each year. More info: www.dragonride.co.uk/.
Start/Finish // Margam Country Park near Port Talbot
Distance // 186 miles (300km)

© STEPHEN FLEMING / Alamy Stock Photo

WEST CORK'S WILD COAST

Jasper Winn cycles above cliffs, around peninsulas and beside beaches along West Cork's coastline to discover big Atlantic seascapes, a maze of country lanes, and whales.

When I'm back home in County Cork and feel like a break I'll often stuff a sleeping bag, a few harmonicas, some rain gear and a pair of sunglasses into my bike's venerable panniers and pedal west for a week or so. I'm prepared for all weathers, ready to join in pub music sessions and able to sleep out if that's the way things go. Navigation? All I have to do is keep the sea on my left. It's an easy approach to cycle touring.

Three times, so far, I've ridden the 186 miles (300km) between Clonakilty and the tip of the Beara Peninsula to the west, following in the tyre tracks of Irish travel writer Peter Somerville-Large. In the snows, rains and wind of early 1970 Somerville-Large set off on a 3-speed bike, carrying a canvas tent and an umbrella, to research his book *The Coast of West Cork*. His writing ranges across history, conjuring up cattle raids, sword-'n'-shield battles, pirate fleets and eccentric landowners, as he pedals between ancient ring forts, medieval castles, ruined manor houses and village ports. Cycling half a century ago he describes a rural Ireland still focused on small farms and close-tied villages. Food then was, by his account, far from inspiring.

Cyclists in West Cork today – far better fed – can still enjoy the meandering spirit of Somerville-Large's inspiring trip, not least

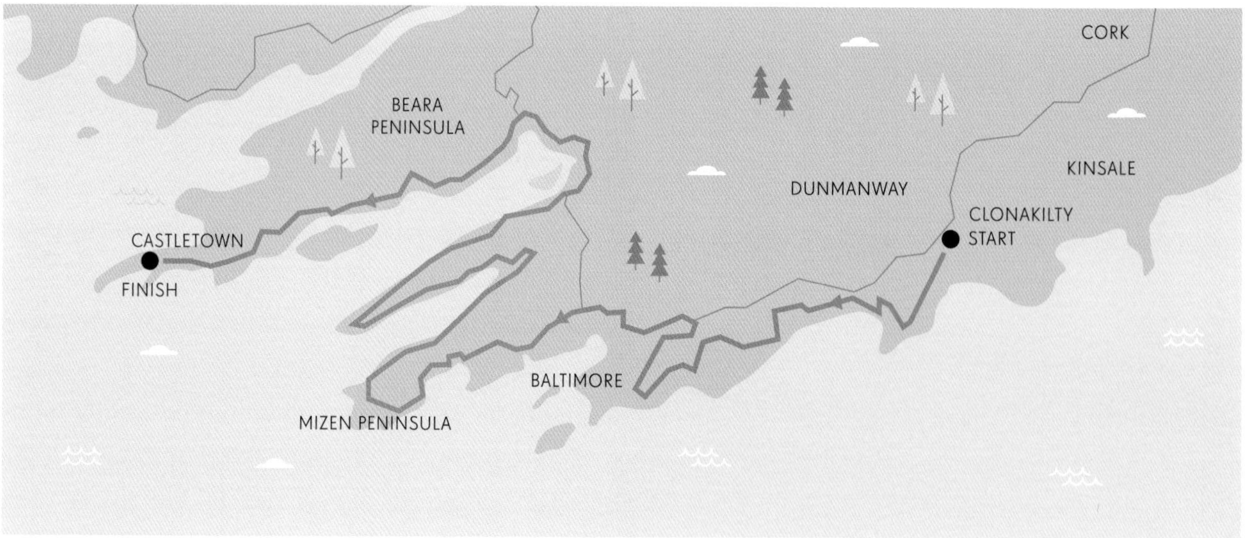

© jackie ellis / Alamy Stock Photo, hughrylands / 500px

An Teach Beag
GUINNESS
GACH LÁ

because the small roads of coastal West Cork now form the most southerly section of the Wild Atlantic Way, a 1533-mile (2500km) 'signed route' designed to lure travellers off busy arterial roads and into the quiet veins and capillaries – the country roads and *boreens* (lanes) – that network the 'Next Stop America' seaboard of Ireland's west.

West Cork attracts and rewards cyclists of all stamps. A peloton of hard-cranking English friends raced the route from west to east in miserable summer weather that drove them into one pub after another for shelter; they loved it. At different times I've lent an old single-speed bike, and the Somerville-Large book, to a guitar-toting Frenchman, to an Israeli student and to a German woman. Each disappeared for a week or two and each had totally different adventures; one sitting in with musicians and cycling from gig to gig, another camping out on remote beaches cooking self-caught fish, and the third island-hopping across Roaringwater Bay before ending up in a Buddhist retreat centre on the Beara.

It's all about the quality of the distractions rather than the mileage, I reckon. Will Clonakilty's street music, or guitar- or cycling festivals change your plans? Will you be tempted by country-market day in any one of the towns along the coast, with stalls of local cheeses, home-baked breads, organic vegetables and cakes? Or a day heading out to sea on a whale-watching boat? An evening sea-kayak trip while phosphorescence lights up the waters? A pub lock-in, as accordions, fiddles, pipes and banjos pepper the air with machine-gun-fast riffs? Things happen when moving at pedal-speed in West Cork.

On the most recent of my cycle 'de-tours' – so-called because of their haphazard nature – to the Beara, I started by riding through a chill autumn night to watch the dawn sun rise over the eastern sea and light up the miniature Stonehenge of Drombeg Stone Circle. Then I freewheeled – mostly – down to Union Hall for a full-Irish breakfast in The Coffee Shop. Bacon, sausages, eggs, toast, and famed Clonakilty black pudding, as well as apple

WHALE WATCHING

Harbour porpoise, common and bottlenose dolphin are present year round in West Cork, blue whale and orca are rare sightings, but it's the minke, fin and humpback whales that are the real attraction. Though they can sometimes be seen from high cliffs with binoculars, for the full marine Jurassic Park experience take a specialist boat trip (www.whalewatchwestcork.com) to get out among the whales as they lunge, dive and breach spectacularly while feeding.

Clockwise from top: Bantry Bay and the town; near Crookhaven, on the Mizen Peninsula. Previous page: Guinness for strength, in Clonakilty; the coastline of West Cork

© Rick Marshall, David Naton Photography / Alamy Stock Photo

tart: the heavy fuel I needed for a day of grinding up hill after hill.

As always, I was making route choices as I rode. If the early morning sun hadn't given way to drizzle, I'd have cycled on to Baltimore to take the ferry across to Cape Clear Island, where Irish is spoken, traditional jigs and reels (Irish folk dancing) played, and I could have pedalled out to the seaward cliffs, where I'd been told there was a good chance of seeing a pod of minke whales feeding close inshore. But with visibility poor I headed around Roaringwater Bay, across the Mizen and onto Sheep's Head instead. By evening I was sitting in a friend's clifftop cabin sipping tea and watching the sunset.

For cyclists, the Sheep's Head is like the whole coast of West Cork, or even the Wild Atlantic Way, in miniature. A coast-teasing 50-mile (80km) circuit following small roads, many so little used they have a strip of grass down their centre. Big cliffs and, in storms, even bigger seas. Hidden stone circles, smaller than Drombeg. Pubs where conversation easily sparks into song. The 'needle-to-an-anchor' old-style shop, post office and sometime wine bar that is J F O'Mahony's in Kilcrohane. Few cars. Perfect riding country.

The next morning from the Sheep's Head I could see the length of the Beara Peninsula far across Bantry Bay. On a big-engined rigid-inflatable boat you'd be across, tip to tip, in 20 minutes, but by bike there's another couple of relaxed days to go, and more distractions. Bantry, with its Friday market. Cafes in touristy Glengarriff. The Caha and Slieve Mishkish mountains inland, Hungry Hill wreathed in cool mist. A pint of Beamish in MacCarthy's in Castletownbere, enjoyed among fishing crews from half a dozen nations' trawlers. Then the long haul to the peninsula's end, cranking out mile after mile, until finally there was only air and water ahead and I'd run out of land. All I had to do now was turn around and head back home. This time keeping the sea on my right. **JW**

"I'd been told there was a good chance of seeing a pod of minke whales feeding close inshore"

TOOLKIT

Start // Clonakilty
Finish // The tip of Beara Peninsula
Distance // 186 miles (300km)
Getting there // Fly to Cork Airport, cycle 12 miles (20km) to Kinsale and you're on the Wild Atlantic Way. Irish buses will usually take one, maximum two, bikes if there's room.
Bike hire // O'Donovan Cycles in Bantry (www.bikenbeara.ie/hire.php) offers rental bikes. See also www.ireland.com/what-is-available/cycling/bike-rental/destinations/republic-of-ireland/cork/all.
When to ride // Early autumn offers good weather, enough evening light, open restaurants, cafes and accommodation, and less tourist traffic.
Where to stay // For hotels, B&Bs and campsites, see www.ireland.com; for independent hostels, see www.independenthostelsireland.com
Where to eat // See www.westcorkmarkets.com for details on country markets.

© Peter Unger / Getty Images

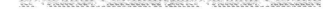

Opposite: the Gap of Dunloe on the Ring of Kerry

MORE LIKE THIS IRISH RIDES

DUBLIN & THE BARROW

This classic three-day journey traces the Grand Canal Way from central Dublin, wending west along the historic waterway to Robertstown in County Kildare. Hang a left here and cycle south along the towpath of the Barrow Navigation, which skirts Ireland's second longest river. Hug the banks of the much-storied and beautiful Barrow as it meanders betwixt several counties, past castles, around woodlands and through ancient towns, including Monasterevin, Athy, Carlow, Borris and Graiguenamanagh, until you reach the last lock in St Mullins, where the river becomes tidal and the towpath evaporates. As you'd expect from a canal-based route, there's no climbing, but there are muddy sections, so a hybrid or mountain bike is recommended.

Start // Dublin
Finish // St Mullins, County Carlow
Distance // 93 miles (150km)

CONNACHT CLASSIC

There's been a huge surge in the popularity of cycling in Ireland over the last decade, but nowhere has embraced the bike revolution more than the beautiful and charismatic County Mayo town of Westport. Myriad routes meander along the coast and into the Connacht countryside from here, including the popular Greenway, but the loop out towards Connemara and delightful Doolough and back is arguably the perfect cycling circuit, taking in the super scenic Sheeffry Pass, Tawnyard Lough and 585m of climbing en route. The outride is mostly along quiet country lanes, past several tempting pubs, while the return route sidles past Croagh Patrick – a stunning peak where St Pat apparently sat for 40 days of fasting in the 5th century. It's a rapid finish along an R-road and then a cycle path back into the embrace of Westport, where Matt Malloy's legendary bar awaits.

Start/Finish // Westport, County Mayo
Distance // 42 miles (67.5km)

RING OF KERRY

A back-route version of the famous Ring of Kerry starts from Killarney, heading out along the quiet country lanes and ultra-remote roads of the Iveragh Peninsula to the wild west coast. The outbound route rolls past Lough Acoose and Glencar, traverses the Ballaghasheen Pass and hits the Atlantic at Waterville, opposite the Gaeltacht (Irish-speaking) village of Ballinskelligs. If you have the legs for it, return via Castlecove and Sneem, pedalling alongside delightful Derrynane Beach, across the Coomakista Pass (a Ring of Kerry highlight) and through the Gap of Dunloe, a gorgeous glaciated valley, on your way back to the many welcoming pubs of Killarney. Examples of ogham stones (standing pillars engraved with an early Irish alphabet), lie close to this route, as does the Staigue Stone Fort. With over 1500m of climbing, and scenery that refuses to be rushed, this ride is best spread across two or three days.

Start/Finish // Killarney, County Kerry
Distance // 95 miles (153km)

© Peter Unger / Getty Images

A TOUR OF LAKE CONSTANCE

One bike, two wheels, three countries… This ride bundles Europe's best into one neat package, with history, lakeside loveliness and Alpine views on every corner.

Morning sunlight bounces off Lake Constance as I pedal along Friedrichshafen's promenade, the mist slowly rising to reveal tantalising glimpses of the Swiss Alps across the water. It's a crisp late-autumn day to kick off a bike tour of Central Europe's third largest lake, which dips into Germany, Austria and Switzerland as it hugs its shores.

As I trundle along the waterfront, I hear snatched conversations in Italian, German, French – a reminder that the lake sits bang in the heart of Europe. And because of its tri-country location, the lake feels like Europe in a nutshell, with Roman forts, Benedictine abbeys and medieval castle-topped villages ripe for a kid's bedtime story, forested mountains tapering down to vineyards and wetlands teeming with birdlife.

You don't need to be a Lycra-clad pro to give it a shot either: bar the odd minor incline, the 168 mile (270km) Bodensee Cycle Path circumnavigating the lake is mostly flat and well-signposted, making it doable for cyclists of every fitness level and age. Then, of course, there is the sheer novelty of it: where else can you freewheel through three countries, enjoy Alpine views without the uphill slog and tick-off multiple Unesco World Heritage sites in the space of a week?

Should time be an issue, ferries make hopping across the lake a breeze, so the trail highlights can be covered in a long weekend. I've allowed myself four days for a loop beginning and ending in Friedrichshafen, a place that has been synonymous with the Zeppelin ever since Count Ferdinand von Zeppelin launched the first of these humungous airship beasts in 1900. They are still used for sightseeing spins to this day – and one floats above me, casting long shadows across the lake, as I pedal out of town.

I ease into my ride as I roll southeast on a trail that weaves among quiet meadows, skirts the yacht-clogged harbour of Langenargen and passes through fruit orchards and vineyards. Like many of the dinky hamlets on the lakefront, Wasserburg sports an onion-domed church, a castle and a handful of gabled houses. It's a restful place for a breather before continuing to one of Lake Constance's most enticing towns: Lindau.

As medieval towns go, Lindau fits the fairy-tale bill nicely. A bone-shaking ride through its cobbled lanes takes me past gabled houses in a fresco painter's palette of pastels and a town hall ablaze with fancy murals, through a square filled with market bustle and down to the prettiest of harbours. Here

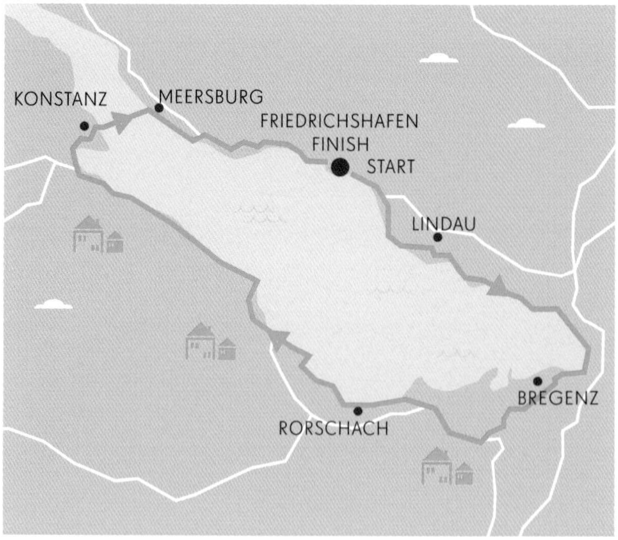

© Westend61 / Getty Images

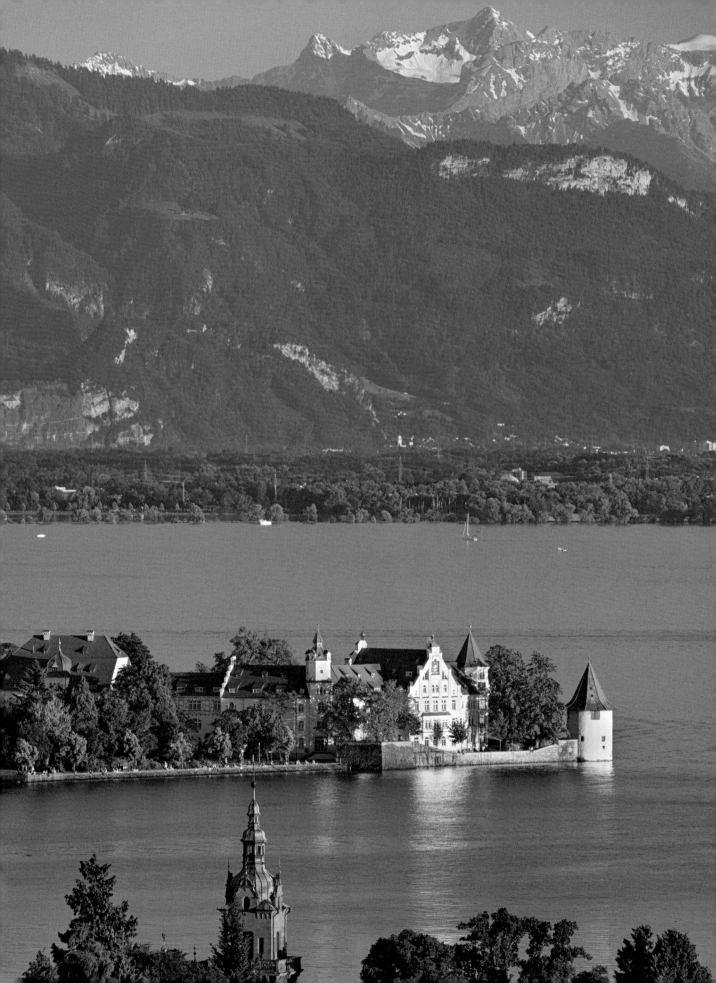

camera-toting day-trippers pose for selfies in front of its two lighthouses and a Bavarian lion sculpture, endeavouring to squeeze the Alps on the horizon into the frame. It's hard to do its beauty justice with a smartphone.

Lindau is just a short pedal from the Austrian border and, on the approach, hills rise steep and wooded above me – the first flush of autumn apparent in their colour-changing foliage. Within no time I reach Bregenz, an affluent town with a couple of striking galleries and a world-famous summer opera festival. I'm particularly drawn, however, to the Pfänder, the 1064m peak that rears above it. I haul my bike into the cable car to the summit. From the top, Bregenz seems toytown tiny and the lake spreads out before me. The Alps feel so much closer here, with views of the already-snow-capped Arlberg and Silvretta ranges, and walking trails leading through a park that's home to ibex, deer and whistling marmots.

After picking up speed downhill, I find the bike path seems remarkably gentle as it threads west of Bregenz, passing pockets of sun-dappled woodland and lakefront beaches now devoid of sunbathers. I pause on the banks of the Bregenzerach, a river that flows swift and glacially cold, pummelling moraine and boulders as it makes its way down from the lush spruce forests of Vorarlberg.

Close by is the Rhine Delta nature reserve, one of the region's most important wetlands for migratory birds. A grey heron darts across the water as my bike casts late-afternoon shadows across the reed-fringed trail. The route heads on into Switzerland from here, where I spend a day happily riding

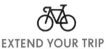

EXTEND YOUR TRIP

Tag on an extra couple of days to tour the northeast shore of the lake in Germany – see the exuberant Rococo pilgrimage church of Birnau and the prehistoric pile dwellings in Unteruhldingen, which form part of an extensive Unesco World Heritage site. Another worthwhile detour west of Konstanz and on Swiss shores is Stein am Rhein, with its showpiece medieval Rathausplatz, where houses embellished with frescoes and oriel windows vie for attention.

© LaMiaFotografia / Shutterstock

Clockwise from top: approaching Birnau Basilica near the lake; the university town of Konstanz; Wasserburg, on the lake's north shore, as is Lindau (previous page)

"The route heads into Switzerland where I spend a day happily riding through late-medieval towns, orchards and fields"

through late-medieval towns, fruit orchards, and fields where wheat ripens come summer.

Hopping back over the Swiss–German border, Konstanz is next on my radar. Once the seat of the 15th-century Council of Constance, the town has kept a tight grip on its history while simultaneously clicking into the groove of a laid-back university town. Presided over by a 1000-year-old cathedral, its alley-woven centre was mercifully spared from the WWII bombings that obliterated other German cities, and its plane-tree-lined promenade is a pleasure to stroll and cycle at leisure.

If I had time to linger, I could easily tag on a detour to the Mediterranean-style botanical gardens of Mainau nearby, or the Unesco-listed island of Reichenau, home to a former Benedictine Abbey founded in 724 by a missionary named Pirmin. But I have a ferry to Meersburg to catch.

I can think of nowhere more fitting to spend the last evening of my tour than this astonishingly lovely lakefront town, crowned by a twinset of castles – one medieval, one Baroque – and backed by vine-striped hills. Snug in the interior of a low-beamed wine tavern, I raise a toast of the local Pinot Noir to what has been a terrific few days on the trail. Outside, the water laps against the shore, as the fading light paints the sky pink. It is back to Friedrichshafen tomorrow and I know I will miss this view of the lake. **KC**

TOOLKIT

Start/Finish // Friedrichshafen

Distance // 168 miles (270km) for the Bodensee Cycle Path, but the route can easily be broken down into shorter chunks.

Getting there // Regular ferries operate between major towns on the lake, including Konstanz, Friedrichshafen, Meersburg and Bregenz. The main operators are BSB (www.bsb.de) and Vorarlberg Lines (www.vorarlberg-lines.at). The nearest airport is Friedrichshafen, served by airlines including British Airways, Lufthansa and easyJet.

Bike hire // Bikes can be hired in towns locally for between €10 and €20 per day.

When to ride // Come in spring or autumn for seasonal colour and fewer crowds. The route gets busy in summer and accommodation can be sparse.

More info // www.bodensee-radweg.com

© Image Professionals GmbH / Alamy Stock Photo, Maurizio Rellini / 4 Corners

Opposite: pausing to take in the view over Lake Como

MORE LIKE THIS
LAKE RIDES

LAKE GENEVA, SWITZERLAND

With the French Alps on the horizon, vineyards staggering down to glittering shores and countless petite villages, a spin of Lake Geneva bundles some of Europe's most sensational scenery into one neat package. Largely flat and suitable for most levels – families included – the 124-mile (200km) Tour du Léman follows Cycle Route 46. Bidding Geneva au revoir, it weaves largely along country tracks, with views of the lake opening up as you pedal past beaches and hamlets to the Olympic city of Lausanne. From here it gets incredibly scenic, dipping into the Unesco World Heritage vineyards of the Lavaux, before descending to skirt the lake and take in Vevey, Montreux and the turreted romance of medieval Château de Chillon. The route then swings clockwise back to Geneva, via the Rhone delta and small market towns straddling the French-Swiss border. More info: www.schweizmobil.ch/de/veloland/routen/route-046.html.

Start/Finish // Geneva
Distance // 124 miles (200km)

LAKE ANNECY, FRANCE

Even in a land blessed with sublime lake and Alpine scenery, the French have to admit this lake is special – shimmering an extraordinary shade of turquoise (from the minerals in the meltwater that flow into it) and rimmed by oft-snow-capped peaks. A leisurely day's pedal makes a loop of the lake – its western shore has a dedicated bike route, while minor, sometimes busy, roads follow its eastern shore. It's rare to get big Alp views like this without the uphill slog, but if you're hankering after more of a challenge, take a climb up to 1660m Crêt de Châtillon. Otherwise, you'll be passing picture-book pretty harbour towns, sleepy villages and beaches where locals come to swim, row and kayak, such as Sévrier, Talloires, castle-crowned Menthon-Saint-Bernard and Veyrier-du-Lac. More info: en.lac-annecy.com.

Start/Finish // Annecy
Distance // 29 miles (46.5km)

LAKE COMO, ITALY

Freewheeling along the shores of Lago di Como on this 99-mile (159km) route is a little slice of Italian heaven. Comprising scenic paths and roads reaching from flat to more demanding, this is a moderate to challenging ride, best avoided on summer weekends when the streets are rammed with traffic. What's the draw? Mountains that rise sheer and wooded above campanile-dotted villages in a fresco painter's palette of colours, lakefront promenades, beaches, gutsy Lombard food – in short, a pinch of everything that makes Italia bella. Go clockwise from Como to stick closest to the lakeshore and you'll pass postcard-worthy Cernobbio, Tremezzo with its waterfront villa and botanical gardens, and Menaggio. On the eastern shore, you'll pass through the tranquil Pian di Spagna Nature Reserve, before dipping into such enchanting villages as Varenna on the return stretch to Como. More info: www.lakecomo.is.

Start/Finish // Como
Distance // 99 miles (159km)

© Cultura Creative / Alamy Stock Photo

INTO THE OUTER HEBRIDES

This other-worldly odyssey by road and water through Scotland's Atlantic archipelago offers stark beauty and unforgettable, windswept cycling.

The Western Isles tempt those of us who plan journeys by tracing fingers along roads on maps. An easy-to-follow line of land and sea runs all the way from Vatersay (Bhatarsaigh), at the southern tail of the chain, to the Butt of Lewis (Rubha Robhanais), at the northern end of the chain. The individual islands are linked by causeways and ferries and seem, from afar, a very mysterious prospect. What is to be found on what are, by definition, the furthest flung islands in the archipelago off Scotland's north-west coast? And what better way to find out than by taking advantage of the island-hopping ferry service and the endless liberties offered by a bicycle, a pair of panniers and brimming overenthusiasm?

The Western Isles are a very long way from the bright lights of the UK. To best make the trip by public transport, you must first get to Glasgow, then an onward train to Oban, one of the west coast's great transport hubs. Ferries buzz to Mull and various smaller islands from here, but the ferry to Barra (Barraigh) still feels like a big deal. The thrill of walking my steel tourer into the body of the boat added to the excitement. Over the next few days I would board several more boats in this fashion and each time I felt the same thrill.

It takes just under five hours to cruise through the Sound of Mull, passing the Summer Isles and other green, rocky specks of land before Castlebay (Bàgh a' Chaisteil) looms into view. By Scottish standards, this is a very long journey indeed.

My own schedule didn't allow for too much dawdling on Barra, so I was grateful that the late summer's evening sun gave me time to catch a little of Vatersay's beautiful beach before bed, with hardly a glimpse at the weather forecast. The next day dawned drizzly and progressively got worse until things were resolutely

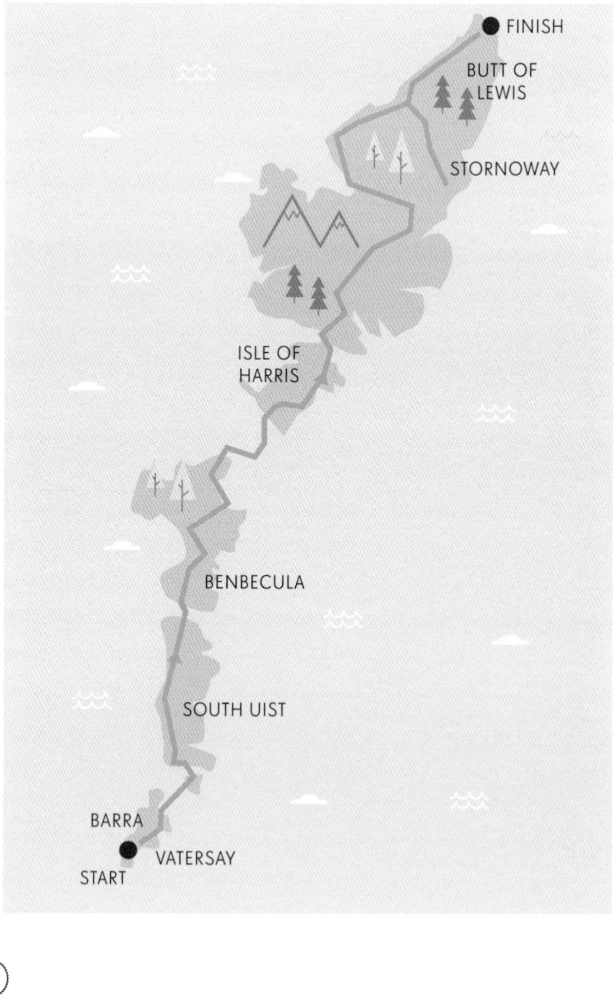

© Carl Bruemmer / Getty Images

North Atlantic. I reasoned I could not complain about it raining, given where I was and that I'd been given one priceless gift: a vigorous tailwind. Over the next few days I passed numerous cyclists battling in the opposite direction who feigned disinterest in my sympathetic waves.

Barra's road network is essentially circular, so there are two ways around it. I took the route to Ardmhor (Aird Mhòr) that passed Barra Airport, voted the most scenic landing in the world for its cockle-strewn beach runway. I didn't see any planes. There weren't any cars for that matter until a few minutes before the Eriskay (Eiriosgaigh) ferry turned up.

This short hop took me onto a chain of islands – Eriskay, South Uist (Uibhist A Deas), Benbecula (Beinn Na Faoghla) and North Uist (Uibhist A Tuat) – with other-worldly landscapes. From the main road in South Uist, a ribbon of single-lane tarmac where few cars passed, the route was flat and watery. Hundreds of tiny *lochans* dotted the horizon. The water world was only broken by the looming peaks of Beinn Mhor (620m) and Hecla (606m), the highest points on South Uist, away to the east of the road.

Dawdling a little, my turns to the west took me to a strip of beach that was backed by machair, much-celebrated coastal grasslands, which were dotted with wildflowers. That said, with the wind and the oddness of the landscape, I gave in to the urge to ride and ride, sprinting across the causeway to Benbecula, and in turn to North Uist, rather than pausing and being a proper cycle tourist. The only distraction breaking the rhythm of the turning wheels, the rain in my face, and the splash of the road, were signs on the causeways warning of otters crossing.

EXPLORE THE REGION

The islands can be traversed in as little as three days, but more time allows for detours and to explore alternative routes on Barra, to detour to the west of Benbecula and pause at Balranald RSPB Bird Reserve on North Uist. A convenient overnight stop is at the hostel on Berneray (Bearnaraigh), from where the ferry across the Sound of Harris (Caolas na Hearad) leaves.

Clockwise from top: Callanish standing stones on the Isle of Harris; a weaver's loom on Lewis; the Golden Road of Harris (and previous page)

© Ashley Cooper / Alamy Stock Photo, Glowimages / Getty Images

Once on Harris (Na Hearadh) I returned just a little to civilisation, the island being well-connected to the mainland via Skye (an t-Eilean Sgiathanach) and the ferry to Tarbert (An Tairbeart). I turned right along the Golden Road, so named for the high cost of its construction, to yellow-sand beaches and sweeping views on the west coast.

The climb out of Tarbert over to Lewis (Leodhais) is one of the finest rides in the British Isles, an initially tough haul giving way to a glorious rolling pedal through mountains, past sea-lochs and hugely tempting roads snaking off, mainly (according to the map) to long-distance dead ends. Somewhere, quite unexpectedly, I passed a sign saying that I had arrived in Lewis: in name an island, in reality a distinctly different part of the same piece of rock. Weavers' cottages started to appear by the roadside, where the Hebrides' most famous export – tweed – is still produced.

There's more to the Hebrides than just quiet roads and wildlife. The islands have millennia-old history that's easily explored, such as the Barpa Langass chambered cairn on North Uist. On Lewis there's Garenin (Na Gearrannan) Blackhouse Village and, most remarkable of all, the Callanish Standing Stones.

The last leg to the Butt involved an out-and-back run to the end of the island before returning to Stornoway (Steornabhagh). After so much solitude the size of the islands' largest settlement came as a shock, but being able to have a pint or two was a fine reward for wonderful, hard miles in the rain.

I rode the high road over the mountains to Inverness to pick up the sleeper train home. My bike travelled with boxes of fresh crab bound for London restaurants. **TH**

"The only distraction breaking the rhythm of the turning wheels were signs on the causeways warning of otters crossing"

TOOLKIT

Start // Vatersay (Bhatarsaigh)
Finish // Butt of Lewis (Rubha Robhanais)
Distance // 150 miles (241km)
Getting there // Caledonian Macbrayne (www.calmac.co.uk) offers a Hopscotch ticket covering ferry travel from Oban to Barra, up through the islands and from Stornoway back to Ullapool. Cyclists can generally turn up and go.
When to ride // March to September, while not necessarily dry, are the brightest and warmest months. They're also the most popular, so book accommodation in advance.
What to take // This route is all on paved roads, but a touring bike is best for long days in the saddle and will allow for the carrying of pannier bags.
More info // www.visitouterhebrides.co.uk.

© Jeff J Mitchell / Getty Images

Opposite: Gimsøystraumen Bridge links Austvagoy with Gimsøya in the Lofoten Islands

MORE LIKE THIS
ISLAND RIDES

SARK, CHANNEL ISLANDS

On Sark all motor vehicles are banned, except tractors, so the only way to get about is by horse and cart, walking or cycling. Which goes a long way to explaining the island's bike-friendly credentials. As does the fact it's virtually flat, super mellow and only 3 miles (5km) by 1.5 miles (2.5km). It has 9 miles (14.5km) of coastline, which you can ride around enjoying views of the other Channel Islands and France. Kids will enjoy a detour to see the secret garden at La Seigneurie and the Window in the Rock, which is exactly what it sounds like and a great spot for a picnic. Older children can give coasteering and sea kayaking a go. Sark was the first designated Dark Sky Island so, if it's not cloudy, a night cycle should guarantee an awesome starry sky backdrop. More info: www.sark.co.uk/getting-around.

Start/Finish // The Avenue
Distance // 9 miles (15km)

LOFOTEN ISLANDS, NORWAY

Not one for winter, when the islands will be covered in snow and ice, but a dreamy summer trip, where families can enjoy cycling in the magical Arctic light, never-ending days, and even take a ride under the Midnight Sun. This narrow chain of islands has more mountains than the rest of Norway put together, which makes for a dramatic panorama, yet, surprisingly, much of the cycling is on flat, easy terrain. Enjoy a landscape of jagged peaks, moorlands, lakes and fjords, while sea birds and eagles soar all around. You'll find plenty of beaches to relax on and, if you're feeling hardy, you can have an extremely refreshing dip in the icy sea. More info: www.lofoten.info/.

Start // Svolvær
Finish // Henningsvær
Distance // 16 miles (26km)

THASOS, GREECE

One of Greece's greenest and most gentle islands, Thasos lies just 6 miles (10km) from the mainland. Its climate, vegetation and forested mountain interior recall northern Greece, yet it boasts enviable sandy beaches, all of which make for stress-free cycling – a 60-mile (100km) circumnavigation of the island is easily doable in three days. Thasos is quite inexpensive by Greek-island standards, and is popular with families and students, with frequent ferries from the mainland and an excellent bus network. The island's main draws are its natural beauty, beaches, inland villages and historical attractions. On a tour of the island's coast, take in the highlights: the excellent archaeological museum in the capital (also called Thasos and the main ferry port); the Byzantine convent Moni Arhangelou, with its clifftop setting; and the Ancient Greek temple at Alyki on the serene southeast coast.

Start/Finish // Thasos
Distance // 60 miles (100km)

© Matt Munro / Lonely Planet

A FLAVOUR OF BAVARIA

Cycle through the greatest concentration of breweries on Earth – and as in the saddle, at the bar it pays to pace yourself.

As I pedal through the Aisch Valley in Bavaria, the bars I'm thinking about are not handlebars. In this quiet, seemingly sober valley, things aren't quite as they seem.

Beyond the facade of neat villages and cornfields is what's said to be the highest concentration of breweries in the world – the equivalent of about one brewery every 0.6 miles (1km) through the valley. This is one ride in which I'm not being slowed by headwinds or hills, but by temptation.

I'm midway through a three-day cycle trip from Nuremberg to Rothenburg ob der Tauber that's almost entirely defined by liquid: the Main Danube Canal, the Aisch River and, most importantly, the amber stream known as beer. The Aisch Valley is the ride's centrepiece, but in this part of Bavaria, beer is a recurring theme.

I begin my ride in Nuremberg, following the Main Danube Canal north. Hovering high above the water is the canal towpath, peering down onto canal boats as they slip through a series of locks. Flowering canola fields colour the land, and towns betray themselves by the sudden presence of joggers and other cyclists on the unfailingly flat path.

This day I have the pick of around 40 beer gardens that sit beside, or near to, the canal. I choose the town of Forchheim, once part of the Franconian royal court and now a cobblestoned monument to beer. Though there are a couple of breweries at the heart of the town, I pedal to its outskirts and the forested hill of Kellerberg.

Burrowed into the slopes of Kellerberg are more than a dozen caves used over the centuries to store beer at a constant temperature of 6°C to 10°C. Today the cool caves serve as cellar pubs.

Beneath Kellerberg's tall trees, those in search of beer nirvana wander up the slopes to the pubs. I pedal past them all, parking my bike against the wall of one cellar pub. It's fair to say that when I ride back out an hour or so later, I'm a little less steady on the bike than when I arrived.

The Aisch River is a just few miles ahead, pouring into the canal, but this day I ride on past its mouth, continuing beside the canal,

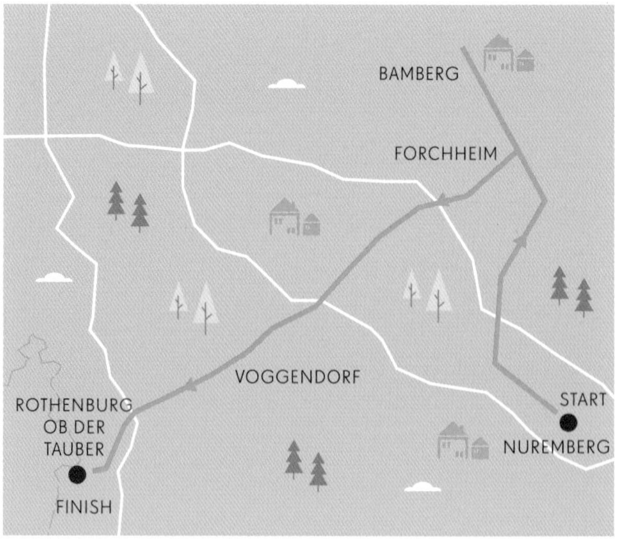

© Andreas Strauss / Getty Images

Hotel Markusturm
Brotkultur im
Kaffeehaus
SCHLECKER

"The route switches between bike paths and undulating country roads that weave between cornfields and beer gardens"

© Sina Ettmer / Getty Images, Prisma Bildagentur / Getty Images, Lonely Planet Images / Getty Images

which points north like a compass needle to Bamberg. Bike paths lead to the heart of this beautiful medieval city, where the World Heritage-listed old town is like a Shakespearean stage set.

Bamberg might just as well be called Bambeerg. At the start of the 19th century there were said to be 68 breweries. The city now has the Franconian Brewery Museum, hillsides drilled with cellar caves, and a Bamberg Brewery Trail that guides visitors between the 11 remaining breweries and their brewery pubs. I consider it carb loading for my next day of riding (see page 48 for more on Bamberg).

Cycling is a cure for hangovers, or so I'm claiming, as I return slowly back along the canal the next morning, turning west into the Aisch Valley after about an hour. Here I link into the Aisch Valley Bike Route, a marked 73-mile (117km) ride that will take me all the way to Rothenburg.

For the first time there are roads and hills, as the route switches between bike paths and gently undulating country roads that weave between fields of corn and more brewery beer gardens. Squirrels bounce across the trail, their jaws locked around acorns, and small birds of prey hover over ploughed fields. The Aisch River is my guiding line, though it's rarely in sight.

I stop for lunch in Hochstadt, the largest town I'll pass through this day, but my eye is really ahead to Voggendorf, a tiny village about 6 miles (10km) further down the road. Little more than a cluster of farm buildings, Voggendorf is typical of the Aisch Valley towns I ride through, containing no stores of any kind but possessing a brewery. I feel immediately welcome in the village as I pedal in past a roadside metal sculpture of a cyclist, albeit with its bum being bizarrely bitten by a fish.

On a rise behind the sculpture is Kellerberg Voggendorf, the beer cellar for the Prechtel Brewery in neighbouring Uehlfeld. Cloud has rolled in and the day outside is as damp as the inside of my stein as I sit under cover, staring out over fields and the surrounding towns, each one pierced by church spires.

After a night in a centuries-old brewery turned guesthouse on the banks of the Aisch River in Neustadt an der Aisch, I'm beginning to think that cycling might actually be bad for me. How else to explain this morning headache and dry mouth once again? But I ride on, albeit slowly, for one of Europe's most beautiful medieval towns is my goal this day. The spread of breweries thins past Neustadt, even as the scene gets more beautiful when I cross from the Aisch to the Tauber Valley. Tiny wooded hills punctuate the horizons, and I'm again winding through fields painted yellow with canola crops. The town of Ipsheim advertises a few wineries – heathens! – but there's barely a beer to be seen.

A wind tows me forward towards my ride's end in the cobbled squares of Rothenburg. As I near the city, beams of sunlight mark the occasion by suddenly breaking through the cloud cover, making Rothenburg's roofs glitter like gold. It feels almost as though I'm riding towards some sort of heavenly welcome at the end of a pilgrimage. But really, there's just another beer ahead. **AB**

BAMBERG BEER WAR

In 1907 Bamberg breweries upped the price of their beer, pushing the cost of a half-litre from 11 pfennigs to 12. Bamberg drinkers weren't amused. In what became known as the Bamberg Beer War, innkeepers went on strike and patrons boycotted local brews. People power won the day. A week after the price hike, the breweries capitulated – the price remained at 11 pfennigs, as it had been for the previous 110 years.

Clockwise from left: Bamberg, where a bike trail links its 11 remaining breweries; souvenir beer steins; Nuremberg. Previous page: Rothenburg ob der Tauber on the Aisch Valley Bike Route

TOOLKIT

Start // Nuremberg
Finish // Rothenburg ob der Tauber
Distance // 124 miles (200km)
Getting there // The nearest major airport is in Munich; trains run to Nuremberg and Rothenburg.
Ride details // The ride follows the Main Danube Canal towpath and the Aisch Valley bike route. A 211-mile (340km) circuit can be cycled by following roads and bike paths along the Franconian Rezat River from Rothenburg to Nuremberg.
Bike hire // Hire from Partner of Sports (www.pos-nuernberg.de) in Nuremberg.
Where to stay // Kohlenmühle Gasthof in Neustadt an der Aisch has a guesthouse attached to a working brewery.

Opposite: roughly 7 million litres of beer are consumed at each Oktoberfest in Munich

MORE LIKE THIS
RIDES TO RAISE A GLASS TO

BASEL TO MUNICH

Oktoberfest is one of the biggest parties in Europe: a time when hordes gather to drink beer from outrageously large glasses and really do slip into *lederhosen* and *dirndl*. If you really want to earn those steins of beer in Munich, catch a train to Basel (on the high-speed rail network), follow EuroVelo 15 as it tracks the Rhine down to Konstanz on the beautiful Lake Constance (see p92). Then pick up the Bodensee-Königssee bike path heading east through southern Bavaria. At Bad Tölz, hop on to the Isar Cycle Route all the way to Munich, with beer gardens a feature of this last section. A veritable tour of the southern German borderlands. Do remember that the Oktoberfest lasts two weeks so you don't need to rush! More information: www.germany.travel/en/map-of-germany.html
Start // Basel, Switzerland
Finish // Munich, Germany
Distance // 280 miles (450km)

PRIORAT, SPAIN

The wines from the Catalonian region of Priorat are among Spain's finest. Rich, with a lingering, concentrated mineral-like essence, they are made from Garnacha and Cariñena grapes, which are grown on rugged hills in a dark, slaty soil sprinkled with quartzite. Thanks to those sparkling hills, the riding in Priorat is very fine too. Quiet roads swoop up gentle gradients, diving down into the shade of scrubby forests, before rising again through the vines. From the coast near Cambrils, venture inland via Montbrió del Camp and Duesaigües to Porrera, before looping back via Falset, La Torre de Fontaubella, Colldejou, and Mont-roig del Camp to the sea. The roughly 45-mile (75km) loop will take you past some of the region's best vineyards and most picturesque villages. In the summer, you'll want to jump in the water to cool off when you get back.
Start/Finish // Cambrils
Distance // 45 miles (75km)

THREE DISTILLERIES PATHWAY, SCOTLAND

Islay is famous for its smoky whiskies, which contain notes of iodine, seaweed, and salt, thanks to the peat, which is burned in order to dry the malt. The windswept Hebridean island is a wonderful place to explore by bike. Twenty-five miles (40km) from top to bottom, and 15 miles (24km) broad, its east coast is rocky and mountainous, while the west is flatter and fertile. Quiet roads join the small villages that are scattered across the island. For a start, try Port Ellen's Three Distilleries Pathway, which joins the white-washed, seaside premises of Laphroaig, Lagavulin and Ardbeg, among the island's most renowned whisky manufacturers. At 7 miles (11km) there and back, you will have plenty of time for a few drams. All three distilleries offer tours and tastings.
Start/Finish // Port Ellen, Islay
Distance // 7 miles (11km)

© Jimmy R / Shutterstock

PAULANER
PAULANER MÜNCHEN
PAULANER
Münchner Genuss
Heisse Nüsse
Ecke
Frische Mandeln
Coca-Cola

WESTERN EUROPE

Riding the Rocacorba in northeast Spain (see page 216)

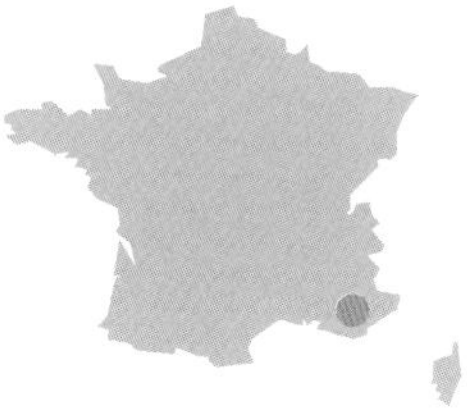

A TRAVERSE OF THE PROVENÇAL ALPS

Cass Gilbert follows a demanding route across the southeast corner of France, packed with technical singletrack. But the rewards – geology, history, pastries – are spectacular.

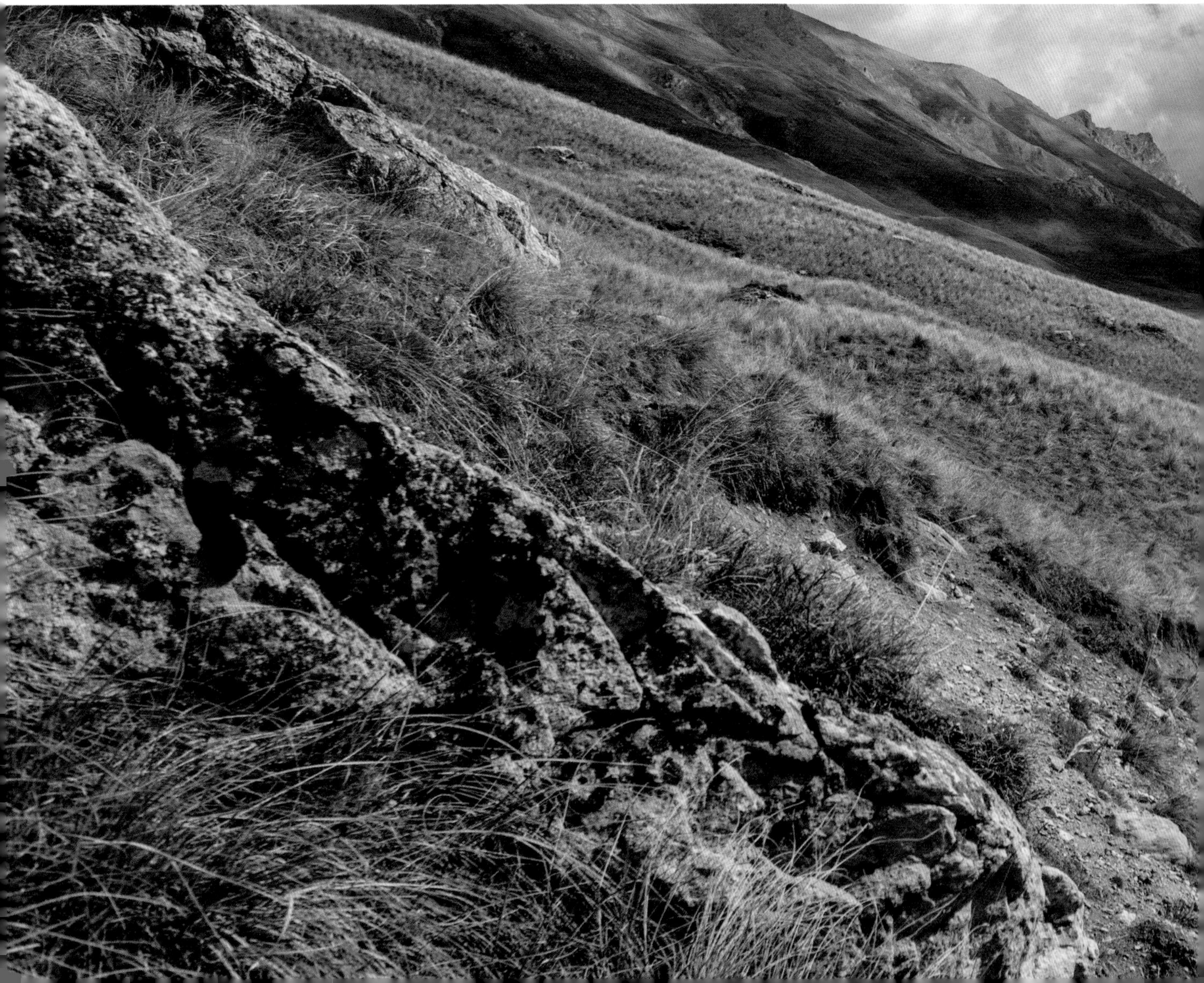

This classic mountain-bike route more than lives up to its rather lofty name. It leads riders from the very highest reaches of southeastern France's Alpes-de-Haute-Provence all the way down to the picturesque villages, lavender fields, olive groves, and bucolic countryside for which the region is famed.

In fact, it begins on the border of France and Italy, at the very tip top of the Col de Larche no less, a mountain pass that seesaws local cyclists between the Cottian Alps and the Maritime Alps; while you're there, take advantage of a pre-journey shot of espresso at the rifugio that's conveniently perched on the col.

If you were hoping this elevated start point might promise an immediate descent, think again. The signposted Grande Traversée L'Alpes-Provence climbs higher still, peeling away above the paved pass on to a rough two-track that's completely devoid of traffic. And it's not long before the true character of this decidedly challenging route reveals itself in the form of

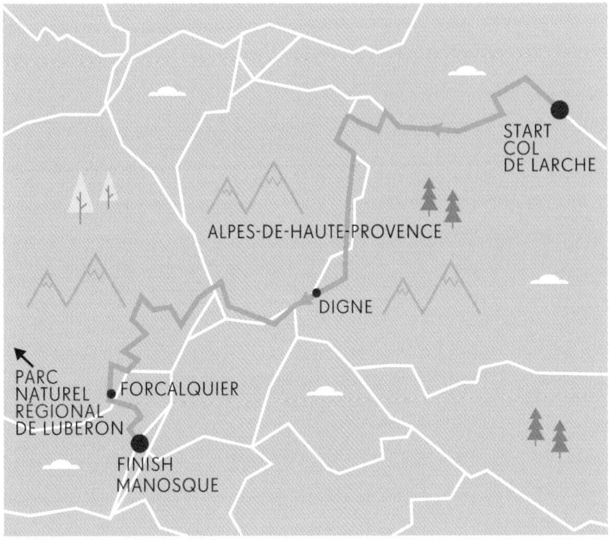

Previous page © Tristan Cardew & The Service Course, this page © Cass Gilbert

a faint, rough and tumble, rocky singletrack descent towards Barcelonnette, with some hike-a-bike style scrambling thrown in for good measure. This is no gentle, backroad meander.

Still, a mountain biker's toil is invariably worth the effort. In the case of this route, rewards come thick and fast, framed by the Haute Provence's snow-capped mountain peaks, its lush forests, its high altitude pastures, and eventually the bizarre, and appropriately named 'Terres Noires'. A jigsaw puzzle of ridges and escarpments, it's definitely the place to hone your bicycle balancing skills, as you enter a network of trails that teeter-totters through this polished-black landscape, a draw for local mountain bikers and hikers alike – which is just as well, because with a loaded bike, hiking is what you'll probably be doing in places.

But as stellar as the riding is, crossing the region isn't solely about railing around sweet singletrack, bouncing along rough doubletrack, and hurtling down whirlygig, switchback descents. It's also a taste of the good life, Provence-style. Punctuating the many overgrown, tumbled-down 'doer-upper' farmhouses, nestled along the most beautiful of backcountry walking trails and old cart tracks, comes a succession of medieval villages straight from the pages of a Marcel Pagnol novel; thankfully, each offers guaranteed spring water to quench your thirst, unlike the experiences of the poor hunchback, Jean de Florette. Time your visit right and resupply for the miles ahead courtesy of Provence's famous village markets, where bountiful produce is guaranteed,

"The 'Terres Noires', a jigsaw puzzle of ridges and escarpments, is the place to hone your bike-balancing skills"

be it delicate pastries, refreshing pears, peaches, and apples, or cheese boards that will impress the fussiest gourmet.

I could go on, of course, just as the trail does, in its meandering route to Manosque, some 186 miles (300km) from the Italian border. And I should certainly mention the beguiling Rochers des Mourres, in the Unesco-listed Parc Naturel Régional de Luberon, the largest geological reserve in Europe. There, bizarrely-shaped limestone rocks tower several metres high, dotted across a vast and open plateau; it's said that once they were a meeting point for witches, though nowadays they're a popular spot for families to picnic amongst, providing tempting outdoor furniture on which kids can clamber.

But I'll leave the rest of the riding to reveal itself to you, and simply suggest you allow ample time to really enjoy this Grande Traversée. Indeed, this is not a ride to rush, no matter how strong a rider you may be. By way of example, the journey took us seven days, including the various logistics of getting to the start point and the train back to Nice, the French Riviera city that's so close in distance, yet a world away from the mountains of Haute Provence. Even then, we'd happily have allowed another half day

© Cass Gilbert

LE PARC NATUREL RÉGIONAL DE LUBERON

This is one of seven protected parks in Provence Alpes Côte d'Azur. Noted for both its living history and its ancient geology, it reaches a lofty 3700ft (1125m). Impressively, there are almost 1250 miles (2000km) of hiking trails and around 300 miles (500km) of cycling routes, which means there's no shortage of potential for those who want to extend their holidays.

From left: Haute Provence is a trove of singletrack; carry a simple shelter, but there are plenty of accommodation options; cafes abound en route. Previous page: descending from the Col de Larche

en route to rest our legs or delve deeper into Provence's nooks and crannies, or just linger in its shady groves. Wandering narrow village backstreets, replete with immaculate displays of flowers and elderly locals catching up on the day's gossip, is a Provençal pastime in itself. If you end up behind schedule, there are plenty of chances to shortcut the official route using minor, low-traffic D roads, circumventing a number of indirect loops designed into the ride. Usefully, the associated website also grades each segment, so you can pick and choose as need be.

Besides, the riding itself is challenging enough that you're best off covering relatively modest distances, especially when taking on the bouts of singletrack that are interspersed throughout. In fact, some of the trails are extremely committing: think steps, tight switchbacks, and narrow corridors of 'babyhead' rocks. For this reason, you'll definitely want to be a confident mountain biker to make the most of the flow of the Grande Traversée L'Alpes-Provence. There are a number of very technical descents, especially before the department's capital, Digne-Les-Bains, which will need extreme care with a loaded bike.

Still, the hike-a-bikes are mostly short, with a few longer grafts that offer a full body workout for aspiring bikepackers. It pays to have a light setup; a simple shelter and room in your framebag for all your picnic kit. Then, release the brakes and allow yourself to be carried away by the sublime singletrack, and the sense of enchantment, that infuses France's Haute Provence. **CG**

TOOLKIT

Start // Col de Larche
Finish // Manosque
Distance // 186 miles (300km); the ride takes 5-7 days.
How to get there // Barcelonnette can be reached from the coast by bus, or by train and bus from Cuneo, in Italy. Manosque, its terminus, has a train station.
What to take // A mountain bike with front suspension; full waterproofs are recommended. A water filter – not all the fountains we encountered were *eau potable*.
When to ride // Autumn, after the summer heat has softened; bear in mind shorter days will impact your riding. Spring is possible, depending on lingering snow.
Where to stay // There are plenty of campsites en route, or stay in accommodation and save some weight.
More info // The Alpes de Haute-Provence VTT website is comprehensive: www.vtt.alpes-haute-provence.fr/

© Cass Gilbert; Camille Moirenc / Getty Images

Opposite: hike-a-bike on the TransVerdon, a more committing ride than the Grande Traversée L'Alpes-Provence

MORE LIKE THIS
MIGHTY TRAVERSES

TRANSVERDON, FRANCE

The multi-day TransVerdon mountain bike route offers an alternative take on crossing Provence, steering further south to take in the impressive, steep side Verdon Gorge, a stunning river canyon popular with climbers, hikers, and rafters alike. Despite comparable conditions and the shorter length – 162 miles (260km) – the TransVerdon is a more committing ride, as it stays higher in the mountains, following often faint and challenging singletrack that clings to the mountainscape, high above treeline. Its starting point, at the top of the Col d'Allos, is close to Barcelonnette, which can be reached by bus, and the route's terminus, Gréoux Les Bains, is a short ride from Manosque, where train connections are available. You can find a full data sheet for the route, including accommodation along the way if you don't wish to camp, at www.vtt-montagne.com.

Start // Barcelonnette
Finish // Gréoux Les Bains
Distance // 162 miles (260km)

TRANS ALP

The venerable Trans Alp is an undoubted classic when it comes to European mountain traverses. There are various routes to choose from: if epic singletrack descents are what you're after, then the Alpencross Extreme is the one to go for. Loosely split into seven stages, it runs from Garmisch-Partenkirchen, a German ski resort in Bavaria, to the azure waters of Lake Garda in Italy, dipping into both Austria and Switzerland along the way. Don't be too put off by the name though. Although the Alpencross Extreme is undoubtedly a tough ride in places, forest roads and quiet mountain lanes form the bulk of the crossing, connected with remote, high-mountain and testing singletrack. Be sure to bring your climbing legs – you'll gain a lung-busting 46,000ft (14,000m) of ascent over the 300-mile (480km) ride. Find more details via Komoot.com.

Start // Garmisch-Partenkirchen, Germany
Finish // Lake Garda, Italy
Distance // 300 miles (480km)

TUSCANY TRAIL, ITALY

The 337-mile (543km) Tuscany Trail is another journey across one of Europe's signature landscapes: it runs from Massa via Florence, Tuscany's capital, to the diminutive village of Capalbio Scalo, from where you can return to your start point by train. The route can be tackled independently or you can sign up and ride it as part of the Tuscany Trail event in May or June each year. Expect lots of camaraderie; with over 700 riders the group ride purports to be the largest bikepacking event in the world. But it's not competitive. Everyone rides at their own pace, choosing their own places to spend the night and places to eat. The route is varied, consisting of dirt roads, asphalt secondary roads and paths – as well as the famous *strade bianche* – and winds its way through vineyards and dense forest. Only a third is paved, so a gravel bike or a mountain bike are both suitable. More information: www.tuscanytrail.it/

Start // Massa
Finish // Capalbio Scalo
Distance // 337 miles (543km)

© Cass Gilbert

THE WHITE ROADS OF TUSCANY

Set out from Siena on a spring sportive that follows the region's cypress-lined 'strade bianche' a day after the professionals race the route.

'Pssshht!'
'Psssshhht!'

The sound is contagious. Soon more of the 5000 amateur cyclists around me are letting a spurt of air out of their tyres. It's early morning in central Siena on a Sunday in March and some of us are realising what lies ahead: 86 miles (139km) of riding through Tuscan hills, 19 miles (31km) of which will be on the white gravel roads that lend this Gran Fondo its name – Strade Bianche (white roads). A little less pressure will lend a little more traction on the loose surfaces.

As Unesco writes in its description of this World Heritage site, 'the whole city of Siena, built around the Piazza del Campo, was devised as a work of art that blends into the landscape.' The city (and much of the art and architecture still within it) developed between the 12th and 15th centuries over three hills south of its great rival, Florence. We're all penned at the start of this sportive beside the 16th-century Fortezza Medicea, a fort built by Florentines to prevent the Sienese taking back control of their city. As the motivational music swells, there's the customary sight of a crowd of chilly cyclists shuffling across bleeping timing mats before starting our anti-clockwise loop around this medieval city.

However, the weekend proper begins the day before with the professional race. The first UCI-sanctioned event (see panel) was in 2007 and it quickly became a favourite of the pro peloton. 'I always look forward to Strade Bianche as it's one of the most beautiful races of the season,' said 2016 Olympic road race champion Greg Van Avermaet. The 2017 women's winner, Elisa Longo Borghini, agrees: 'This race is fascinating due to the cultural and artistic level of the surroundings.'

After registering and collecting a goodie bag that contains a commemorative jersey, a buff and a box of the best pasta that I have ever tasted – at €55 the entry fee is good value – we have a pizza at Il Pomodorino (great views of Siena's historic skyline, lousy service). Then, alerted by the approaching helicopters, we rush up some steps and along an alley just in time to see the bobbing helmets of Julian Alaphilippe, Jakob Fuglsang and Wout van Aert speed up the steep Via Santa Caterina, seconds before Alaphilippe attacks and drops into the Piazza del Campo as the 2019 winner. The crowd along the narrow street is six-deep and spectators are hanging out of townhouse windows, cheers

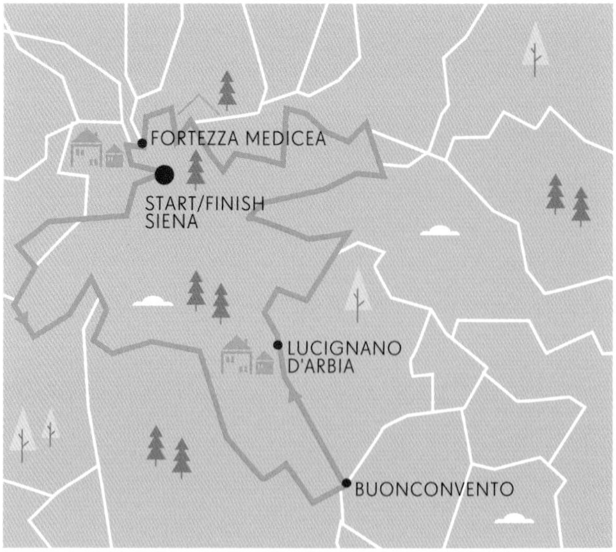

© Tim de Waele / Getty Images

CAPS
lotto
letsgo
Jayco
Ridley

bouncing off the medieval walls: the city is an astounding arena.

The following day it's my turn. Sportives or Gran Fondos are often maligned as a group of well-upholstered, middle-aged men playing at being professional racers for a day. But the start line of Strade Bianche suggests a far more diverse appeal, with plenty of women among us. And it's an international affair: there are groups of Germans in sleek, coordinating kit on state-of-the-art gravel bikes, Brits in obscure regional club strips, and local riders in the most lurid Lycra imaginable, straddling Italian racing bikes with skinny 23mm tyres.

Together we will be following the route of the elite women's race (the men do roughly an extra 30 miles (50km) of racing with 39 miles (63km) of *strade bianche* in total). The route heads out west of the city, down from its hilltop vantage point and out to the first sector of *strade bianche* after 11 miles (18km). It's an easy warm-up, being a gentle descent, but causes a lot of brake levers to be grabbed in panic. The gravel is unsettling, with loose larger stones sinking into ruts. However, as someone who has spent the winter riding England's rolling, chalky South Downs, I'm in my element.

A pattern emerges. I power ahead on the increasingly hard gravel climbs and descents – I don't speak Italian but I'm sure those were shouts of encouragement – and then lose ground on the tarmac roads in between. The scenery spurs me on: cypress-lined white roads zigzag up hills to terracotta hilltop villages such as Buonconvento. At one photo stop I meet a couple of American

"This is why we are here: pedalling up the 14th-century flagstones of Via Santa Caterina and then into Pizza del Campo"

L'EROICA

If you feel a yen for the golden age of cycling, with its steel frames, friction shifting, woollen jerseys and a spare tyre slung bandolier-style about your shoulders, then L'Eroica is the amateur event for you. It was founded in the Sienese province of Chianti in 1997 and rules stipulated no bikes made more recently than 1987 were to be ridden. The vintage cycling festival spawned a race in 2007, Monte Paschi Eroica, that became Strade Bianche (modern kit permitted).

Clockwise from top: poplars and dust, two features of Strade Bianche; the author on the home straight; Julian Alaphilippe wins the 2019 edition. Previous page: first run in 2007, the race is now a favourite of the pros

© Luc Claessen / Getty Images, MARCO BERTORELLO / Getty Images

cyclists. 'Strangely, we found it easier to convince our wives to come to Siena in spring than go to Belgium,' they confide. There's talk of Strade Bianche joining the five Monuments of cycling, those great races such as Milan-San Remo and Paris-Roubaix, and although it doesn't share their century-old histories, the sense of an occasion is no less.

In the final quarter of the route, steeper gravel inclines appear, the most notable being Colle Pinzuto, with an average gradient of 15% and the 18% climb to the top of the Tolfe. Traditionally, these are springboards for long-range attacks by racers who don't fancy duelling it out in the streets of Siena. There's a sheepish thrill to see the top 10 of Strava's leaderboard for the Colle Pinzuto climb filled with names like Wout Van Aert, Tiesj Benoot, Vincenzo Nibali and king of the mountain Greg Van Avermaet, all marginally ahead of me.

In smaller groups now, we dive down into a valley on tarmac roads before Siena rises ahead of us. The finale of our ride, and the reason many of us are here, is the spine-tingling sensation of pedalling up the flagstones (first laid in 1349) of Via Santa Caterina at 16%, then rounding a couple of corners to emerge into the Piazza del Campo. Yesterday, Alaphilippe, Fuglsang and Van Aert had disappeared up this slippery street in the blink of an eye. Today, we exhausted amateurs, caked in white dust, weave up at walking pace having tested ourselves on the same playing field as the pros. **RB**

© Sportograf.com

TOOLKIT

Start/Finish // Siena
Distance // 86 miles (139km)
When to ride // The Strade Bianche race weekend is in early March, but you can ride the route at any time; autumn is a particularly lovely time of year in Tuscany.
Where to stay // Book early for accommodation during race weekend; there are good Airbnb options but beware of bringing a car into the old part of the city.
Where to eat // Osterias and pizzerias abound; we stocked up on take-home meals at DAL5 Stazione Gastronomica, just outside Porta Pispini.
What to ride // A road bike with the maximum width of tyre that will fit (28mm or more, ideally); modern gravel bikes (road bikes with clearance for tyres of 35mm-45mm).
More info // www.gfstradebianche.it; there's a downloadable GPX file to follow the route any time.

Opposite: Dirty Reiver wends some 125 miles off-road through Kielder forest in Northumberland

MORE LIKE THIS
GRAVEL EVENTS

NOVA EROICA, ITALY

Unusually, the Strade Bianche pro race evolved out of an event for enthusiasts called L'Eroica, which was staged on the white roads around Siena; it had a dress code of period costume and permitted only bicycles built before 1987. L'Eroica has spread its wings (see sidebar on previous page) but the contemporary incarnation, Nova Eroica, still takes places on Tuscan gravel roads in late April each year. The festival is based at Buonconvento and, unlike the retro events, it is open to modern road, gravel and cyclo-cross bikes. Distances range from a family fun ride of 9 miles (14km) to the full-length route along as many white roads as can be squeezed into 81 miles (130km). Copying modern enduro mountain bike events, there are four timed stages on the 81-mile option. You can download a GPX file to follow the route at any time. More info: https://eroica.cc/en/nova-eroica

Start/Finish // Buonconvento
Distance // 9 miles to 81 miles (14km-130km)

GRINDURO, UK & SWITZERLAND

Timed stages also appear in the Grinduro family of gravel rides, so participants can enjoy a relaxing ride with their friends and then open the taps for a climb or a descent. The OG (Original Grinduro) was hosted by the Sierra Buttes Trail Stewardship in Quincy, northern California, sending riders up then down Mt Hough. In 2020, five more Grinduros were inaugurated around the world, including two in Europe, in Switzerland and the UK (exact locations may vary from year to year). Like their parent event, Europe's Grinduros feature timed sections over a distance of around 50 miles (8km), offering, in the organisers' words, the perfect 'party-to-race ratio'. The race entry fee includes camping, food and beer. More info: www.grinduro.com

DIRTY REIVER, UK

South of Scotland's border with England, the Dirty Reiver gravel race takes its name from the brigands that roamed these parts until the 18th century. And it too should be approached with caution: the route traces 125 miles (200km) of gravel tracks through Kielder forest in Northumberland each April, with riders braving river crossings, incessant undulations and whatever the often inclement weather can throw at them. It's an event where a survival blanket and a warm hat are on the required kit list. If you prefer to sample the gravel riding Kielder has to offer first, the forest roads are usually open (and free from logging traffic at weekends), and there are downloadable route files available online. The visitor centre also provides maps of cycling routes, including the Cross Border Trail that connect Kielder with Newcastleton, one of the 7stanes mountain bike centres. More info: www.dirtyreiver.co.uk

Start/Finish // Kielder, Northumberland
Distance // 125 miles (200km)

© Andy Heading / Dirty Reiver/ Focal Events

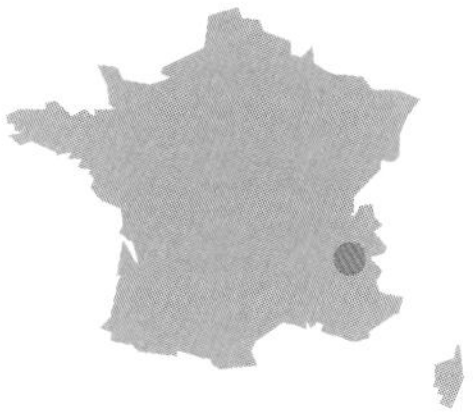

TWICE UP THE GALIBIER

Three brutal ascents, two historic cols, one truly epic day in the Alps. This high mountain stage tests aspiring Grand Tour champions and cycle tourists alike.

When Tour de France founder Henri Desgrange first included the Galibier in the 1911 edition of his race it wasn't certain the riders would even make it to the top on their heavy, single-speed bikes. In the end, just three reached the col without being forced to walk.

The road up the Col du Galibier is austere and desolate, providing a vital connection between the Savoie and Hautes Alpes regions. It's usually open from early June to the end of October – if you arrive early enough in the year you'll find the road's highest reaches hemmed in by banks of snow. There's no gift shop or cafe at the top, and upon reaching its highest point at 8668ft (2642m) the road simply turns and heads into the next valley. It is one of cycling's most storied mountains and remains the scene of the highest ever Tour de France stage finish.

This testing 124-mile (200km) route follows much of the *parcours* of the historic cyclosportive La Louison Bobet – it takes in twin ascents of the Galibier, along with its similarly grand and historic neighbour, the Col d'Izoard, a climb forever associated with cycling's 1950s heyday. A loop of the Galibier and the Col d'Izoard can be formed via the spectacular Gorges du Guil; even with copious cafe stops, it's a tough day out.

The northerly ascent of the Galibier begins outside Valloire (which is a good base for a riding trip, high in the Auvergne-Rhône-Alpes). The scrawl of names across the road surface is testament to its place in road-racing history. Decades of fans have risked the wrath of the local gendarmerie to paint the names of their favoured racers on its tarmac: 'Bardet' and 'Froome', in block letters, compete for space with more faded characters such as Wiggo and Contador. On the concrete walls of the lower corners,

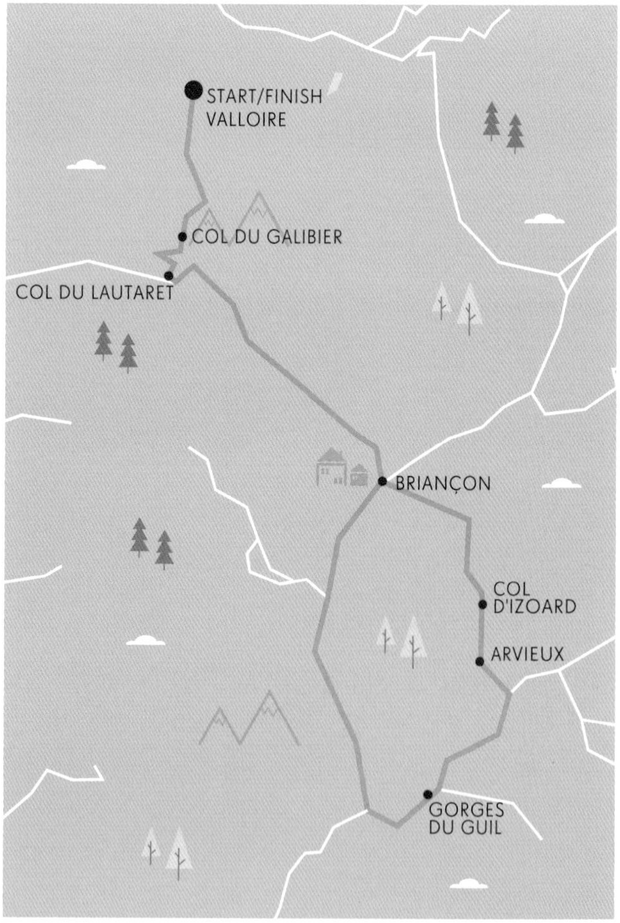

© Biagio Anselmi / Getty Images

you can even find 20-year-old tributes to the Italian Marco Pantani.

Yet, even without any history, the Galibier still would be a star attraction. The road drapes over the barren landscape as if intended to show off the mountain's contours. Never too steep, and coming right at the beginning of the day, all that's required to make it up this first time is patience and pacing. Along with sufficient red blood cells to deal with the thin air at the top.

On the col, pausing alongside the famous sign marking the boundary between the Savoie and Hautes Alpes regions, it's best not to dwell on what the two coming ascents will do to your legs. There was a time when the TV coverage used to cut away from the racing once the leaders crossed the summit. But the descent off of the Galibier is one no cyclist should miss. Wide, sweeping corners and open lines of sight mean you can shoot down with as much abandon as you dare, or the speed limit allows, whizzing past the monument to Desgrange as you do so.

After what seems an age heading south down the N94, it's only once you're way past Briançon that the descent peters out and the route then turns east at Les Isclasses towards the spectacular Gorges du Guil and the day's second climb.

If the Galibier is forever associated with racing's heroic early years, the Col d'Izoard is synonymous with its golden era. In the '50s, film cameras started to follow the race into the mountains and photogenic stars such as Fausto Coppi and Louison Bobet made the Izoard the backdrop to their legendary exploits. Even today it retains an aura of high glamour.

However, down in the sheer-sided Gorges du Guil there's little

"In the 1950s, stars such as Fausto Coppi and Louison Bobet made the Col d'Izoard the backdrop to their exploits"

GALIBIER DUELS

In 1911 Émile Georget slogged up unpaved roads and between banks of snow to become the first racer to cross the Col du Galibier. Since then it's been the scene of many era-defining contests, such as Fausto Coppi escaping his rivals in 1952, and Jacques Anquetil and Raymond Poulidor going head-to-head in 1966. However, Marco Pantani overhauling Jan Ullrich on a murky stage in 1998 might be its most spectacular. That duel also marked the highpoint of a now-discredited era in which illegal substance abuse was rife.

Clockwise from above: Fausto Coppi (right) brought glamour to the Col d'Izoard, and, with Louison Bobet, is commemorated there; fans before and during a Tour de France stage on the Galibier

© LB / Getty Images, Universal / Getty Images

indication of what the Izoard holds in store for the rider. Almost imperceptible at first, only the counterflow of the river gives an indication that the gradient is no longer in your favour. With the entire climb measuring 19.5 miles (31.5km), this sapping first section seems to gain little height; it's almost a relief when it ramps up properly at the town of Arvieux. Now at least there's an obvious reason for the fatigue in your legs. Yet from here 6 miles (10km) remain to the summit.

Through the woods, and then out above the treeline, a short descent provides a moment of respite before depositing riders on to the mountain's weathered upper reaches. Known as La Casse Déserte, this expanse of scree is punctuated by contorted pillars of rock yet to succumb to the wind and snow that blast these high slopes. There are monuments to both Coppi and Bobet, the ghosts of cycling's past still haunting this weird landscape. Not a place to be caught pushing your bike; a mile or so more and the climb is done.

Two *hors catégorie* climbs in, you'd be forgiven for blanching at the prospect of now heading north, via Briançon, to the Galibier once more. The landmarks will be familiar, but where you previously flew past them in a blur, you'll be able to examine them in excruciating detail this time. Past the abandoned tunnel beside Le Rif Blanc, then the still current avalanche tunnel just below the Col du Lautaret, then the monument to Desgrange. Once up top for the final time, all that's left is to sink down the last familiar miles back to Valloire. **JD**

TOOLKIT

Start/Finish // Valloire, France
Distance // 118 miles (190km)
Getting there // The Gare de Saint-Michel Valloire train station (which sits at the foot of the Col du Télégraphe) is a cab ride away from Valloire. The nearest airport is Chambéry, although Geneva, Lyon, Grenoble are also within driving distance.
Bike Hire // There are at least four quality bike rental outlets in Valloire, including two branches of Snow and Bike.
When to ride // The road over the Col du Galibier is normally open from the beginning of June to the end of October.
Where to stay // Summer is the off-season here, so there are always plenty of rooms. The Hotel Les Mélèzes in Valloire, from €69 per night, is comfortable and has secure bike storage.

© Tim de Waele / Getty Images, Agence Zoom / Getty Images

Opposite: the Col des Aravis which featured in the 2020 Tour de France

MORE LIKE THIS
FRENCH ALPINE LOOPS

COL DE LA COLOMBIÈRE AND COL DES ARAVIS

What the feared Col de la Colombière lacks in height it makes up for in difficulty. When approached from Cluses in the north, it climbs for 11 miles (17.3km) and gains 3700ft (1127m) of elevation. As it gets higher, it gets steeper – its upper slopes hit 13% in places. The col has featured more than 20 times in the Tour de France, and its wide-open sides and steep slopes provide stunning but vertigo-inducing views. This route then proceeds to the nearby Col des Aravis, another familiar Tour climb, which, thankfully, is less demanding. You'll have over 6500ft (2000m) in your legs by the time this challenging but not outrageous loop delivers you home via Flumet, Megève, and Sallanches along the Arve Valley.
Start/Finish // Cluses
Distance // 62 miles (100km)

GLANDON, TÉLÉGRAPHE, GALIBIER, ALPE D'HUEZ

If you have only one day in the Alps you might as well make it a big one. Delivering as many mountains as most people will need in a lifetime, this 116-mile (187km) route packs in four famous climbs and 17,000ft (5180m) of ascent, and twice takes riders above 2000m. After the opening descent from Alpe d'Huez, the first 6781ft (2067m) summit comes on the pretty and little-travelled Col du Glandon. Next, circling round to the Col du Télégraphe, then the Galibier via its hardest, northern approach. Topping out at 8677ft (2,645m), from here the route descends over the Col du Lautaret, before heading west towards Alpe d'Huez and its famous hairpins. A long day by any standards, once done you'll have banked almost double the climbing of even the toughest Tour de France stages.
Start/Finish // Alpe d'Huez
Distance // 116 miles (187km)

TWICE OVER THE COL DE LA MADELEINE

The Col de la Madeleine is contender for the most beautiful mountain in the Alps, and there are multiple ways to climb it. All are stunning, but some are also almost deserted. This loop takes in perhaps the most famous route up from Feissons-sur-Isère, before descending to La Chambre and returning via the little-used D76 road. Familiar to Tour devotees, the opening ascent passes the forests and waterfalls that make the Madeleine famous. Above these, once the views open up, the sense of exposure is immense. Arriving at the top for the first time a sign declares the altitude to be 2km (6562ft) exactly. That the actual elevation is some seven metres shorter seems churlish to mention, especially given the 11,033ft (3363m) of climbing this route takes in. The foot of the descent in La Chambre is a good point to take lunch, you'll be heading straight back up via the parallel road to the west, before returning the way you came.
Start/Finish // Feissons-sur-Isère
Distance // 56 miles (91km)

© Justin Paget / Getty Images

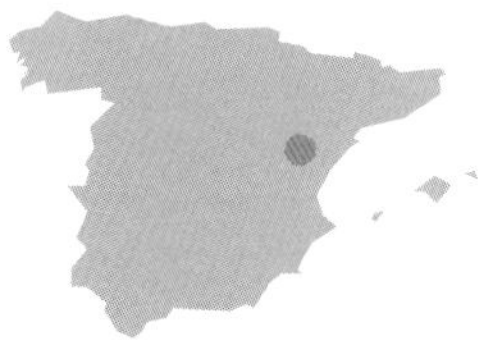

INTO THE MONTAÑAS VACIAS

Ernesto Pastor experiences Spain's sparsely populated eastern interior on a route that reveals the sights, smells, and sounds of this little-known bikepacking paradise.

Sharing stories with fellow cyclists is one of the many charms of exploring by bike. The motivations and plans are inspiring – and can provide an endless source of ideas for trips of your own. Before long, it becomes clear that we're all searching for similar things in our bikepacking experiences: adventure, wild nature and a sense of remoteness. It was shortly after this realisation that the idea for the Montañas Vacías (Empty Mountains) route hit me.

Nestled deep within Spain's eastern interior lies a far-reaching mountainous region known as Serranía Celtibérica. Twice the size of Belgium and occupying around 13% of the country's total footprint, it boasts vast landscapes and high peaks, made all the more dramatic by its incredibly sparse population. In certain areas, there's just one person for every square kilometre. A figure similar to that of the equally sparse Finnish Lapland – giving rise to Serranía Celtibérica's unofficial nickname, the Spanish Lapland.

Teruel, the high-altitude town I call home, could be considered Serranía Celtibérica's centre. It's the perfect launch pad to discover the surrounding mountainscapes, and was my chosen start point for the 430-mile (700km) Montañas Vacías route I designed to showcase Spain's most adventurous – and little-known – riding destination. From here, paved roads and human company rapidly recede, and the region's wilderness begins to impose upon your senses.

As you leave Teruel headed west in the direction of Sierra de Albarracín, the 17-mile (28km) long mountain range reveals its red cliffs, dotted with medieval villages and impressive viewpoints like the 4900ft (1500m) Peña de la Cruz. A short section of hike-a-bike on part of the Camino del Cid trail then draws you up above Albarracín for a breathtaking panorama of the village, one of Spain's most beautiful, complete with its towering ancient walls.

From here, the route enters the Alto Tajo Nature Reserve, home to the source of the Iberian Peninsula's longest river, the Tagus. This meandering forest stream belies the mighty body of water it will become, eventually stretching out over more than 625 miles (1000km) across Spain and into Portugal. The route hugs its banks on gravel tracks for the next 60 miles (100km) until, on its journey to the Atlantic, it bends westwards at Puente de San Pedro, where the opportunity for a farewell dip in its icy turquoise waters is too good to pass up.

© Ernesto Pastor @Montanasvacias

Whether you choose to ride this route in five days or 15, travelling through the quiet hills and villages of the region has a profound effect. Soon you find yourself adapting to the rhythms of the territory's people, scarce though they may be. Pack a little Spanish and talk to them, ask about their customs, their traditions, their foods. I find that one of the best times to do so is during *almuerzo*, a heavy brunch usually taken mid-morning, consisting of a big sandwich, some olives, and a coffee. Most towns and villages in the region are brought to a standstill by *almuerzo*, which makes it the ideal time to catch the locals at their most conversational. Nor should you miss the opportunity to refuel, all the better to knock off those miles before lunch – and on into the province of Cuenca, to the heart of the Serranía.

Roe deer, wild boar, foxes and vultures outnumber human inhabitants by some margin here, and the region's dense pine forests begin to rise up before you. Here, the remoteness of Spanish Lapland hits home: from Beteta to Beamud, there are no

"In certain places, the mountainous Serrania Celtibérica has a population of just one person per square kilometre"

more options for replenishing supplies, with only a mountain refuge for respite should you need it.

There's nowhere better to experience the appeal of a quiet bivouac. My favourite spot is a tiny stone structure atop the Collado del Buey, sitting at 5640ft (1720m), with no facilities beyond a roof and four walls. The first time I camped here I barely slept. Not for lack of comfort, but for the draw of the stars outside lighting up the night sky.

Aside from the isolation and the ever-changing mountain climate, it's the elevation that provides the biggest challenge – accumulating more than 42,500ft (13,000m) across the 430-mile (700km) journey. Until now, most of the climbing has been short, sharp inclines with little in the way of flat riding. But ahead lies the Pico de Peñarroya – our highest point at 6653ft (2028m). A perfect, albeit steep, gravel road leads to the summit, and rewards your efforts with unspoiled views across the neighbouring Maestrazgo region and the Sierra de Javalambre.

From the dizzying heights of Peñarroya, our route begins its meander back towards Teruel, towards real life. We leave behind the ancient communities that we've passed through, many of which are suffering from the effects of depopulation. For while the quiet and peaceful villages serve as a beautiful backdrop for our bikepacking adventures, their cultures are disappearing. It is my hope that in establishing this route, we can turn the threats of depopulation into opportunities. We could see this land not as empty or without a future, but as a remote place worth visiting, that has all the isolation, intrigue, and adventure we usually search for in far-flung exotic cycling destinations. **EP**

STARRY NIGHTS

Serranía Celtibérica boasts some of the clearest skies in all of Europe. The population scarcity, coupled with a lack of flight paths crossing the region, makes for minimal light pollution and a night sky illuminated only by the stars. One of the best places to gaze is the Javalambre plateau, where a simple stone shelter provides the perfect setting for a night spent in the elements watching the skies.

Clockwise from left: the so-called 'Spanish Lapland'; a bed for the night; the fortifications of Albarracín; Previous page: Laguna da Taravilla, near the Tagus river

TOOLKIT

Start/Finish // Teruel
Distance // 430miles (700km)
Getting there // Fly or take the train to Valencia or Zaragoza, then catch a regional train (which allow bikes) to Teruel.
When to ride // Spring and autumn. Summer can be punishingly hot, and winter is a little too like the real Lapland.
What to take // A rugged adventure touring bike with at least 2-inch tyres. You'll need to be an experienced bikepacker if you're riding the full route: take a comfortable bivvy set-up and enough water-carrying capacity to get you through those long sections without resupply points.
More info // www.montanasvacias.com

© Ernesto Pastor @Montanasvacias

MORE LIKE THIS
SPANISH BIKEPACK ADVENTURES

PIRINEXUS

Looking for your first bikepacking trip in Spain? Pirinexus is a 217-mile (350km) loop that takes riders from north Girona through both Spanish and French Catalonia, and along the Costa Brava, never straying far from 'green ways', rural gravel roads and low-traffic tarmac roads. Not as demanding as the Montañas Vacías, or as remote, this well-signposted loop is open to riders of all abilities. As you pass from village to village, be sure to take enough time to sample the local gastronomy: from the rustic to the very best restaurants (plenty of places in the region boast a Michelin star). Along the way, you'll find campsites, hostels and other accommodation options – which add to the route's simple and accessible appeal. More info: www.viesverdes.cat/en/routes/pirinexus

Start/Finish // Girona
Distance // 217 miles (350 km)

BURRALLY

Continuing our theme of remoteness, you're more likely to encounter a boar than a BMW on this 435-mile (700 km) adventure through Valencia. The route begins on the Mediterranean coast and heads inland as it proceeds south to the west of the city of Valencia. The region is incredibly mountainous and hosts the annual Burrally ride through its beautiful landscapes, including the Penyagolosa Natural Park, Sierra de Espadán, the Chera-Sot de Chera Natural Park, and the Canal de Navarrés. Dubbed as a challenge, not a race, this small event is limited to just 30 people, and is inspired by the Torino-Nice Rally (see page 240). Taking anything from four to 10 days to complete, the route can be ridden throughout the year, but as temperatures soar here in summer, it's often ridden as a winter getaway. More info: burrally.wordpress.com

Start // Vinaroz, Castellón
Finish // Xàtiva, Valencia
Distance // 435 miles (700km)

CAMINO DEL CID

A dense network of trails crossing Spain from Burgos, about 150 miles (240km) south of Bilbao, to Alicante's Mediterranean coast, the Camino del Cid follows the steps of Rodrigo Díaz de Vivar, also known as El Cid Campeador, a medieval knight from the 11th century. It's the ideal starting point from which to plan your next Spanish cycling tour, and features alternative tracks for mountain bikes or touring bikes which are signposted across its entire length: around 869 miles (1400km) of tracks and 1240 miles (2000km) of roads. Experience the contrasting cultures of the myriad medieval villages and towns that dot the route, as you travel through the provinces of Burgos, Soria, Guadalajara, Zaragoza, Teruel, Castellón, Valencia and Alicante. More info: www.caminodelcid.org

Start // Vivar del Cid, Burgos
Finish // Orihuela, Alicante
Distance // 932 miles (1500 km)

© Luis Cordon, Thomas Owen

Above: the mountainous interior crossed by the Burrally bikepack event. Left: a pause at Camprodón on the Pirinexus

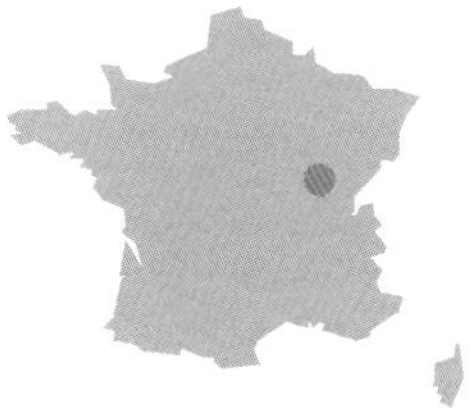

A TOAST TO THE VINES OF BURGUNDY

A delicious two-day spin through 'the stomach of France' will bring out the wine-loving gourmand in anyone, says the food writer Felicity Cloake.

However fussy you are about what you put in your glass I maintain it is impossible not to fall in love with the elegant Chardonnays and silky Pinot Noirs of this superstar wine region – or indeed its legendary cuisine. Burgundy is a land of remarkable richness, famous for its Bresse chicken and Charolais beef, juicy blackcurrants and glorious cheese, and, of course, its many dishes cooked in wine (hey, if you've got it, flaunt it). As one wine expert put it: 'Let Paris be France's head, Champagne her soul; Burgundy is her stomach.'

Happily, its vine-striped valleys and handsome villages also make Bourgogne, as it is in its native tongue, a lovely place to ride – but I'd be lying if I said the cycling was what drew me to take a train from Lyon to Chalon-sur-Saône with a bike and a gaggle of friends one fine June morning; this was very much an expedition fuelled by greed.

Though I'd blown in from the High Alps, where I'd been busy conquering cols and eating tartiflette, my peloton flew into Lyon from the UK; you can arrive by rail too but do consult the SNCF website about provision for bike transport if you want to bring your own. With just two days to play with, and a leisurely pace imposed by the summer heat, Chalon-sur-Saône, 90 minutes away by train, seemed a good place to start our expedition: long enough to allow for a decent picnic after a visit to the celebrated Les Halles de Lyon indoor market. (If you'd prefer to extend the ride, then you can get off at Villefranche-sur-Saône to take in the Beaujolais region too, or Mâcon for the whites of the same name.)

After picking up rental bikes at the station, we skip town and head north on the wide gravelled towpath of the Canal du Centre. Though pedalling along this placid waterway doesn't feel much

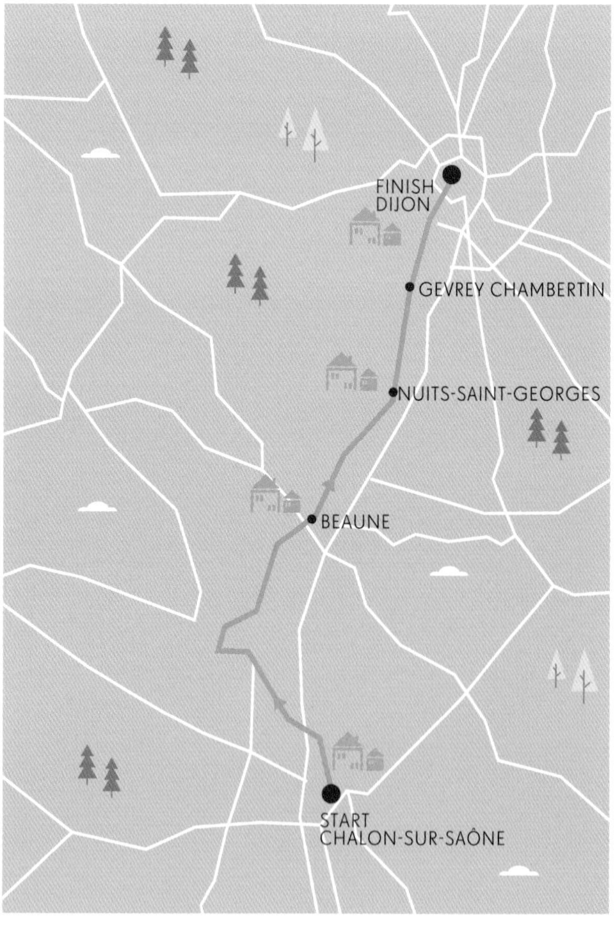

© Alain Doire / Bourgogne-Franche-Comté Tourisme

like being in wine country, as we approach Santenay the modest hills of the Côte d'Or put in an appearance on the horizon to the audible dismay of those faint hearts behind me. No, I say, without turning my head, don't worry, we're not going up them. Nevertheless, we stop for some emergency chocolate anyway, 'just in case'.

Appropriately fortified, we abandon the towpath for the thrillingly named Route des Grands Crus, where there are more than enough vines to keep everyone happy as we pass through names familiar from the bottom end of the wine list, like Puligny-Montrachet and my own particular favourite Mersault. Unlike Bordeaux, this is not a land of grand chateaux, however – Burgundy saves the razzmatazz for its towns, as we quickly realise as we finally roll into Beaune, some 24 miles (40km) later, having stopped for a photo at almost every bend.

The centre of the Burgundy wine trade, Beaune is a truly charming place with plenty to detain the thirsty tourist, from its wine museum to the riotously tiled Hospices de Beaune, the 15th-century almshouses that now play host to a very serious charity wine auction each November – and some excellent restaurants, including a good sprinkling of Michelin stars. It's also pretty busy, as we find to our cost when we try to score a table for six without a reservation; eventually a brasserie in the centre takes pity on us and plies us with rich, sticky boeuf bourguignon and carafes of entry-level local red. Really, I reflect tipsily as we wobble home through its medieval streets to our charmingly rickety Airbnb flat, it's hard to go too far wrong in France.

Nursing some slightly sore heads the next morning, we self medicate with Paris Brest buns, oozing praline cream, eaten on the

"In a brasserie we are plied with rich boeuf bourguignon and carafes of local red. It's hard to go wrong in France"

WINE TASTING IN BURGUNDY

Although you won't see as many roadside adverts for free tastings as in less celebrated wine regions (frankly, most producers don't need the business) there's more than enough in Burgundy to keep the committed oenophile happy. Tourist offices in Beaune, Nuits-Saint-Georges and Dijon will have a list of those who welcome visitors; unless you're buying enough to ship home, remember to make room in your panniers for some souvenirs (chuck clothes out if necessary).

Clockwise from above: the riotously tiled Hospices de Beaune; the author working up a thirst; avoid riding in September, the busy harvest month. Previous page: Burgundy, 'the stomach of France'

© Felicity Cloake, fotoluk1983 / Getty Images

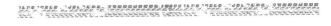

sunny wall outside the Boulangerie Bouillot, and then get on the road, passing through our first photo stop, the 18th-century stone Porte St Nicolas within minutes. Fortunately, there's a mere 15 miles (24km) to cover before lunch, leaving plenty of time to meander along the narrow tracks through the vines used by *viticulteurs*, who are much in evidence today, bent double with concentration over their secateurs, or, as lunchtime approaches, hurrying home in their shiny Mercedes.

We're heading for the bustling town of Nuits-Saint-Georges, where we attack the excellent value €14 menu at the Cafe du Centre with such gusto we have to have a little snooze on the sunny terrace afterwards. Nothing to do with the glass of wine that came with it, obviously. Refreshed, we head on to Dijon, through the pretty village of Gevrey Chambertin and past the magnificent Chateau du Clos de Vougeot, stopping at the Cave des Vignerons (winemakers' co-operative) in Morey-Saint-Denis to choose a bottle for pre-dinner drinks, a process which involves a fair bit of tasting (and spitting, naturally). In fact, we buy so much that madame behind the counter is quite taken aback to discover we intend to stick it all in our panniers – 'Oh là là!'

Perhaps surprisingly, we still make it to Dijon, renowned for its architecture and its mustard, in time to enjoy a glass or two before heading out for a victory feast of plump, garlicky snails, coq au vin and a beautifully boozy blackcurrant sorbet made with local *crème de cassis*. After all, we've cycled here, we reason, merrily toasting ourselves with a final, budget-blowing glass of wine – we've earned it. **FC**

© Richard Taylor / 4 Corners, Lucy Smart

TOOLKIT

Start // Chalon-sur-Saône
Finish // Dijon
Distance // 54 miles (88km)
Getting there // Fly or take the train to Lyon, then take a local train to Chalon-sur-Saône (90 minutes).
When to ride // Summer, when there is fruit on the vines, but before the September harvest, when roads are busy with vitícultural traffic. There are wine festivals year-round.
What to eat // Everything, but particularly dishes cooked in wine like coq au vin, boeuf bourguignon and their vegetarian equivalent, *oeufs en meurette*.
Where to stay // There's no shortage of accommodation, from grand chateaux to cheap and cheerful hostels, but to meet locals, rent rooms through Airbnb.
What to take // A corkscrew... and plenty of water.
What to read // *One More Croissant for the Road*, my account of my 1400-mile bike journey around France in search of culinary perfection.
More info // www.burgundy-by-bike.com

MORE LIKE THIS
FRENCH WINE JOURNEYS

ALSACE WINE ROAD

Not only is heavily forested Alsace, on the Franco-German border, one of the prettiest parts of France, with its rolling hills and half-timbered villages, but the vineyards on those wooded slopes produce some of the finest Rieslings, Gewürztraminers, Pinot Gris and Pinot Blancs in the world. The Véloroute du Vignoble d'Alsace follows a Roman road parallel with the Routes des Vins, and passes through 100 winemaking villages and 50 different Grand Cru winemaking areas, complete with stunning churches, medieval ruins and some of the cosiest restaurants you've ever hung up your helmet in. *Winstubs*, often translated as taverns, feel more like a home from home where you can enjoy local wine and hearty, distinctly Germanic dishes such as *choucroute garnie* (fermented cabbage with an eye-popping array of pork products) and delicious fruit tarts. More info: cyclinginalsace.com

Start // Marlenheim
Finish // Thann
Distance // 83 miles (135km)

CHAMPAGNE

Champagne is popularly known as the king of wines, and the wine of kings – possibly because only royalty can afford the eye-watering prices commanded by some of the Grandes Marques. Fortunately, however, the visitor to the region cannot help but discover lesser-known, but often more interesting wines at rather more attractive prices thanks to the many smaller producers in villages such as Le Mesnil-sur-Oger and Verzenay, some of whom will helpfully ship wine back home for you too. Starting in Reims with its stunning Gothic cathedral, this 99-mile (160km) loop takes you through the Grand Cru village of Aÿ, home of Bollinger, the ancient villages of Baulne-en-Brie and Vertus in the Côte des Blancs, and finishes in pretty Épernay, home to many of the fanciest names in fizz. More info: tourisme-en-champagne.com

Start // Reims
Finish // Épernay
Distance // 99 miles (160km)

BORDEAUX

Bordeaux is the world's largest fine wine region, which means you could spend months pedalling around its grand chateaux enjoying some of the best wines on Earth. But this whistlestop tour, which takes in the appellations of Pessac-Léognan, Graves and Sauternes, offers a satisfying greatest hits compilation of crisp whites, bold reds and golden, almost nectarous stickies. If you're in a rush, it can easily be done in a day from Bordeaux (there's a train back from Langon), though to sample any wine en route, it would be wise to take your time, not least because the region is also well served by restaurants offering vast platters of briny Atlantic oysters and *entrecôte à la bordelaise*. If you can't manage dessert, take a few gooey little canélé cakes home in your pocket. More info: bordeaux-graves-sauternes.com

Start // Bordeaux
Finish // Sauternes
Distance // 30 miles (48km)

© Cultura Exclusive/WALTER ZERLA / Getty Images, Route des Vins / phlabeguerie, FreeProd33 / Shutterstock

Clockwise from top: on the Alsace Wine Road; the harvest in Bordeaux; wine of the Graves region matures in its barrels

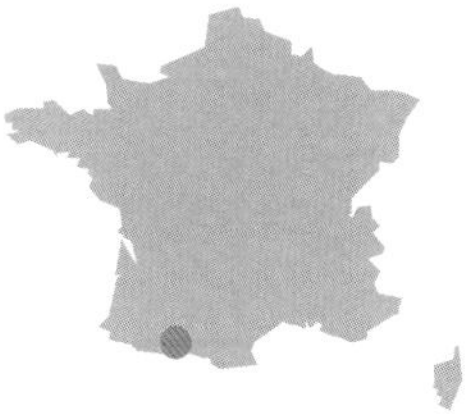

HOW TO RAID THE PYRENEES

Rob Penn embarks on a mighty road traverse of the mountain range from the Atlantic to the Mediterranean – with the added challenge of completing the ride in under 100 hours.

The Pyrenees figure highly in the imagination of cyclists. They have done for over a century. Their inclusion in the Tour de France for the first time in 1910 was a turning point not just for the Tour, but for all cycle racing. Henri Desgrange, then Tour organiser and editor of a French sporting newspaper (he had originally developed the idea for a great bicycle race to outsell a rival daily), immediately grasped the significance of sending cyclists over mountain eyries where mere mortals feared to tread. Famously, the eventual 1910 race winner, Octave Lapize cycled past a team of marshals on a Pyrenean pass and exclaimed the words 'Vous êtes des assassins!' The Pyrenees have featured in the Tour ever since, in turn drawing amateur cyclists to these epic mountains like moths to a flame.

In 1950, five riders from the Cyclo-Club Béarnais in the town of Pau first rode the length of the Pyrenees. They then instigated the creation of the Raid Pyrenean as a *randonée permanente* – a long-distance cycle route. Tens of thousands of fit, amateur cyclists have since followed in their tyre tracks. Today, you can contact the Cyclo-Club Béarnais and, on receipt of a modest fee, they will send you a *carnet* or booklet, which you then have to get stamped at various 'control' points (generally cafes and shops) along the way. Cyclo-Club Béarnais also arrange a medal and certificate to

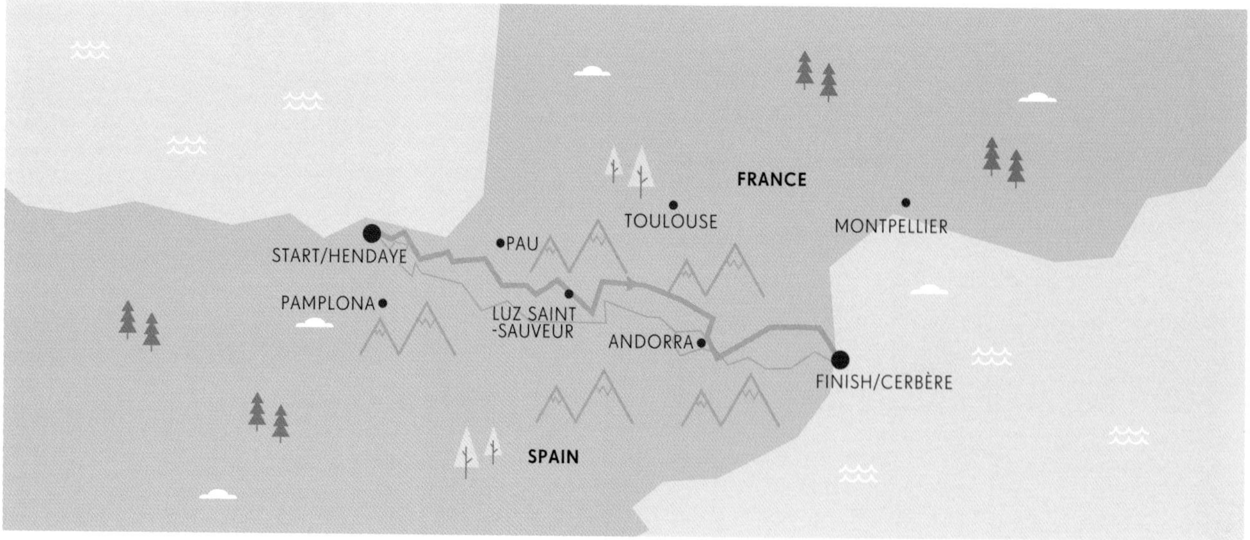

© PHILIPIMAGE / Shutterstock

be waiting for you at the end, on completion of the challenge.

The Raid Pyrenean traverses the length of the range through France, shadowing the border with Spain, from the Atlantic Ocean to the Mediterranean Sea – 450 miles (720km) with 36,000ft (11,000m) of ascent over 18 cols. The challenge is to complete the Raid Pyrenean in 100 hours, or four days and four hours.

Of course, you can plot the route yourself and just set off, or even pay a cycle tour operator to organise the whole thing for you (and carry your luggage). As someone who respects the lore and history of cycling, though, I chose to write to the secretary of Cyclo-Club Béarnais, pay my fee and receive my booklet. Somehow it adds to the experience. I rode a lightweight steel bike and carried my own kit in bikepacking panniers. Crucially, I had the right gearing – you need it. There is a lot of climbing.

The prestigious cols – Peyresourde, d'Aspin, Portet d'Aspet and Puymorens as well as the legendary trio of Aubisque, Soulor and Tourmalet (known as the 'Circle of Death' in Tour de France lingo) – together make up the meat of the Raid. The lesser known cols, however, surprised and delighted me. Some are hidden deep in great forests, others are tucked away on quiet backroads, while a few hardly warrant their designation as a col, they are so low. From one to 18, I bagged them all gladly.

The route officially starts on the Boulevard de Mer, overlooking the Bay of Biscay in Hendaye. The first day is a gentle opener; there are three low cols to cross. After that, traversing the central Pyrenees, the following three days are arduous. Where you stay is not proscribed, so you're free to choose when and how you take

"The prestigious cols are known as the 'Circle of Death' – but the lesser-known are often delightful surprises"

THE CRUX OF THE RAID

The Hautes Pyrenees is magnificent cycling country; a fantastic place to submerge yourself in the invigorating, mysterious and occasionally spiritual experience of riding in the high mountains. At the heart of it is the Col du Tourmalet (6939 feet, 2115m), the most visited col in the world's most famous bike race. Following the Raid route from west to east, the climb begins in Luz Saint-Sauveur and goes on for 11.3 miles (18.2km) with 4604 feet (1404m) of ascent. In places, the scenery is spectacular; other spots are very exposed.

Clockwise from above: riders gain 36,000ft over 18 cols, including the Tourmalet (and previous page); Le Géant du Tourmalet sculpture by Figure Studio Métais of Octave Lapize; Cerbère, journey's end; Octave Lapize

© Roger Viollet / Getty Images, Isa Fernandez Fernandez / Shutterstock

the pain. I tried to even the climbing out, but on day four, I covered 101 miles (162km) with 9600ft (2926m) of ascent, including a 17.5-mile (28km) climb to Col de Puymorens into a withering headwind.

As much as the Raid is about climbing, do not discount the descending. Some of the descents are fast and, in the sort of adverse weather conditions the Pyrenees are famous for, tricky. Staying focused on long descents from high cols like Tourmalet or Peyresourde in the wet is exhausting. But flying down the same descents in good weather, at least when you are feeling at one with your bicycle, can also be profoundly exhilarating.

I knew from studying the route that Col de la Perche was the denouement. If I made it over the top at the end of day four, the Raid was in the bag. The last 80 miles (130km) or so to Cerbère are downhill, tumbling out of the eastern Pyrenean mountains, or flat, with a whiff of the Mediterranean and the prospect of a cold beer urging you on. Exhausted, I rolled over the col as the heat of the day leached away, the sun sinking behind me.

Then I was freewheeling; the grind of the day was finally over. Then I was speeding down through a red canyon and fizzing through sleepy villages, sinking the bike into each bend, wearing a fixed grin with hands clamped into the drops, with elbows bent and my weight spread evenly over the frame. I eased the bike left and right with the tiniest shifts in balance, breaking early, carving hard through the radius of each bend, and accelerating back to top speed, owning the road, honouring the Pyrenees. **RP**

© Tom Irvine / Alamy Stock Photo, Hemis / Alamy Stock Photo

TOOLKIT

Start // Hendaye
Finish // Cerbère (the majority ride west to east)
Distance // 450 miles (720km)
When to ride // Early June until the end of September, when the highest passes are generally clear of snow.
The time limit // 100 hours is four days and four hours; most riders set off at 9am and finish before 1pm on day five.
Getting there and back // There are airports at Bilbao, Biarritz, Toulouse and Perpignan. Research the tricky logistics of getting your bike box from the start to the finish; or use a tour operator.
Where to stay // Whether you use hotels, Airbnb or chambres d'hôtes, the Pyrenees is a busy tourist destination in summer, particularly around the Tour de France; book your accommodation well in advance
More info // https://ccb-cyclo.fr/

Opposite: in Gran Sasso, just one of the national parks to ride through on a traverse of the Apennines

MORE LIKE THIS
RANGE BAGGING

INNSBRUCK TO LAKE COMO

This five-day ride starts in Innsbruck, the unofficial capital of the Tyrolean Alps, and ends beside the turquoise waters of Lake Como. It crosses the mountainous region of South Tyrol, or Alto Adige, where distinct peoples and languages overlap, where frontiers have changed over the centuries and where customs collide. The highpoint is Passo dello Stelvio (9045ft, 2757m), one of the greatest Alpine passes, but you also need strong legs to get over Passo Giovo, Passo di Foscagno and Brenner Pass (one of Europe's most important trade routes since the early Middle Ages) as well as up the hill to the cyclists' chapel of Madonna del Ghisallo, on a promontory above Lake Como. There is a lot of climbing, but there are also endless, wonderful Alpine views, ruined castles on rock promontories, forests, dashing white rivers and good food.
Start // Innsbruck, Austria
Finish // Lake Como, Italy
Distance // 280 miles (450km)

BREVET DES SEPT COLS UBAYENS, FRANCE

To complete the Brevet (another word for a *randonnée* or long-distance cycling event) des Sept Cols Ubayens you simply have to climb the seven cols that surround the Ubaye, a beautiful valley in the southern Alps. I say simply: the seven cols include Vars (6916ft, 2108m), Allos (7372ft, 2247m), Cayolle (7631ft, 2326m) and the lofty La Bonette (8907ft, 2715m). Starting and finishing each col in the unspoilt town of Barcelonnette, the whole brevet amounts to 250 miles (400km) with a whopping 23,600ft (7200m). However, there is no deadline; you climb them all at your pace; no matter how long it takes, you get a certificate. If you want to range beyond the Ubaye Valley, the cycling is superb in neighbouring territories too. More info: www.ubaye.com/GB/summer-activites/cycling.html
Start/Finish // Barcelonnette
Distance: 250 miles (400km)

THE APENNINES, ITALY

The Apennine Mountains form the backbone of Italy from Sicily to northern Tuscany, extending almost the entire length of the country. This ride winds up and over them, from the Abruzzo region, passing through Umbria and Le Marche to reach Tuscany, crossing several national parks including Maiella, Gran Sasso and Monti Sibillini. There are quiet roads, tough climbs, hanging villages, dramatic peaks, dashing rivers, dark woods and arid, high plains, but the little-visited towns – Santo Stefano di Sessanio, Camerino, Gubbio and San Sepolcro, for example – will also delight. Avoid the heat of summer; May and September are the best months. More info: https://italy-cycling-guide.info/cycle-routes/lakes-and-mountains/national-parks-apennines/
Start // Sulmona
Finish // San Sepolcro
Distance // 442 miles (708km)

© N Eisele-Hein / Getty IMages

DOWN THE DANUBE

Clover Stroud and her family meander along the efficient bike path on the Danube's Austrian banks and enjoy a vivid snapshot of the thriving river, the longest in Europe.

My husband and I chose Linz as our starting point, as we headed out along the Danube River, although many cyclists start the Donauradweg upstream in Passau, a German city on the Austrian border. But since we are both amateurs, and reaching our destination of Vienna inside a week would mean covering 43 miles (70km) a day, we jumped to Linz, ensuring our daily cycle was closer to a more leisurely 30 miles (45km).

We lingered in Linz, enjoying ice creams in Hauptplatz, the elegant central square surrounded by baroque buildings painted the colours of strawberry and pistachio. But the river soon tugged us onwards, and as the city's industrial suburbs gave way to verges of nodding daisies, and fields of clover and campion, I realised for the first time, but certainly not the last, that the joy of this holiday lay in the journey.

The Danube was strategically important to the Romans, since it provided a watery barrier against invading barbarian hordes.

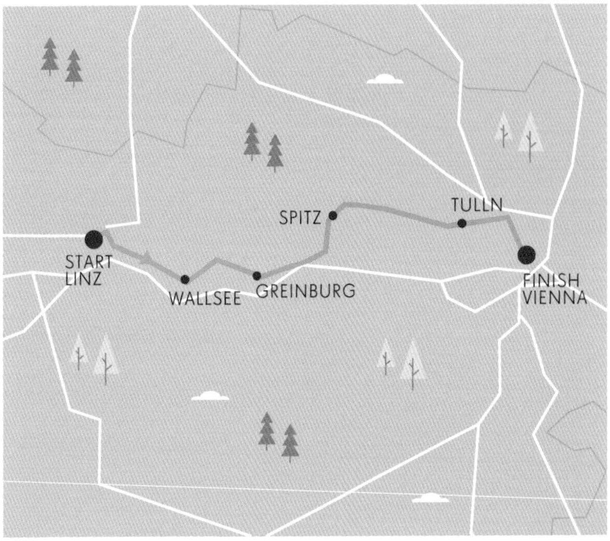

© Julian Love / Lonely PLanet

But where the waters were later used to shift salt barges along this trade route, now the cargo you're more likely to spot will be gleaming new cars, or excited tourists.

The river is a reassuring travelling companion and covers some of the defining ages in Austria's history, from its Celtic roots, which we found at Mitterkirchen Celtic village, to the castles of the mighty Habsburg Empire, to a more difficult, recent past, which we sensed most keenly in Mauthausen, where 120,000 people died in a concentration camp.

The route was flat, our main obstacles not hills but Lycra-clad cyclists who bombed along the path, head down, like sleek bullets, or in jovial groups, shouting encouragement to us amateurs, easily distinguishable from the pros in our denim shorts and Converse trainers.

By dusk, we were cycling through the sticky scent of poplar trees, with all stages of life parading along the river's banks. We passed a teenage couple, eating pizza between drags on shared cigarettes. Further up, a young family paddled, their picnic of rolls and broken biscuits left behind them. Later, a group of men with beards and paunches cradled bottles of beer while cooking foil-wrapped potatoes on a campfire, their fishing rods momentarily forgotten. And in the twilight, as the 16th-century castle of Wallsee rose ahead, an elderly couple, four walking sticks between them, tottered along, swans on the water escorting them home. That night, after cycling 30 miles (48km), the Austrian diet of fried meat and piles of carbohydrates suddenly made great sense.

From Wallsee we cycled through the orchards of the Mostviertel,

"We were cycling through the sticky scent of poplar trees, with all stages of life parading along the river's banks"

where apples and pears are harvested for flat local cider called *most*. An hour later, flagging before lunch, we were rewarded with the silhouette of Greinburg Castle on the northern bank. Loading our bikes onto a tiny wooden ferry, which wouldn't look out of place chugging up the Amazon, we joined tourists bussed into this Disney-like Habsburg town for the castle and kitsch curiosities of Austria's oldest theatre, built in a granary in 1563.

That evening in Persenbeug, apricots played a starring role on the menu, cooked with pork and used to stuff sweet pancakes, reminding us we were entering the jewel in the fruit-growing necklace of the Danube, the Wachau, or wine district of Lower Austria.

The next day, we saw vines criss-crossing the banks, and the cycle route left the river to meander through orchards, passing gardens ripe with huge courgettes, shiny tomatoes and lines of elegant runner beans. We stopped to stuff a few euros into an honesty box selling bags of apricots, while tumbling pear trees created moments of shade in the 40°C heat, and our bike wheels slipped on the plums and greengages littering the track.

Before Spitz we wiggled through Willendorf, famous for its voluptuous Paleolithic Venus found in 1908, and then Schwallenbach, where a honey-coloured tower, crimson roses and fluttering white doves transported me to Provence.

© Julian Love / Getty Images, Florian Werner / Getty Images, © Tupungato / Shutterstock

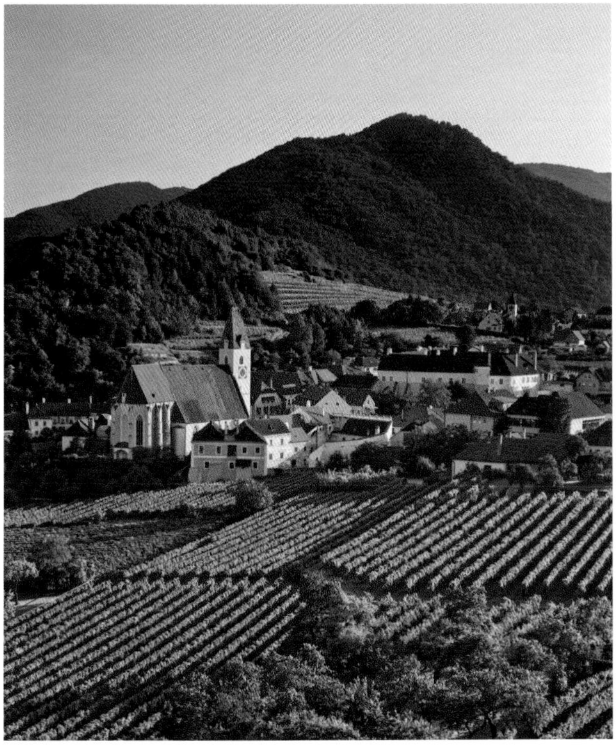

SNACK STOPS

There are very few cafes or snack bars en route, so be sure to pack a picnic every morning. But there are some small stalls selling whole mackerel grilled over an open fire. There's a particularly nice one at a bar called Piratenknetpe, just beyond Grein on the southern bank, opposite St Nikola. The mackerel is delicious, served with thick slices of rye bread and butter: very welcome after a long cycle ride.

From left: riding the Danube cycle path; Austrian energy food; Linz; the town of Spitz in the Wachau Valley. Previous page: the 'Danube Loop', an oxbow bend opposite Schlögen, near Passau

In Spitz, our resting place for two nights, we stretched out by the pool, but we soon became restless, hungry for the unexpected adventures we were sharing on the journey. We found these in the medieval castle at Dürnstein, where Richard the Lionheart was imprisoned in 1192. Krems an der Donau, 12 miles (20km) on, was less appealing, heaving with tourists gorging on chips and knocking back gigantic beers at 10am.

The bucolic beauty of the Wachau vanished as we cycled on past gas power stations. It wasn't pretty, but we spotted real, local Austrian life in the mothers gossiping as their children paddled along scraps of beaches, and the excitable teenagers on waterskis showing off to leggy girls on rollerblades who sliced down the cycle path, futuristic in goggles and knee pads.

At Tulln we raced around the Egon Schiele Museum, posing for pictures beside the elegant, surprising sculpture of Attila the Hun greeting his bride Kriemhild on the waterfront. But there was little time for sightseeing, and when we hit the fringes of the Vienna forest, we passed Russian boats from the Black Sea lining the river as the skyscrapers grew taller, and the huge city bridges of Vienna itself loomed above us.

Suddenly we lost the familiar Donauradweg as we left the river, instead joining evening commuters and ladies walking their dogs after a day in the office. I missed the bobbing ducks who seemed to have accompanied us all the way from Linz, and the rattle of trams and taxis startled me.

I didn't want the journey to end. I wanted the river to flow on beside my spinning wheels forever. **CS**

TOOLKIT

Start // Linz
Finish // Vienna
Distance // 150 miles (241km)
Getting there // International flights arrive at both Linz and Vienna.
Tour // Macs Adventure (www.macsadventure.com) offers a Danube Family Cycling package from £495 per person.
When to ride // April until October is the best time of year, but check ahead with the Austrian Tourist Board (www.austria.info) about flooding.
What to take // Mosquitos are rife during wet and warm months, so pack plenty of repellent.
Where to eat // Weinhotel Wachau (www.weinhotel-wachau.at).

© Rainer Mirau / LOOK-foto Westend61 | Getty Images

Opposite: the Rhine Cycle Route, which passes through nine Unesco World Heritage sites, in Basel, Switzerland

MORE LIKE THIS
RIVER TRAILS

CAMEL TRAIL, UK

Once the railway track that linked the Southwest to London, carrying sand and fish inland, and immortalised in Betjeman's Cornwall as 'the most beautiful train journey I know', the Camel Trail is now a super family-friendly cycle path. It cuts through some of Cornwall's prettiest countryside. From Rick Stein's famous fishing port of Padstow to Wadebridge, it hugs the vast Camel Estuary before heading through the woodland of the Camel Valley and onto Bodmin. The trail then heads inland to the foot of Bodmin Moor, finishing up at the moorland village of Blisland. The route is mostly traffic-free and includes both a Site of Special Scientific Interest and a Special Area of Conservation. The estuary section is especially great for birdwatchers, look out for peregrines, ospreys and mute swans. More info: www.sustrans.org.uk.
Start // Padstow
Finish // Blisland
Distance // 18 miles (29km)

CANAL DE LA GARONNE, FRANCE

The Romans first entertained the idea of a canal connecting the Atlantic and Mediterranean. The Canal du Midi between Sète and Toulouse was constructed in the 17th century, but it wasn't until the 19th century that the cash was found for its western extension, between Castets-en-Dorthe, just east of Bordeaux, and Toulouse – whereupon the railway pilfered much of its goods traffic. As a tourist destination, it has finally found its footing. It's also an easy, family-friendly 160-mile (260km) cycle route (mostly along green ways) that you can fit into a week, beside a waterway shaded by beautiful plane trees, enjoying quiet villages, well-known wine regions and enjoying all the canal's opportunities for fun on the water. Finally, it's bookended by two of France's most attractive cities.
Start // Bordeaux
Finish // Toulouse
Distance // 160 miles (260km)

THE RHINE CYCLE ROUTE

The Rhine Cycle Trail is suitable for cyclists of all levels of fitness and ages. And it's also part of a EuroVelo route, in this instance 15. Riding along one of Europe's longest rivers isn't something that many people will do in a single trip. Instead, pick out the tastiest portions of Switzerland, France, Germany or the Netherlands and spend a week or two on them. Choose from nine Unesco World Heritage sites, including the city of Strasbourg, Dutch windmills, Cologne's cathedral, and the entire Middle Rhine Valley between Bingen and Koblenz. And why not stop to sample some Riesling wines around Colmar in Alsace? More info: www.rhinecycleroute.eu
Start // Andermatt, Switzerland
Finish // Rotterdam, Netherlands
Distance // 765 miles (1231km)

© Westend61 / Getty Images

THE 24 HOURS OF FINALE LIGURE

A day and night of madcap riding on Italy's Ligurian coast, this 24-hour mountain-bike event is half-race, half-festival.

I confess I only agreed to ride the 24 hours of Finale Ligure race because I wasn't paying attention. My friend had been making enthusiastic noises about it, and there's a case to be made for Liguria being the best spot in Europe to ride a mountain bike. Plus he'd offered to drive me there from the UK. It was only when he started discussing sleep strategies and contingency plans in case one of us got injured that I began to realise this wasn't the holiday I'd imagined.

Just over the border from France, Italy's Ligurian coast benefits from a maritime climate, meaning its hills and mountains are more verdant than those of the High Alps. Its winding trails aren't defaced by ski-lifts, and post-ride drinks at most osterias come with a complimentary serving of *farinata*, an olive-oil-and-rosemary-infused chickpea pancake. Basically, it's a kind of cycling paradise. Like all the most enjoyable things in Italy, it also remains largely untroubled by English speakers.

The 24 hours of Finale Ligure has been running for over two decades. It involves riding a a loop typical of the area's superlatively good singletrack. The route teases its way through twisty forest trails and a series of steep climbs and technical descents, before bursting out on to the rocky slopes above the waters of the Ligurian Sea and traversing the headland separating

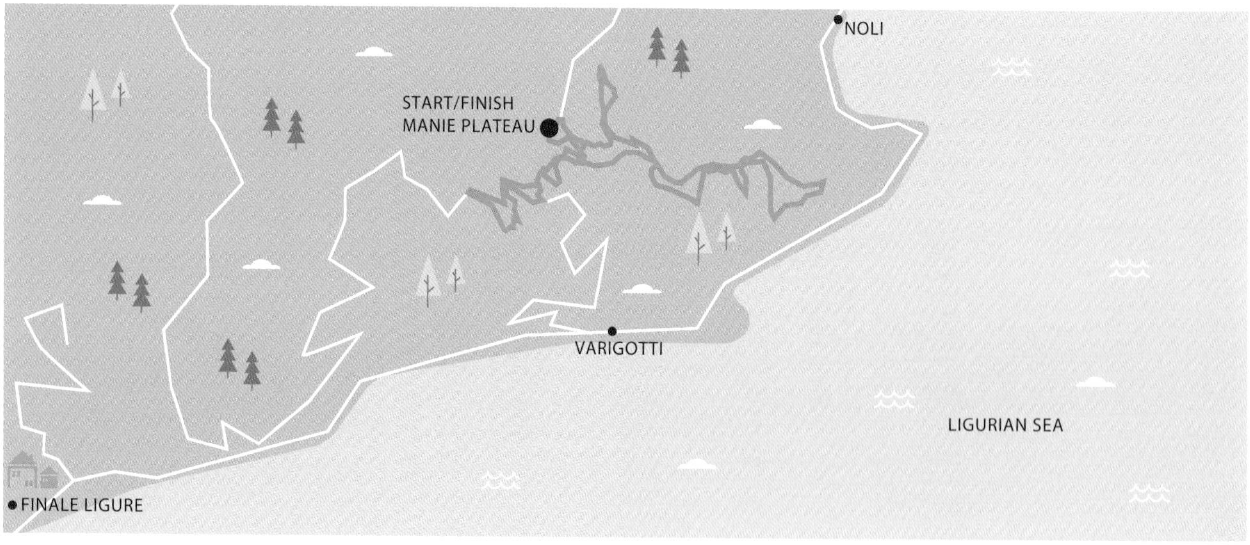

© Sportograf.com

Finale and the fortified town of Savona. In centuries gone by, ships would have set out from here to pillage up and down the coast. However, negotiating these tricky and rock-strewn sections, riders will have to make a decision: enjoy the views or stay upright.

The 7.5-mile (12km) course takes around an hour to complete, and is as perfect a slice of riding as you could wish for. Wonderful. Except the 24 hours of Finale Ligure demands that you (or your team) ride this loop non-stop for 24 hours.

It's open to solo riders, or teams from pairs up to 12 racing in a relay. To break up the field, there is a Le Mans-style start in which riders make a kilometre-long dash to their bikes. From then on it's a case of pacing yourself and hoping your teammate is ready and waiting when it's time to change over at lap's end.

How to kill time when you're not turning yourself inside out in the saddle? Thankfully, the 24 hours of Finale Ligure also functions as a mini-festival. Thousands arrive with tents and motorhomes, while the most organised teams bring gazebos and generators, stationing themselves beside the course, or tucked away in quieter fields nearby. Riders not catching up on sleep can watch the bands playing. In fact, the course takes racers pass the front of the music stage each lap, so it's possible to rock out and heckle fellow competitors from the same spot.

Three pasta meals are included for racers in the solo and duo

"As the sun goes down, riders fire up their lights to navigate the deepening gloom and the fans on the course get rowdier"

categories. Otherwise, the onsite Ferrin restaurant is good but can get very busy. Better to trek the kilometre down to La Grotta. Local specialities include wild boar, rabbit, walnut sauce, and pasta alla Genovese which comes with potatoes, beans and pesto. While there you should also check out the caves below.

As the day wears on and the sun goes down, riders fire up their lights to navigate the deepening gloom and well-lubricated fans out on the course get rowdier. However, in the handover pens, the atmosphere is more serious. Riders peer into the darkness in the hope their teammates haven't had a crash, mechanical problem or some other mishap. When they do appear, there's barely time for a hug and a few words of encouragement before handing over the transponder that records the team's time and dashing back into the fray.

A stint on the graveyard shift is a terrifying prospect. On the course, it's possible to go for miles without seeing the light of another competitor. During these hours the glow of the marshal stations dotted around the hills are beacons in the darkness.

© Sportograf.com

FINALE LIGURE AND FINALBORGO

The town of Finale Ligure itself has a split personality. On the seafront, it offers the beachfront restaurants and bars you might expect of a resort where many Italians take their holidays. Tucked in behind is the older, charming community of Finalborgo. Home to a picturesque palazzo, along with the medieval Convent of Santa Caterina and Basilica of San Biagio, it's watched over by the imposing Castel San Giovanni.

From left: the Le Mans-style start to the race; a spectacular descent on the course overlooking the Ligurian Sea. Previous page: how to corner at night

As physical fatigue and lack of sleep start to cloud your brain, sections you'd mastered during the day are suddenly unfamiliar. Animals skitter away from the track upon your approach; shadows in the undergrowth take on weird proportions. On several occasions, I convinced myself I was about to get charged by a *cinghiale*, one of the area's ferocious wild boars.

Of course, if you assemble a large enough team you can share the load, and get yourself a decent amount of sleep between laps. Those on squads of four seem to be enjoying themselves, but riders on the largest teams of 12 need only smash out two or three fast laps between watching the bands, barbecuing, and drinking spritzes.

Still, no matter how many laps you're putting in, when the sun does finally come up over the sea the feeling is magical. From here it's only a few bleary hours more as everyone tries to wring the last drops of energy from their legs. Then the klaxon sounds. Finito.

On stage, the solo category winner stares at the crowd through red eyes, thanking them for keeping him motivated in a voice so devoid of emotion as to be genuinely chilling. Other finishers stumble about in an equally zombie-like state. From a distance it would be hard to imagine any of these people had fun. But I promise you they did. It might just take them a day or two and a long nap to realise. **JD**

© Flow Mountain Bike

TOOLKIT

Start/Finish // Manie plateau, Finale Ligure
Distance // the course is 7.5 miles (12km).
Getting there // Fly or take the train to Nice, France or Genoa, Italy, then catch a train or drive along the coast to Finale Ligure.
Bike Hire // Finale has many good hire shops. Try Soul Cycle: www.soulcyclesfinaleligure.com
When to ride // The race is in early June, but the well-signposted course is open year-round.
Where to stay // Camping is included with your race entry. The pitches away from the race village are quieter. There's also permanent camping beside the Ferrin restaurant outside of the race. weekend: www.terrerossecamping.it
More info // www.24hfinale.com

Opposite: the hair-raising mass start from 8530ft at Megavalanche

MORE LIKE THIS
MOUNTAIN-BIKE RACES

DOLOMITI SUPERBIKE, ITALY

With over 20 years of history behind it, this tough off-road circuit through the Dolomite Mountains in northern Italy is a scenic challenge for rough riders. Setting off from Villabassa in South Tyrol, the epic 70-mile (113km) course rolls through a Unesco World Heritage-listed mountainscape before finishing back at Villabassa. Around 80% of the race route travels along gravel roads, so the pace is fast, and there are sections of singletrack and sealed surface in between. Along the way, riders have to contend with 12,540ft (3822m) of climbing, and the course tops out at 6607ft (2014m). If all that sounds too much, there is a half-distance option of 37 miles (60km). More info: www.dolomitisuperbike.com/
Start/Finish // Villabassa
Distance // 70 miles (113km)

GLENTRESS 7, SCOTLAND

Solos, pairs, or teams of three racing for seven hours in Glentress Forest in the Scottish Borders – whoever has completed the most laps by the end wins. Comparatively short in duration, and taking place on a fun and challenging course, this is a race for riders that prize enjoyment over suffering. It's part of the longstanding Tweedlove festival, which includes a huge range of races and events to suit all tastes. It's worth entering even if you're well acquainted with Glentress as the course takes racers into parts of the forest not usually open to riders. Camp onsite and make the race part of a long weekend of riding – the location is in the heart of the UK's largest network of trail centres, the 7 Stanes, which encompass everything from national-standard downhill courses to family-friendly blue routes. More info: https://tweedlove.com/
Start/Finish // Glentress, Scottish Borders
Distance // 7 miles (11km)

MEGAVALANCHE, FRANCE

The Megavalanche in Alpe d'Huez is the world's longest continuous downhill race – and arguably the world's most spectacular race, descending 8530ft vertically (2600m) from the glaciated summit of Pic Blanc in the French Alps at over 10,800ft (3300m) to the valley below. Riders line up for a berserk high-speed mass-start down a snowfield, and those that survive these opening minutes will be in for 12 miles (20km) of technical riding as they compete elbow-to-elbow with around 350 other riders. The best professional riders in the world will be there; qualification takes place a day or two earlier on a separate and shorter course. Do well in your heat and you might find yourself gridded next to one of the sport's big names come the weekend. Either way, you'll be in for a few days of intense racing. More info: www.ucc-sportevent.com/en/megavalanche-alpe-dhuez-en/
Start // Summit of Pic Blanc
Finish // Allemond
Distance // 12 miles (20km)

© Hoshi Yoshida

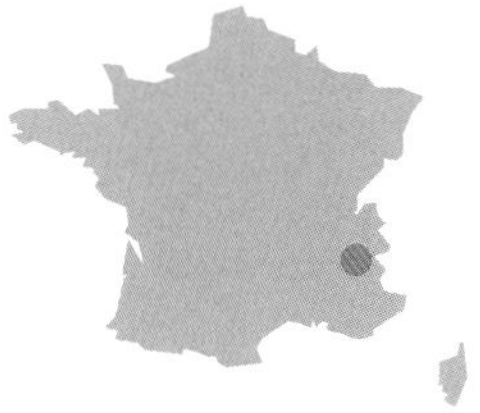

LA ROUTE DES GRANDES ALPES

Pedal the highways that give the French Alps their riding reputation and discover the titanic military face-offs that led to their creation.

The Pyrenees were the first 'proper' mountains to feature in the Tour de France, but the numerous high passes of the Alps are now more celebrated, and a ride from north to south is a dream trip for many cyclists. For over 100 years an official tourist route, the Route des Grandes Alpes, has linked Lake Geneva and Nice, on the Mediterranean coast. In some 435 miles (700km), it crosses the Cols de Colombière, Aravis and Saisies, then the Cormet de Roselend and the highest road pass in the Alps, the 9068ft (2764m) Col de l'Iséran. From there, it descends to the foot of the Col du Télégraphe and the oppressively mighty Galibier – and then hits the cols of Izoard Vars, Cayolle, Valberg, Couillole, Saint Martin, Turini and Castillon, before one last bump, the 1663ft (507m) Col d'Èze, before the official finish in Nice.

Phew.

This roll call of iconic passes totals around 65,000ft (20,000m) of climbing, enough to ignite fear and desire into the heart of any wannabe Fausto Coppi or Bradley Wiggins. But although these perfect ribbons of tarmac are a cyclists' playground, they were not made for us. So what on earth are they doing up in these inhospitable, lonely places?

The Alps divide countries, peoples, languages, food and much more. Yet, formidable as these high borderlands are, they are nonetheless contested. The Route des Grandes Alpes, which takes in so many of the Tour de France's favourite battlegrounds, is in many parts a product of these geopolitical skirmishes.

The history starts with Vittorio Emmanuele II of the Savoy dynasty, who in the 1850s, from the family seat in Turin, spearheaded the political movement to unify the city states

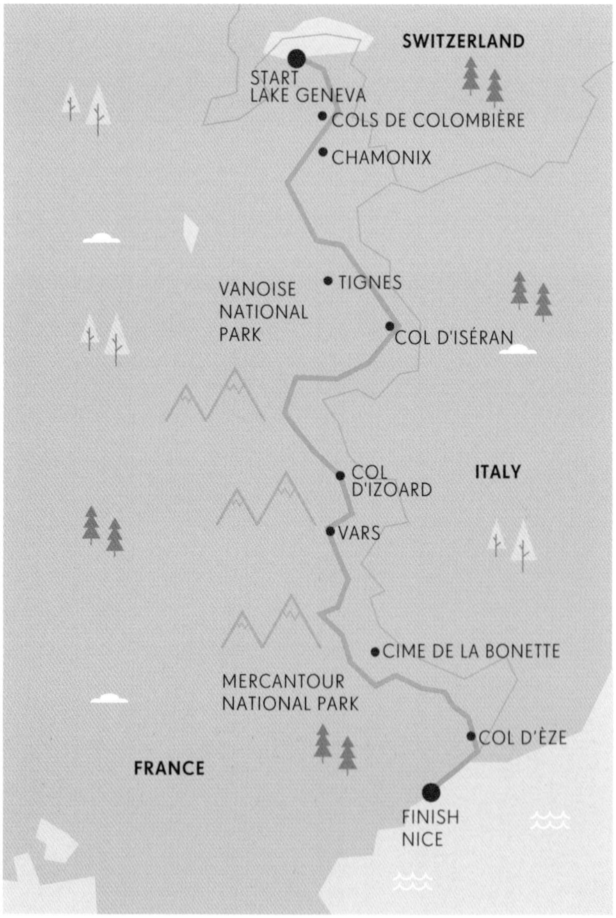

© Antton Miettinen

that made up Italy. In this he received the support of the French Emperor Napoleon III and, when the modern Italian nation was being born, a large chunk of the Alps was gifted to France in return. From 1860, the Savoie region, as well as Nice and its environs became French.

Napoleon III had already been doing some 'hearts-and-minds' PR work for Paris in the Alps, building refuges for travellers on some of the major passes, and many locals were happy to be French. But as Italy grew more confident, these new territories began to present France with a problem – a long, undefended border with a powerful new nation. Indeed, the major road-building projects in the Alps – Montgenèvre and Mont Cenis – undertaken by Napoleon Bonaparte (Napoleon III's uncle) to speed access to his conquests in the east, now seemed like major weaknesses.

What France needed was a backbone of roads running through the Alps from north to south so that, in the words of General Baron Berge, military governor of Lyon and commander of the Army of the Alps: '... heavy convoys of the modern army are no longer the prisoners of the valleys and can rise into the mountains, crossing the cols.' And, at the end of the 1880s, he set about building some. The most northerly of the famous cycling cols to owe its existence to these *routes stratégiques* is the Col du Galibier, long a passage for merchants and animal herders. It was improved and opened

"General Berge attacked the Izoard, the Aravis, Allos, Champs and Cayolle, turning mule tracks into solid carriage roads, along which artillery could move"

in 1879. General Berge then attacked the Izoard, the Aravis, Vars, Allos, Champs and Cayolle, turning mule tracks into solid carriage roads and creating an Alpine spine along which heavy artillery and troops could easily move.

Transalpine tensions remained high until after the outbreak of WWI, when Italy sided with the Allies and officially made friends with France. At a stroke, the impetus to make mountain paths into passable roads was gone. Luckily for cyclists, the Touring-Club de France, a tweeds-and-moustaches motoring organisation, was pushing for a scenic route to link Évian and Nice, respectively France's biggest summer and winter spas. The inaugural voyage by automobile on the 'Route des Alpes' departed from Nice in 1911, though it detoured out of the mountains at times. By 1912, thousands of people a year were signing up to travel the Route in open-top buses.

Development was halted by WWII, but continued apace

© Antton Miettinen

THE HIGHEST PAVED ROAD IN EUROPE?

One variation to the official Route takes in the Cime de la Bonette, which, at 9192ft (2802m) claims to be the highest road in Europe. There are dirt roads in the Alps and a couple of paved ones in Spain and in Austria that go higher. But they are dead ends, so the Bonette can boast only of being the highest-paved *through* road. Still, the 16-mile (25km) northern ascent is perhaps the most beautiful in the Alps.

From left: the author exploring the Col du Parpaillon (and previous page); a bike-friendly property rental near the Parc des Écrins; early motorists were quick to explore the sealed high roads

afterwards. The Col de l'Iséran was inaugurated in 1937, and the final section to be tarmacked, the Cormet de Roselend, opened in 1970.

Cycling the Route des Grandes Alpes is an unforgettable journey – one that every serious road cyclist should think about making, whether it's with a company taking your luggage from hotel to hotel, or more purely touring. Days can be idyllic, full of camaraderie and hard graft, water stops at old fountains and ice-cream breaks by the side of the road. And it's possible to simply sweat up and glide down these majestic highways, in the tyre tracks of heroes, and enjoy the huge climbs, sweeping descents and the stunning views of snowy peaks and Alpine meadows. But if you're taking on the Route, you'll be spending a lot of time pedalling uphill – so why not, as you're attempting this physical journey, take a mental journey back in time, too.

The Alps are famous for the welcome they give cyclists, but there are only a few letters' difference between 'hospitality' and 'hostility'. Think about that as you eat a local cheese-and-ham baguette and sip on a coke at a cafe on top of one of the famous cols. Look past the cows and the sheep in the meadows, past the waterfalls and the glaciers, to the forts above the roads, and to the tarmac beneath your feet, and think, just for a moment, of all the history that brought you to this point and made it possible. **ML**

TOOLKIT

Start // Thonon-les-Bains, Lac Léman (aka Lake Geneva)
Finish // Nice
How to get there // The closest airport to the start is Geneva; Nice too has an airport.
Distance // 448 miles (722km), with options to extend. At least a week's riding, not including rest days.
When to ride // The passes are generally free from snow from mid-June to mid-October, but early September is probably the latest you'd want to set off.
What to take // Mountain weather is unpredictable, so be prepared with everything from factor 50 sun cream to leg warmers and a good rain jacket.
More info // www.cycling-challenge.com/route-des-grandes-alpes-stage-1/

© Antton Miettinen, Science & Society Picture Library / Getty Images

Opposite: the Passo dello Stelvio, which took 2000 workers five years to construct

MORE LIKE THIS
RIDES INTO HISTORY

THE PASSO DELLO STELVIO, ITALY

The Stelvio Pass is the jewel in Italy's Alpine crown, a 9045ft (2757m) jumble of switchbacks in the Ortler range hard near the border with Switzerland. The pass was used as far back as the Bronze Age to get from what is now the Tyrol to Italy, but after the Napoleonic Wars the region fell under the control of the Austro-Hungarian Empire. However, in between the ruling Habsburgs and this new, rebellious territory lay some impenetrable Alps, and in 1820 they began to build a road over them. In only five years, 2000 workers under a master engineer called Carlo Donegani constructed a miracle: the north side, famously, has 48 hairpins, and there are 75 in all. During WWI it marked the westernmost point of the *Guerra Bianca*, the 'White War' in the mountains between Italy and Austria-Hungary, but it is now completely in Italian territory.

Start // Bormio
Finish // Prato
Distance // 27 miles (45km)

THE MASSIF CENTRAL, FRANCE

The Massif Central are France's 'lost' mountains, found between Clermont-Ferrand, a few hours south of Paris, and the vineyards of the Mediterranean. OK, the highest roads might only just scrape over 5000ft (1500m), but the terrain of this huge region is varied. The Pas du Peyrol (5213ft, 1589m) crowns the extinct volcanoes which burst higgledy-piggledy skywards in the north (think Volvic: this is where the water's from). The Col de Finiels (5056ft, 1541m) journeys through the rolling dairy pastures and thick forests of the centre, and Mont Aigoual (4944ft, 1507m) presides over the high limestone plateaux of the south and the stunning Gorges du Tarn. Folk tales such as the fearsome 'Beast of the Gevaudan' abound here, and it was a stronghold for the Resistance in WWII. Expect hearty local rustic food (Puy lentils, sausages, Roquefort) that's perfect for cyclists, and no shortage of good cheap wine.

LA VIA DEL SALE, ITALY

La Via del Sale is Italian for 'the salt road' – a 22-mile (35km) stretch of high gravel road that used to form part of one of the many routes by which salt, a valuable commodity, was transported from the coastal flats over the mountains to the Savoy stronghold of Turin. It's now a recognised mountain-bike trail, but it's passable on a gravel bike with big tyres, and there's a *rifugio* half way along if you want to stop for a slap-up meal, a glass of wine and a night in a dormitory. The Via del Sale is accessed from the Col de Tende, on the French/Italian border, and hopscotches either side of the line before running down to Monesi, in the province of Liguria. The road was improved by the army in the 18th century to service several forts overlooking the frontier. It's a beautiful piece of engineering that winds along above 6562ft (2000m) and affords incredible views over a high, desolate karst landscape.

Start // Col de Tende
Finish // Monesi
Distance // 22 miles (35km)

© Neil Emmerson / robertharding / Getty Images

INTO THE VALLEY OF DEATH

Beware. Fedaia Pass, the climb that was the scene of a legendary Marco Pantani victory in the Giro d'Italia, begins comfortably – and then turns into 'the graveyard of champions'.

Marco Pantani lit up the 1998 Giro d'Italia like few other cyclists could. The bald wiry Italian they called Il Pirata, thanks to his bandana and earrings, trailed his rivals as the tour of Italy hit the Dolomites. He would have to attack. His first opportunity came on the flanks of the Marmolada, the highest peak in a range that punches through steep meadows in great granite fists. But, as his teammate Roberto Conti recalled in a biography of Pantani, Il Pirata had never tackled the climb. 'And it's hard, very hard,' Conti warned him.

Others have gone further, describing the road from the village of Caprile to the Fedaia Pass variously as the graveyard of champions, the valley of death or the corridor of fear. It seduces first timers with its pleasant lower slopes before wringing them through the gorge at Sottoguda and, heading north, spitting them on to an unbending two-mile ramp towards the final twists. But Pantani felt so strong that when Conti asked him when he was planning to attack, Pantani said: 'When does the Marmolada start?' An incredulous Conti replied: 'We've already ridden half of it.'

The rest is cycling history. Pantani, who would be kicked out of the following year's Giro after doping allegations, duly attacked. Tossing his bandana on to the road in his customary signal of

© Tim de Waele / Getty Images

© Alex Genovese / Alamy Stock Photo

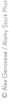

intent, he destroyed a huge time deficit and won the Maglia Rosa (pink jersey). On days like those, cyclists climb into the sporting annals – and so do the roads on which their legends are made.

Almost 20 years after Pantani danced his way up the Fedaia, I too had been warned that it was a very hard climb. I too was unprepared. What I did not need was a teammate to confirm that I was on it. I have climbed Mont Ventoux in a heatwave, ridden the length of Britain with a dodgy knee and taken on the notoriously tough hour record while writing about Bradley Wiggins' 2015 attempt. I know what hard riding feels like. But on the upper slopes of the Marmolada I would buckle. Banned substances? If only.

I was in northeast Italy to write about one of the dozens of high-end cycling outfits now taking wealthy roadies to storied destinations. In cycling, money eliminates any excuses for poor performance; on Marmolada day, I set off from a five-star hotel in the mountain town of Corvara on a bike worth more than any car I'll ever own. I carried nothing but my phone. Support vehicles trailed my group bearing spare wheels and energy bars. Pros of Pantani's era would have blushed at such service.

I had one such pro for company; Eros Poli, who had created his own legend with a stage win for the ages over Mont Ventoux in the 1994 Tour de France. It was Poli who warned me about Fedaia, telling me to take it easy on the first climb of the day,

"'Grinta! Grinta!' the former Italian pro shouted as he overtook me at impossible speed. 'I say to you it's hard, eh?!'"

right above Corvara, to the Campolongo Pass. I ignored him, settling into the kind of fast, satisfying rhythm that can, when a rider is in reasonable shape, fool him into wildly overestimating his true fitness. Right then, I could have climbed Everest on a penny farthing.

After a joyous descent through Arabba to Caprile, the first bit of the Fedaia climb was gentle. The gorge was spectacular. The old road, now closed to cars, wound up along a river beneath towering cliffs, almost permanently shaded and lush with pines and glistening ferns. It was close to the end of the gorge, at Malga Ciapela, where I rejoined the main road, that my early confidence began to wobble. Past the cable car station, the climb takes a right turn and disappears up into the distance as it skirts the forbidding east face of the Marmolada itself. It was as if the road builders had run out of asphalt and, eschewing hairpin bends, had rolled straight up the valley. 'It's like someone's horribly steep driveway,' the 1988 Giro winner Andy Hampsten said of what he described as

THE MARMOLADA MASSACRE

The Fedaia Pass, in the shadow of the Marmolada mountain, has tested generations of Giro champions. In 1987, when the Irish cyclist Stephen Roche mercilessly crushed his own team leader Roberto Visentini, the Italian defending Giro champion, he needed police protection from enraged Italian fans. Undeterred, Roche defended his position on the Fedaia en route to victory for Ireland on a day that went down in history as the 'Marmolada massacre'.

From left: Fedaia Lake, at climb's end; the author (left) with ex-pro Eros Poli; Fedaia Pass was the scene of one of Marco Pantani's great victories. Previous page: remember to deviate up Sottoguda Gorge

one of the hardest climbs in cycling.

They call it 'bonking' when blood sugar levels drop and the body's engine begins – often suddenly – to choke on fumes like a car running out of fuel. Every muscle – including the brain – becomes useless. For me it happened on Hampsten's driveway. The logical thing would have been to stop, but strange things happen to amateur cyclists in pursuit of meaningless glory. Stopping is defeat. I ground on, wishing I had more gears.

Poli had nothing to prove, of course. He had also, shall we say, filled out in retirement and was some way behind me. But then, out of nowhere, he overtook me at impossible speed, clutching the roof rack of the support van. 'Grinta! Grinta!' he shouted the Italian encouragement, which means 'grit'. 'I say to you it's hard, eh?!' I forced my face into a smile. Eventually, the road began to twist again for two more miles until, at last, it flattened for the run in to the eastern end of Fedaia Lake, the end of the climb.

A lone *rifugio* is the place to recover with an espresso. It had taken me almost 90 minutes to ride less than nine miles, probably the slowest and hardest riding of my life. It wasn't even over – my 60-mile (95km) clockwise loop south of Corvara continued past Fedaia Lake and down to Canazei, before the climbs up the Sella and Gardena passes, bringing another 3280ft (1000m) of climbing before the return to my hotel and a late lunch of humble pie. **SU**

TOOLKIT

Start // Caprile
Finish // Fedaia Lake
Distance // 8.8 miles (14km). Fork off the main road up the Sottoguda Gorge (small fee to pay at the gatehouse).
How to get there // Venice or Innsbruck are the nearest major airports. (I travelled with the cycle tour operators inGamba.)
Where to stay // The bike-friendly ski resort of Corvara is an ideal base and is the end of the famous annual Maratona dles Dolomites sportive.
When to ride // Snow can choke high passes into early summer but May-October are generally fine. July and August are busy.
What to take // Wide range of gears, plenty of fuel, extra layer in case of chilly descents.

© Simon Usborne; Franck Seguin / Getty Images

Opposite: the rough trail up to the Colle delle Finestre; the Mortirolo, 'the hardest climb I've ever ridden,' claimed Lance Armstrong

MORE LIKE THIS
GIRO D'ITALIA CLIMBS

COLLE DELLE FINESTRE

The biggest thing in road cycling right now is ditching the road. Not entirely, of course, but gravel riding is booming, recalling the grime-and-sweat glories of a lost age of road cycling, when pristine asphalt was an unknown wonder. Short stretches of unpaved surfaces have appeared in recent editions of the Tour de France and its Spanish sister the Vuelta. The more agricultural Giro d'Italia got there before it was cool, introducing the Colle delle Finestre to Italy's 'tour' in 2005. Until then, it had been off limits as a military access road to the Fenestrelle Fort, in Piemonte's Cottian Alps. Giro fans were immediately bewitched by the forbidding 4921-ft (1500m) climb's lower forested hairpins and its barren upper reaches (no *rifugios* or cafes here), but even more so by the final 8km (of 22km) when the road turns to gravel all the way to the summit at 9003ft (2744m).
Start // Susa
Finish // Colle delle Finestre
Distance // 11 miles (17.7km)

PASSO DI MORTIROLO

It is not the most brutal ascent in Italy, reaching just over 6000 feet (1852m) and covering almost 8 miles (12.5km) but thanks to stretches with gradients of up to 18%, the winding route up from Mazzo di Valtellina in Lombardy through thick forest has earned a fearsome reputation during multiple appearances in the Giro d'Italia. On a spring training ride for the Tour de France in 2004, a perhaps underpowered Lance Armstrong described Mortirolo as 'the hardest climb I've ever ridden'. 'Perfect,' the American added, 'for a mountain bike'. Troubled Italian cycling legend Marco Pantani made the Mortirolo his own in 1994 when he put the dominant Spanish rider Miguel Induráin to the sword, announcing his arrival at the top of his sport (a shrine to 'Il Pirata' remains half way up the Mortirolo).
Start // Mazzo di Valtellina
Finish // Passo di Mortirolo
Distance // 8 miles (13km)

MADONNA DEL GHISALLO

At 2474 feet (754m), it is not more than a steep hill above Lake Como. But its stature in cycling could not be greater. The story goes that the medieval Count Ghisallo sought refuge form bandits at a shrine on the spot. The chapel memorialises the myth but after its regular appearance in the Giro di Lombardia and the Giro d'Italia, the chapel began to attract pilgrims on two wheels. By 1949, the Pope confirmed a proposal by a local priest that La Madonna del Ghisallo should be declared the patroness of cyclists. The chapel has since become a museum of the sport and a monument to late cyclists. Fausto Coppi donated his 1942 hour-record-setting bike and the remains of the bike on which local boy Fabio Casartelli died during the 1995 Tour de France serves as a sober reminder of the risks pros take in pursuit of glory. There are several routes to the shrine; the climb from Bellagio is the toughest and best known.
Start // Bellagio
Finish // Madonna del Ghisallo
Distance // 6.5 miles (10.6km)

© Luigi Masella / Getty Images, Francisco de Casa / Alamy Stock Photo, Tim de Waele / Getty Images

Fedaia Pass

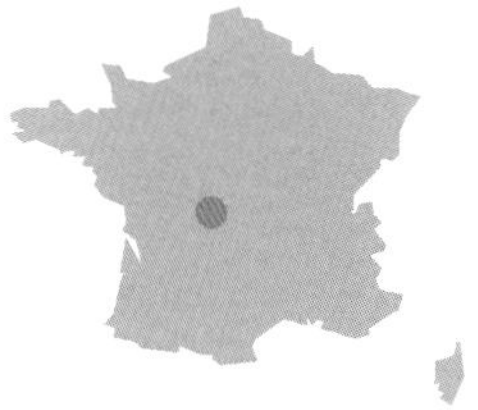

ACROSS FRANCE THE EASY WAY

From the English Channel to the Côte d'Azur, this route wanders through the heart of la France profonde, immersing you in its many flavours and landscapes.

Creating a cycle route is as much a pleasure as riding one. The journey begins not when you first turn the pedal but at home on your kitchen table as you spread out the map for the first time, smoothing out its creases, and start to plot.

When we began preparing the route that would become the basis of our book *France en Velo* it felt a little daunting, the open map a blank canvas. How to cross a country shaped like France is far less obvious than, say, somewhere like the UK with two obvious geographic points to join up. So we started with deciding the start and conclusion, as these are the bookends to the whole experience.

It may well be true that it's the journey not the destination that matters, but a memorable terminus rounds off any trip and adds to the celebration at journey's end. With that in mind, we settled on Nice on the sparkling Côte d'Azur – which seemed very far away as we set off from within the fortified walls of St-Malo, against the backdrop of the grey and turbulent Channel.

With the beginning and ending finalised the fun began. Choosing to cross a country from one coastline to another naturally promises a route that will take you through changing landscapes and culture, but simply drawing a pencil line between two distant geographical points is unlikely to land on the best roads; curiosity, with a sprinkling of research, led the way.

Looking at the map certain place names jumped out, sparking our imagination and painting a picture of long, languid lunches; oysters in Cancale, fragrant truffles in Sorge, fine wine in Chateauneuf-du-Pape. Decisions needed to be made at every turn, selecting the headliners was easy, but the desire to visit

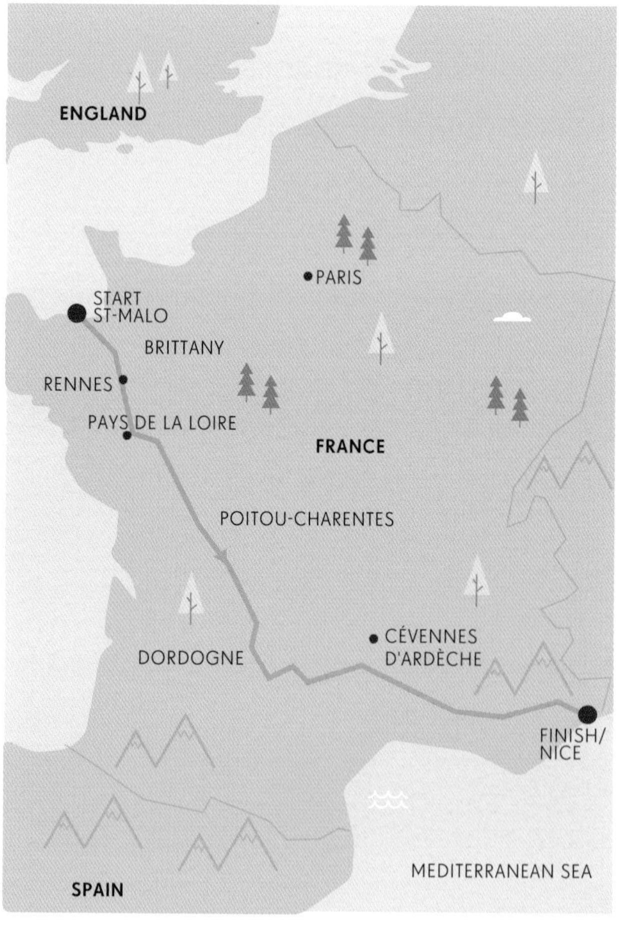

© John Walsh

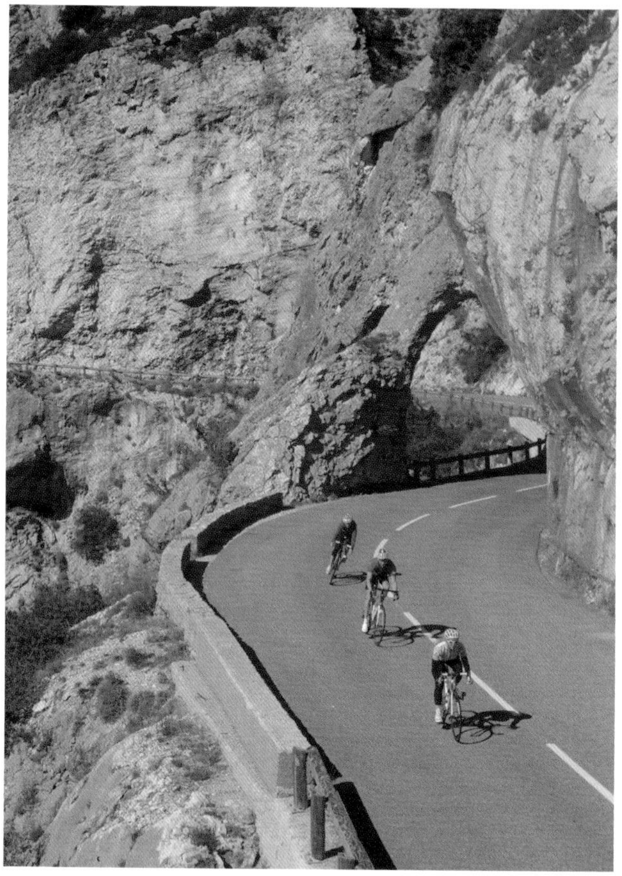

somewhere needed to be balanced against the miles and the climbing, opting for one village means by-passing another. It became a giant game of join the dots, picking out the prettiest and most interesting villages and linking them together with river courses, gorges and scenic roads.

What we ended up with is a *chemin des écoliers*, a winding path that children take to avoid getting to school too quickly, which suited our aims perfectly. The purpose wasn't to ride to Nice as fast as possible but to ensure that every mile was stuffed to the brim with the best cycling, cuisine and culture. We chose to follow the Lot river from its source high up in the Cévennes till it is big enough to cut a deep gorge, to pedal for days beneath the watchful eye of Mont Ventoux and descend between dramatic limestone pillars and through perched villages of the Alpes-Maritimes, whilst ensuring that the route is littered with picturesque villages for food and rest.

Travelling by bike is precisely the right speed for immersing yourself in a country. Even without getting off the saddle you can learn about the region you are passing through, simply by absorbing the scenery, sounds and scents. *Terroir* is a complex term, best understood by the cycling gourmet – we wanted to eat, sip, sniff and taste our way across the country, the landscapes we pedalled through by day reflected in the restaurant menu each

"One of my favourite memories is swimming beneath the limestone arch of the Ardèche at sunset, watching swallows"

evening. In this we succeeded. By the end of the ride we had indelible sensory memories of the places we passed through. If you dropped me blindfolded in southern France I would know where I was by the heady smell of lavender and tinnitus ring of cicadas. Northern France is tangy sea air, crisp apples, farmhouse cider and a particular damp field where garlic bulbs were being lifted.

We mapped our ride in more ways than just miles – every *menu du jour* eaten spoke of where we were; truffle, duck and foie gras in the Perigord region, lamb gorged on woody sage and rosemary from around the limestone plateau near Gramat and the nourishing basil scented, vegetable rich *soupe au pistou* of Provence. Each meal was washed down with local wine; by the slightly stagnant banks of the Loire we lifted elegant glasses of dry, sparkling *crémant* outside turreted chateaux, in the Rhône we drank *pichets* of spicy, full-bodied red wine and chilled glasses of palest pink rosé, beaded with condensation when we reached Provence. Thank goodness that cycling works up an appetite and the need for indulgent calories.

© David Santiago Garcia / Getty Images, Lisovskaya Natalia / Shutterstock, John Walsh

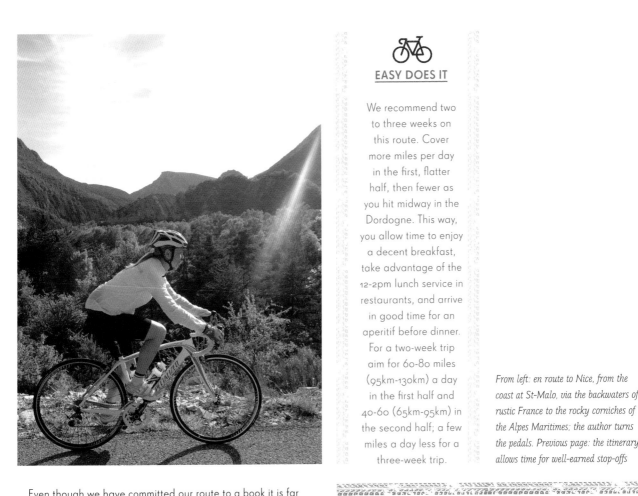

EASY DOES IT

We recommend two to three weeks on this route. Cover more miles per day in the first, flatter half, then fewer as you hit midway in the Dordogne. This way, you allow time to enjoy a decent breakfast, take advantage of the 12-2pm lunch service in restaurants, and arrive in good time for an aperitif before dinner. For a two-week trip aim for 60-80 miles (95km-130km) a day in the first half and 40-60 (65km-95km) in the second half; a few miles a day less for a three-week trip.

From left: en route to Nice, from the coast at St-Malo, via the backwaters of rustic France to the rocky corniches of the Alpes Maritimes; the author turns the pedals. Previous page: the itinerary allows time for well-earned stop-offs

Even though we have committed our route to a book it is far from definitive. A route is a living creation, it is freshly written by each different person who rides it, even if each turn is followed identically. A thousand miles can be ridden as a physical challenge, hammer down, nose to stem, or as a relaxed exploration with time to swim in cool rivers and sleep off the lunch time excesses under a shady tree.

While some places will stand out in everyone's memories – the deep aquamarine of the Gorge du Verdon or the sinuous curves of the Gorge d'Ardèche – it is the smaller and unexpected finds that make each journey unique: a marvellous bakery just at the moment you are pining for a pastry or a perfectly ripe peach from a road-side stall. One of my favourites is swimming beneath the limestone arch of the Ardèche at sunset when all of the kayakers have returned to their campsites, watching the swallows dive through the arch, skimming down to touch the surface of the water.

Our meandering route, led as much by our stomachs as our desire for the best cycling, is not the most direct way to cross France, nor is it the easiest, but we believe it is the most varied and scenic. Follow it and it will lead you through hidden lanes, stunning gorges and beautiful villages but perhaps most importantly it provides an opportunity to write your own story of discovery. **HR**

TOOLKIT

Start // St-Malo
Finish // Nice
Distance // 1000 miles (1600km)
Getting there // By air: Dinard. By train or ferry: St-Malo. Nice has an airport and train station.
When to ride // Late spring to early autumn.
What to take // A touring bike with panniers, and a cork screw and a pen knife for road-side picnics.
Where to stay // In our book we make three recommendations in each town: a campsite, a family run hotel and a chambre d'hôte. Local tourist information offices are helpful too.
More info // www.franceenvelo.cc to purchase *France en Velo The ultimate cycle journey from Channel to Med.*

© John Walsh

Opposite: make time for Eilean Donan Castle, Loch Duich, on your way to John O'Groats

MORE LIKE THIS
CROSS-COUNTRY JOURNEYS

LAND'S END TO JOHN O'GROATS, UK

LEJOG is the popular end-to-end for British cyclists, linking the two geographically most extreme points of the island of Britain, the very southwest tip of Cornwall to the northeast point of Scotland. There are various routes: the one on which speed records are set is 874 miles (1407km) but this takes in some busy roads and misses many of the interesting villages and more scenic riding. There is a perception that the route starts easy and becomes more difficult in Scotland, but some of the steepest climbs and most challenging days are in the Southwest before crossing the border into Wales. The Northwest of England contains the most urban riding, around former industrial areas such as Preston, but also some of the wildest and most beautiful around the Trough of Bowland.
Start // Land's End
Finish // John O'Groats
Distance // varies according to route, but at least 874 miles (1407km)

LES DIAGONALES, FRANCE

The 'shape' of France dictates that there is no definitive geographic 'end-to-end' route. Instead, a network of nine long-distance rides has been created between six points around the French border, criss-crossing the country. The shortest is Hendaye to Menton, 580 miles (940km), the longest Brest to Menton, 870 miles (1400km). Many riders choose to tick them off over several cycling seasons (they are designed rather for the achievement of riding across much of the country than for their inherent interest or beauty). The society L'Amicale des Diagonalistes de France recognises the achievements of riders who have completed at least one of the *diagonales* and publishes the official routes, including designated start and end points.

HIGHLANDS COAST TO COAST, SCOTLAND

Though you'll pass through Cairngorm National Park via Fort Augustus, Kingussie, Tomintoul, Ballater and Edzell, there aren't many more remote or wild routes in the UK. Plan carefully, prepare to be self-sufficient and if not wild camping (as permitted in Scotland), then pre-book accommodation. Anticipate everything from glorious sunshine, to day-long downpours and biting wind. But there are dramatic rewards: jagged crags, majestic peaks, tumbling streams; deer and grouse are in abundance too. The Cairngorm National Park is also home to a quarter of the UK's rare and endangered species, from the golden eagle to the red squirrel. You may even see the herd of reindeer that has recently been introduced. There is a significant amount of climbing and the terrain varies across rough tracks, single-track trails and short road sections. The descent from Mount Keen is one of the longest and most exhilarating in the UK.
Start // Fort William
Finish // Montrose
Distance // 190 miles (306km)

© john finney photography / Getty Images

A TRAVERSE OF THE SIERRA NEVADA

Rob Penn's tour of Andalucía's Sierra Nevada mountains and Las Alpujarras, a quiet and beautiful part of southern Spain, culminates in the culturally dynamic Granada.

From the top of Pico de Veleta – at 11,132ft (3393m), the second highest peak in mainland Spain – the view was astounding. I could see the entire Sierra Nevada range of mountains rolling out to the south and the east in a series of cappuccino brown peaks. Beyond that were the narrow, green, winding valleys of Las Alpujarras. In the distance, the silvery Mediterranean Sea was illuminated by afternoon sunshine. It was a view to die for – and I felt like I had nearly died for it.

The ascent of Pico de Veleta has to be one of the greatest European cycling challenges. It is an extraordinary climb by any measure: the bare statistics are staggering. I had cycled uphill for 31 miles (50km) from the centre of Granada, clocking over 2700m of vertical ascent. The major part of the ride is on a good paved road, which serves the ski resort in winter; the last half-mile (1km) or so is on gravel; the final 300ft (100m) is on foot, over rocks.

Climbing to the top of Pico de Veleta was the culmination of a four-day tour of the Sierra Nevada, Spain's highest range of mountains, and Las Alpujarras, the foothills that roll south from the high peaks towards the sea. It is an enchanting, often overlooked part of Spain. Decent roads, plenty of sunshine and minimal traffic (at least until you approach Granada) make it a wonderful place to ride a bicycle.

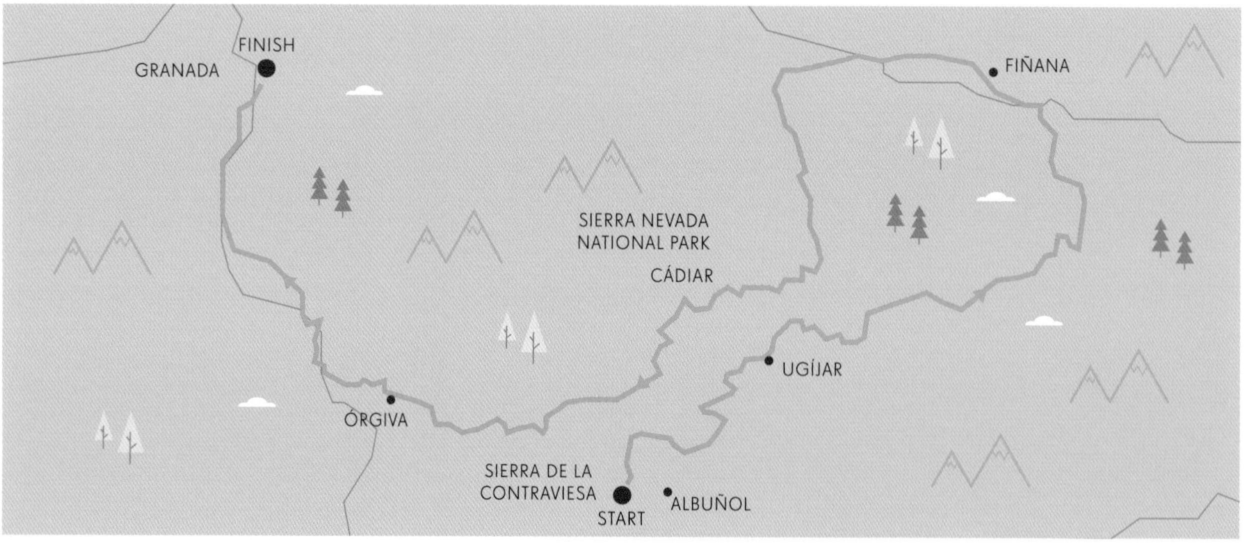

© Szymon Kotowski

The whole area remains profoundly rural – a region of whitewashed villages, arid highlands, terraced hillsides, wooded valleys, almond trees and olive groves. The Berbers from North Africa occupied Las Alpujarras for several centuries, before they were expelled with the Moors from Granada in the 15th and 16th centuries. Remarkably, half a millennium later, their legacy remains – in the labyrinthine villages, the flat-roofed houses and the irrigation systems that are still in use today, taking snowmelt water off the mountains to grow vines, oranges, lemons and pomegranates. The pace of life here is slow, almost otherworldly: for the first two days, I wondered where everyone was. Eventually, I stopped caring.

My ride started in the Southern Sierras, known as the Sierra de la Contraviesa. It is a long ride up from the shores of the Mediterranean: I cheated, and got a lift halfway, to the village of Albondón. After a coffee and a sandwich in a sleepy cafe, I set off along even sleepier roads, winding through vineyards, down to the small town of Ugíjar. After the scalding, white heat of midday, it was a delight to climb up to the village of Laujar de Andarax in the soft, golden light of early evening. In the small square, locals were busy constructing a stage and bars for the annual fiesta.

Because the coast of Spain has been such a magnet for tourists in the last half century, areas like Las Alpujarras have been slow to develop. The region only really began to emerge from the Middle Ages with the demise of the Franco regime and the enactment of a democratic constitution in the 1970s. As a consequence, places to stay are still few and far between and I had to put in a long ride to get over the Sierra Nevada range twice the next day, to reach a delightful hotel, La Alquería de Morayma, near the town of Cádiar.

The road gently rose and fell to the pretty village of Ohanes, before climbing through arid countryside and, higher up, holm

ALHAMBRA ARCHITECTURE

The Alhambra was rebuilt and added to by successive Moorish rulers of Granada from the 9th to the 15th centuries, as it grew from a simple fort to the grand citadel of the Nasrid sultans, rulers of the last Muslim kingdom in Spain. The complex of stately and military buildings set in beautiful gardens represents the glorious climax of Moorish art and culture in Europe. Allow several hours for a visit and book tickets in advance.

Clockwise from top: lots of sun and little traffic in Andalucía; the Albayzín district of Granada; the whitewashed town of Laujar de Andarax in the Alpujarras; a palace in the Alhambra. Previous page: climbing above Orgiva

© David Ionut / Shutterstock, Lucas Vallecillos / Alamy Stock Photo, Szymon Kotowski

oak forests, to reach the first col of the day, Puerto de Santillana (4386ft, 1337m). It was deserted and the descent to the town of Abla was fast, open and memorable.

The main climb of the day, up and over Puerto de la Ragua – 10.5 miles (17km) with 3018ft (920m) of ascent – is a Category 1 climb, which has featured in the Vuelta, Spain's great pro-cycling stage race. The climb starts just outside the picturesque village of La Calahorra. The first few miles wind gently through a sweet-smelling pine forest. At each bend, there are panoramic views down to the 16th century Renaissance Castillo de La Calahorra, one of Andalucía's emblematic fortresses, with its huge, squat turrets. Beyond, the great reddish-brown plain of Marquesado stretches away to the north.

At the top of the col, there is a picnic area and a spring-fed fountain. After a snooze in the shade of the trees and a head bath in the water trough, I sped down on a well-tarmacked road, easing through the bends, savouring the views south over Las Alpujarras. The final part of the day was up and down a beautiful winding road through the villages of Valor, Yegen and Mecina Bombaron to reach Cádiar, as the sun began to sink.

The following day, the sky was a luxurious cobalt blue again. Before the sun rose over the high peaks, I pedalled down through the Guadalfeo Valley. After the wild country at the eastern end of the Sierra Nevada, the towns of Órgiva and Lanjarón felt cosmopolitan. The heat and the traffic intensified as I snaked through canyons and over rivers to reach the Puerto del Suspiro del Moro, the 'Pass of the Sigh of the Moor'. From there, it was a gentle run downhill into Granada; to the mighty palace-fortress, the Alhambra, one of the most intriguing monuments in Europe; to the tapas bars and the riverside cafes; and to my bed, for a long sleep before the gruelling ascent of Pico de Veleta. **RP**

"Decent roads, plenty of sunshine and minimal traffic make Las Alpujarras a wonderful place to ride a bicycle"

TOOLKIT

Start // Sierra de la Contraviesa
Finish // Granada
Distance // 239 miles (385km), with a total vertical ascent of some 28,000ft (8500m).
Getting there // Airports in Málaga and Granada provide plenty of options to get to and from this part of Andalucía.
Bike hire // Rent A Bici (www.rent-a-bici.com; €25 per day, minimum of two days) in Granada.
When to ride // May, early June, late September and October are the best times to cycle the Sierra Nevada: in July and August it's too hot, and busy with holidaymakers.
Where to stay // In Cádiar, La Alquería de Morayma (www.alqueriamorayma.com/en/) is a good option.
What to eat // Thick, meaty stews, charcuterie and black pudding are popular – but the locally grown fruit and vegetables are excellent too.

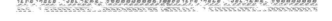

© MATTES RenÃ©Ã / Getty Images

Opposite: Roquebrune-Cap-Martin, near cycling hotspot Menton, on the Côte d'Azur, France

MORE LIKE THIS CROSSING RANGES

PROVENCE, FRANCE

This undulating ride, from the elegant, medieval town of Avignon to the city of Nice on the glamorous and gleaming Côte d'Azur, crosses archetypal Provençal countryside. Along the way you will pass ochre, hilltop villages unblemished by the late 20th century, bustling farmers markets shaded by plane trees, fields of poppies and church spires protruding from row upon row of lavender. There are climbs but they are never back-breaking, while the descents are laid-back, winding and glorious. You'll ride down into the Gorges du Verdon, perhaps the most beautiful river canyon in Europe, and round the Lac de Sainte-Croix, before crossing the oak-covered, red volcanic hills of the Massif de l'Estérel for your first view of the Côte d'Azur. Following the Boulevard du Midi along the coast via Antibes, you can roll lazily past beaches, glamorous hotels and ritzy yachts to Nice.

Start // Avignon
Finish // Nice
Distance // 217.5 miles (350km)

THE AUVERGNE, FRANCE

In the relatively uninhabited heart of France, the Parc Naturel Regional des Volcans d'Auvergne occupies most of the western Massif Central. About 20 million years ago this was one of the most active volcanic areas in Europe. Glaciers then shaved the tops off the cones, resulting in this highland of broad-flanked hills, jade-green valleys, dark-stone villages and vast panoramas. It's a fabulous spot for serious bike riding and the summit of Puy Mary lures many climbing cyclists – who would be wise to remember to pack a warm and windproof jacket. A leisurely three-day, 106-mile (170km) tour starting in Clermont-Ferrand heads south through the natural park to Le Mont-Dore then via Puy de Sancy and the Col de la Croix St-Robert to Condat. The final day is reserved for tackling the 5863ft Puy Mary (1787m), joining the mountain sheep on its alpine pastures.

Start // Clermont-Ferrand
Finish // Murat
Distance // 106 miles (170km)

THE VIA FRANCIGENA, ENGLAND TO ITALY

A pilgrim route, the 1120-mile (1800km) Via Francigena from Canterbury to Rome is known to us thanks to the notes of Sigeric, a 10th-century Archbishop of Canterbury, who detailed the 80 mansions he was accommodated in during his journey in 990. Today, pilgrims still follow its path, as do cyclists, crossing two of Europe's great mountain ranges – the Alps and the Apennines – along the way. That three-week journey to Rome can be abbreviated, by embarking from Besançon in eastern France, to shorten the run-up to the 8100ft (2469m) Saint Bernard Pass. Once over the Alps, the Apennines are not inconsiderable (the Passo della Cisa rises to 3415ft, 1041m). Thereafter, the delights of Lucca and Siena await the devout before the roll into the Eternal City. More info: www.viefrancigene.org/ which has detailed maps.

Start // Canterbury
Finish // Rome
Distance // 1120 miles (1800km)

© Lottie Davies / Lonely Planet

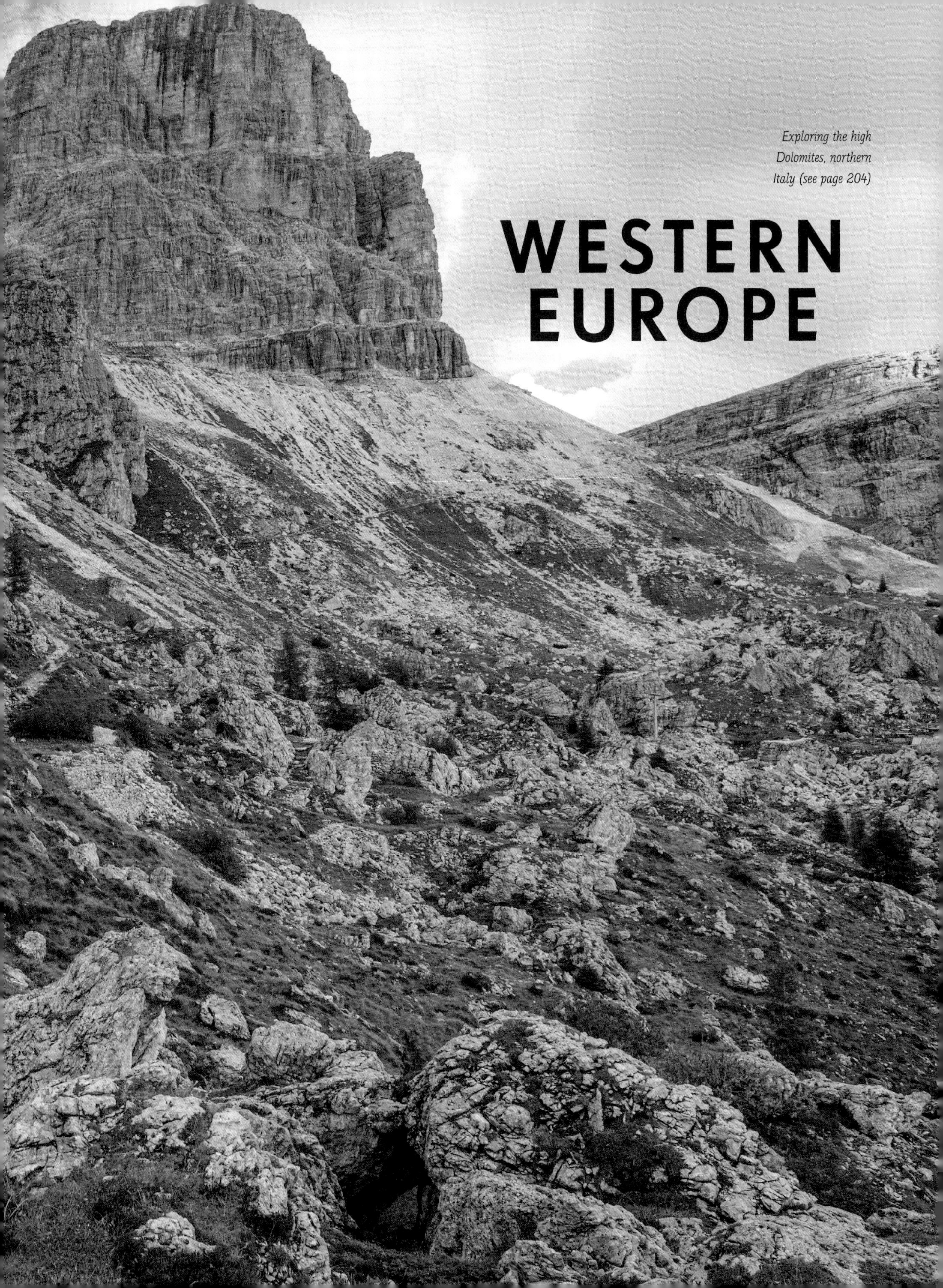

WESTERN EUROPE

Exploring the high Dolomites, northern Italy (see page 204)

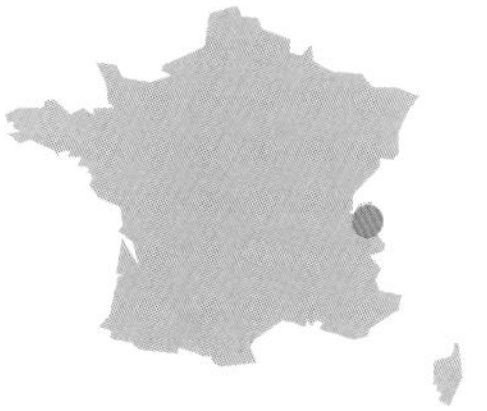

THE TOUR DU MONT BLANC

A grand, multi-day jaunt around Europe's highest peak takes you into France, Switzerland and Italy (while gaining enough elevation to scale Everest).

Dunking my knackered body into the Dranse de Ferret river is refreshing, but perhaps, I realise, a little reckless. A few feet from the bank, the glacial meltwater rushing off the mountain exerts an unexpected pull, and as I don't fancy being swept down the valley I instead have to content myself with splashing about in the shallows.

Three days in, and a little over halfway through the 105-mile (170km) Tour du Mont Blanc (TMB), I'm definitely in need of freshening up. My clothes and limbs attest to the effort of crossing the Col de Voza, Croix du Bonhomme, Col de la Seigne, and Grand Col Ferret. I had just raced the river down from the last of these snow-covered peaks, and the dregs of the day's remaining energy had been spent on navigating a safe path to the valley floor. Now, crashed out on the river bank, the quiet local bar is beckoning. All I need to do is make myself decent enough to be allowed in.

A lap around the white mountain, the TMB includes almost 30,000ft of climbing and also descending. Taking riders somewhere between four and eight days to complete, it also offers a surfeit of Alpine wonders, from rocky peaks and glaciers to inviting rivers and lush green pastures. Originally conceived as a walking route, it's wild and remote in places, yet signposted well enough to be relatively simple to navigate. Still, with multiple peaks above 6500ft (2000m), it's not something to undertake on a whim, as you'll need good physical fitness along with the basic skills to keep yourself safe in the mountains.

Setting off from Chamonix, we'd begun our attempt by hitching a lift on the cable car at Les Houches. The dense mist that we ascended into was an early reminder of the vagaries of mountain weather. We alight with the day trippers at the lift station and begin a climb that seems to go on for hours, the clouds eventually breaking up to reveal the large Refuge de la Croix du Bonhomme.

Refuges (*rifugios* in Italian) are mountain-top staging posts, varying in amenity from the austere to the luxurious, and unless you want to carry camping gear with you, staying in them on the TMB will make an already tough trip far less arduous: you'll get a bunk in a dormitory, a shower and some of the meals to be had are excellent. Even if you don't stay the night, it's almost always worth popping in to eat. Checking in to our first refuge of the tour it

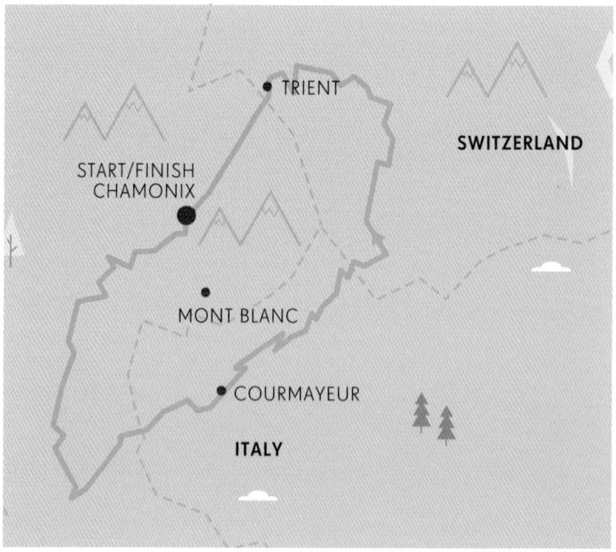

Previous page Cass Gilbert, this page © MontanusWild.com

"After our first night in a refuge, the guardian pours us a coffee and fills us in on what lies head that day"

turns out we have the place to ourselves – so over coffee the next morning the guardian has plenty of time to fill us in on what lies ahead for our small group.

Back on our bikes, the previous day's upwards grind is soon rewarded by the first extended descent. It doesn't disappoint. We howl down almost a kilometre of vertical in one long swoop. When we finally crash-land at the foot of the trail, we're grinning like goons (and nursing our screaming hands).

And so it goes, down and then up, over and over, around the nine peaks surrounding Mont Blanc (about half of the riding is on singletrack). First through France and then into Italy. Each climb following a similar pattern. We hit the bottom full of enthusiasm, and, as the gradient increases, invariably find ourselves pushing the last few hundred metres or with the bike on our shoulders. Yet each time the descent more than compensates for the uphill exertion, as we smash down incredible trails largely free of other riders and walkers (do be careful to slow down and give way to the latter).

For three days this is how we ride, happily sleeping and eating in the refuges. But the sight of the pretty comune of Courmayeur is a welcome one, the first proper civilisation we've seen since Chamonix. In reality this means taking the opportunity to fortify ourselves with pastries before heading back into the wild. After a night at the Rifugio Walter-Bonatti, ahead of us lies the TMB's most elevated point, the Grand Col Ferret.

This dizzyingly high 8455ft (2577m) lump marks the Italian-Swiss border, and it takes an entire morning to grind up. The reward is a descent that takes several hours, the lower part passing in a blur of high-spec holiday homes and rolling trails, before the Alpage de Bovine rears up ahead of us. The huge ferns and similarly ancient-looking plants that line its lower slopes give way to forests of pine which lead to pastures full of pink and yellow flowers. One of our party grew up working in a plant nursery, and he happily stops several times to photograph various orchids.

Unusually for the TMB, the Alpage de Bovine is a climb that can be ridden up in its entirety, but, appropriately enough, we're forced off the bikes by an irate cow just before the summit. Slithering down the far side, there's not a single tyre track to suggest other bikers have ever been this way.

A night in Trient, Switzerland, follows before we're popped back into France the next day via the Col de Balme, the route's last big peaks now finally behind us. For the hikers, the TMB here takes in an ominously named *passage délicat*, a series of ladders fixed to rock faces. For we riders, of course, such a *passage délicat* is impossible.

But I don't resent the climbers scrambling up. As we head for Chamonix, I realise I've had my fill of summits. **JD**

© Hemis / Alamy Stock Photo, Luke Mulder / Shutterstock

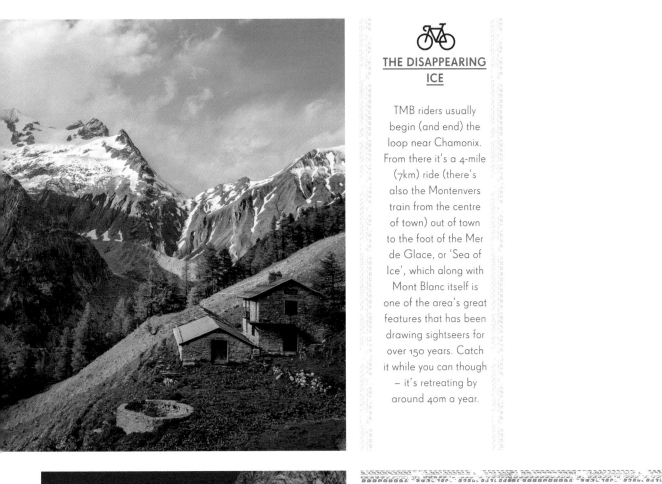

THE DISAPPEARING ICE

TMB riders usually begin (and end) the loop near Chamonix. From there it's a 4-mile (7km) ride (there's also the Montenvers train from the centre of town) out of town to the foot of the Mer de Glace, or 'Sea of Ice', which along with Mont Blanc itself is one of the area's great features that has been drawing sightseers for over 150 years. Catch it while you can though – it's retreating by around 40m a year.

TOOLKIT

Start/Finish // Chamonix, France
Distance // 105 miles (170km)
Getting there // Gare de Saint-Gervais-les-Bains-Le Fayet is the nearest train station to Chamonix, 12 miles (20km) away. Or rent a car or book a minibus shuttle from Geneva airport.
Bike hire // Legend'Chx rent high-end (and pricey) bikes (www.legend-chamonix.com).
When to ride // Early June to early September. In any case, pack warm layers and a good shell.
Where to stay // There are mountain refuges dotted along each stage. Bring a sleeping-bag liner and pre-book: www.autourdumontblanc.com.
What to eat // Re-stock whenever possible. Don't rely on refuges or mountain cafes being open.

Clockwise from top left: shepherds still tend flocks near Mont Blanc; the Walter-Bonatti refuge; the tour is well signposted. Previous page: descending into Italy near Courmayeur

©Ashley Cooper pics / Alamy Stock Photo

Opposite: at Morgins on some of the Portes du Soleil's 400 miles of trails linking 12 mountain resorts

MORE LIKE THIS
MOUNTAIN-BIKE ADVENTURES

CAIRNGORMS DOUBLE LOOP, SCOTLAND

If you think the UK doesn't do wild you should heed the joke that climbers 'go to Everest to prepare for the Cairngorms'. You'll find tundra-like conditions on this vast upland plateau which is home to ptarmigans, eagles, red deer and mountain hare. This double loop takes in the best of the area, via everything from fast-rolling gravel paths to technical singletrack. Accommodation is the bothies that dot the route, or you can wild camp. The route stays largely clear of the area's many summits, so there aren't too many occasions where you'll be forced off your bike (except when fording the occasional river). Take a map, appropriate clothing and spares for your bike – the route is remote. There are multiple variations of the two-loop format; we'd recommend beginning in Aviemore as this means you can catch the train to the start and the town has plenty of places to buy supplies before you head out (along with a place to grab a pint on your return).
Start/Finish // Aviemore
Distance // 186 miles (300km)

BIKE TRANSALP (TASTER), AUSTRIA, SWITZERLAND, ITALY

First run in 1998, the Bike Transalp is one of the toughest and longest-running multi-stage mountain-bike challenges in the world, and it boasts an incredible amount of elevation gain to boot. The route changes each year, but competitors will generally start in Austria and traverse the Alps south, expecting to climb about 60,000ft (18,000m) over about 300+ miles (500km). If you'd like a taster, how about stage three of the 2016 race, from Scuol to Livigno. You'll climb into the Alp Astras, round Alp Buffalora, ascend Passo del Gallo, pass through Stelvio National Park and negotiate the Mega-Flow-Downhill route from Passo Trela, over Trepalle and through the Val Torto to the shores of Lago di Livigno. And if that whets your appetite, you can find out more here: https://bike-transalp.de/
Start // Scuol, Switzerland
Finish // Livigno, Italy
Distance // 45.5 miles (73km)

PORTES DU SOLEIL, FRANCE, SWITZERLAND

For those who prefer to mix up their cross-country runs with some lift-assisted downhill (DH) action, the Portes du Soleil area in the Franco-Swiss Alps boasts 12 mountain resorts with four linked mountain-bike parks and over 50 DH trails. As the resorts are linked, so too are the lift passes, with access to 21 bike-friendly lifts and more than 400 miles (650km) of tracks. This enables you to explore Châtel Bike Park, the 'European Whistler', with 20 DH tracks; the Les Gets Park, with 14 DH tracks, six all-mountain cross-country routes and a freeride slope (plus some trails for beginners); Morzine Bike Park, with further DH tracks and a range of trails suitable for less experienced riders; and Montriond-Avoriaz with a mixture of DH trails. The Pass'Portes du Soleil weekend event kicks off the MTB season, with an epic 50-mile (80km) all-mountain course, featuring 6500m of descent (and only 1000m of climbing). More information: en.portesdusoleil.com/; www.passportesdusoleil.com
Start/Finish // Morzine, France
Distance // 50 miles (80km)

© Ilan Shacham / Getty Images

ROLLING THROUGH BAROQUE SICILY

When an earthquake all but destroyed Val di Noto in 1693, its aristocracy rebuilt – and how. A short tour reveals its architectural (and culinary) hits.

Everybody, I am sure, has their own preferred way of appreciating Baroque architecture. Mine is after a couple of evening beers. It's then that Baroque's excess seems to make the most sense. Why finish a corner with a boring right angle when you can add some curlicues and a gargoyle? At night the shadows seem to accentuate the drama.

Some of the world's best examples of Baroque towns are in Sicily and it so happens that they can be strung together on an easy clockwise loop starting from Syracuse on the east coast over three or more days. The other corners of this compact triangle are Noto and Ragusa (with a side-trip to Modica, famed for its chocolate, and a fly-by through Palazzolo). I'd also heard great things about Sicilian cuisine so this ride was as much about epic food as architecture.

From my base at Hotel Gutkowski on Syracuse's island of Ortigia, I headed south and west to Noto, a short ride of 19 miles (30km). It's a gritty, wind-blown road along the coast to Avola's marina but here I turn inland and then climb up to Noto. I'm staying at Il Giardino del Barocco, a B&B with rooms set around a quiet courtyard in the centre of town.

This region is known as the Val di Noto. On 11 January 1693, a massive earthquake devastated the towns and villages of southeast Sicily. Tens of thousands died and disease and plundering was rampant in the weeks after the quake. But by May of 1693, a reconstruction commenced that was largely funded by the local aristocracy and Benedictine monasteries and led to the most vivid flowering of late-Baroque art in the world.

An innovation of post-quake Baroque urban planning was a linear layout. Noto is arranged along three strata with, naturally, the rich living at the top of the hill and the poor at the bottom. This has the convenient effect of aligning many of the town's Baroque big-hitters along its main street, Corso Vittorio Emanuele. After a Sicilian-style pizza (more like two crêpes sandwiched together) and a Noto-brewed Belgian ale by Birra Vendicari at the *salumeria* Sabbinirica à Putìa d'Ercole, I wander over to the church of San Domenico. It's a pure expression of 18th-century Sicilian Baroque and the masterpiece of Syracuse-born architect Rosario Gagliardi (who died in Noto in 1762), the dominant figure of the Val di Noto, and one of the most original architects of 18th-century Italy.

Further along this pedestrianised street is a fusion of Baroque and Neoclassical at La Cattedrale, dedicated to St Nicholas of

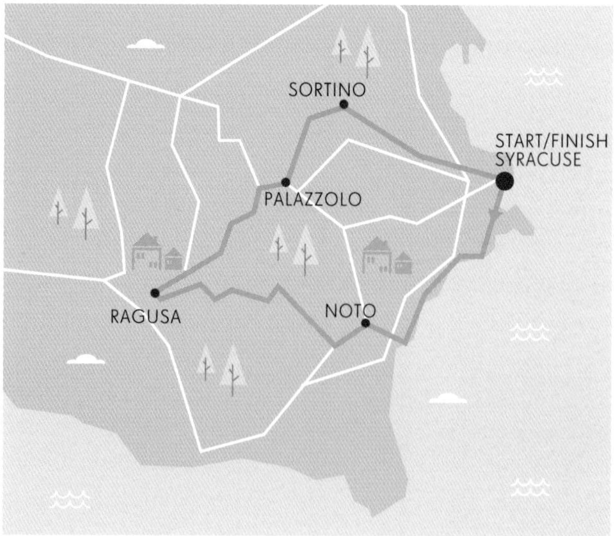

© Westend61 / Getty Images

Myra, the patron saint of a rag-tag bunch including students, brewers, prostitutes, merchants, sailors and children. He was the inspiration for Santa Claus (Saint Nick). At the Palazzo Nicolaci di Villadorata, built in 1737, I get a glimpse of the lifestyles of Noto's nobility on 'Prince's Street'.

The next day, after a breakfast beneath citrus trees, I set out for Ragusa by riding southwest along a main road then turning right on to a road that is wider than the little white line on the map suggests. This is suddenly a more rural Sicily, which means that none of the names nor roadside chapels marked on the map are signposted on the road. But I keep faith and am rewarded with my first signpost to the town of Frigintini, next stop Ragusa.

Ragusa, like Noto, was destroyed during the earthquake of 1693. The Old Town, Ragusa Ibla, was rebuilt on a promontory, now adjoined by suburban Ragusa Superiore. I'm staying in its Baroque heart, with about 60 churches around me. But first things first: food. I park by Salumeria Barocco for a platter of cheese and salami. The star *formaggio* is called *tuma persa*, the 'lost cheese'. Cheesemaker Salvatore Passalacqua found the recipe for a hard, savoury cows' milk cheese that hadn't been made for a century, and resurrected it. As I'm nibbling the last of it, thunderclouds unleash grape-sized hailstones and lightning. A dozen people cram into the tiny shop, surrounded by Sicilian wine, cheese, *salumi*, artisanal ales and chocolate from Modica. An hour later I leave, enlightened but a little heavier.

The spine of Ragusa Ibla is the flagstoned Corso XXV Aprile, which leads from the Giardino Ibleo Belvedere uphill to the

"The star formaggio uses cows' milk and is called tuma persa, the 'lost cheese'. It has been resurrected after a century"

MONTALBANO

Almost as great a pull to southeast Sicily as Baroque architecture and crunchy-oozy *arancini*, is the fictional detective Montalbano. The creation of writer Andrea Camilleri, Salvo Montalbano solves crimes in almost 30 novels, but always finds time for his early-morning swim and a long lunch. The hit TV series uses Ragusa as the setting for many scenes (Montalbano's restaurant is actually A' Rusticana) and his house on the show is, of course, now a B&B.

Clockwise from above: St Nicholas Cathedral, Syracuse; the canyons of Pantalica; the Val di Noto; Modica chocolate, a local speciality. Previous page: Ragusa's old town

© Quanthem / Getty Images,, Choi Mong Lee / Getty Images

Duomo, another of Rosario Gagliardi's masterpieces.

From Ragusa, the route retraces its way up the valley then continues uphill to Giarratana and east to Palazzolo, the next Baroque town on the itinerary. An aggressive feral dog apart, this section offers the most scenic cycling.

Lunch at Palazzolo proves that slow food isn't just about the ingredients. I continue onward to the Anapo Valley, where 15ft tall rushes sway in the humid air. Vincenzo, the host of the Sacre Pietre *agriturismo*, gives me a tour of his farm: he grows numerous varieties of lemon, including one that you can eat raw (delicious with a bit of olive oil, chilli and herbs), kiwi fruit, pomegranate, figs and oranges. After my hot ride he pours me a glass of sweet, home-made (and grown) almond milk. He shows me an ancient Greek well in his orchard, which was part of an irrigation system that took water down to Syracuse, but I'm distracted by trying to find fresh figs in his trees.

The Valle d'Anapo is on the Dell'Antica Grecia cycling route from Syracuse and that's the way I'll return to the Sicilian coast after breakfast: fresh eggs from Vincenzo's hens, bread made from an ancient grain, local ricotta (try it with Vincenzo's marmalade). The final day is generally downhill with a couple of climbs, one to Belvedere for a first sighting of the sea. Back on Ortigia, I refuel with pasta alla Siracusana. Cycling in Sicily has been not only a way of getting from one amazing building to another but from one great meal to the next. **RB**

© Giacomo Augugliaro / Getty Images, siculodoc / Getty Images

TOOLKIT

Start/Finish // Syracuse
Distance // Up to 150 miles (240km)
Where to stay // I travelled with Inntravel (www.inntravel.co.uk) who booked bike-friendly hotels in each town and organised luggage transfers and airport transfers.
Where to eat // In Noto, the Sabbinirica à Putìa d'Ercole at Via Emanuele 93. In Ragusa Ibla, the Salumeria Barocco (www.salumeriabarocco.it) at Corso XXV Aprile 80. In Syracuse Casa Trimarchi at Via Laberinto (www.casatrimarchi.it).
When to go // Avoid June to August due to heat; September and October are ideal.
More info // Book at www.inntravel.co.uk; rental bikes can be provided or bring your own. If you wish to be independent, a pannier or large saddle or frame bag would be sufficient to carry everything.

Clockwise from top: the mosque-cathedral of Córdoba; the Bauhaus school in Dessau, the Duomo of Siena

MORE LIKE THIS
ARCHITECTURE TOURS

BAUHAUS, GERMANY

By convention, cyclists prefer curves, contours and crests to straight lines. But when the straight lines belong to a building designed by the founder of the Bauhaus, Walter Gropius, and constructed in the 1920s, then our hearts skip a beat. The Bauhaus Building in Dessau, a perfect example of the Bauhaus principle of utilitarian harmony, is the destination of this 82-mile (132km) bike ride. After a visit to Berlin's Bauhaus Archive (in its temporary home), pedal southwest out of the capital and pass through pretty Potsdam and continue in a straight line to Dessau: the Komoot app can plot a route that is mostly on cycleways. The prize for reaching the Bauhaus Building is an overnight stay there. Yes, you can sleep very inexpensively in the very studios where the likes of Josef Albers, Herbert Bayer and Gertrud Arndt worked. Breakfast is not included but the bicycle garage is free. More information: www.bauhaus-dessau.de

Start // Berlin
Finish // Dessau
Distance // 82 miles (132km)

GOTHIC ITALY

Gothic architecture – all flying buttresses, ribbed vaults and pointed arches – gestated in the Late Middle Ages in northern France, spreading down to Italy and Tuscany, where it employed Tuscan marble to great effect. The cathedrals of Florence and Siena are classic examples, both built during the 13th century and decorated with frescoes. Inntravel's seven-night tour of Tuscany starts in San Gimignano, where 14 of its original 70 towers erected as status symbols by wealthy families still stand, and ends in Siena. The route passes through quiet valleys and hamlets over five days before arriving in Siena where you can admire the magnificent black-and-white Duomo, dating from the 13th century. Check out the western facade, which features elements of French Gothic, Tuscan Romanesque, and Classical architecture. More info: Tuscany on Two Wheels at www.inntravel.co.uk.

Start // San Gimignano
Finish // Siena
Distance // From 85 miles (135km)

ISLAMIC SPAIN

The Moorish architecture of southern Spain has several headline acts, including Seville's Giralda, Córdoba's mosque-cathedral and the Alhambra of Granada. But Andalucía's smaller towns and villages also demonstrate the influence of the region's Islamic rulers from the 8th century onwards. This tour starts from the town of Antequera, just north of Málaga, the nearest international airport. Head northeast to the Moorish village of Iznájar then make for Lucena and pick up the Via Verde de la Subbética rail trail to Zuheros and its 9th-century Moorish fort. From Zuheros, pedal past the Parque Natural de las Sierras Subbéticas to Priego de Córdoba and its fascinating Islamic quarter. Continue through the hills of the Sierra Nevada to Montefrío and then follow the path of the Catholics as they marched to conquer Granada in 1492. Granada's Alhambra and Albayzín, its Muslim quarter, remain.

Start // Antequera
Finish // Granada
Distance // 165 miles (265km)

© Sean Pavone / Shutterstock, StevanZZ / Getty Images, Cinematographer / Shutterstock

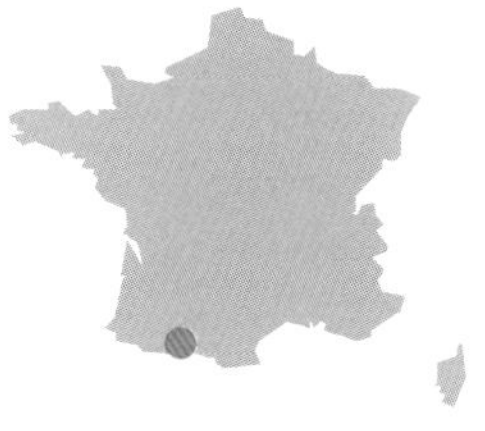

THE COL DE PORTET (ON A FOLDING BIKE)

Tour de France commentator Ned Boulting likes nothing more than to emulate the pros on a Brompton. Here he recalls his toughest day on two (tiny) wheels.

When we are commentating for ITV, former *maillot jaune* of the Tour de France David Millar and I unfold Bromptons every morning and head off towards the finish line of the day's stage, following the actual route of the race over the closing kilometres. Now, it's worth noting that Bromptons are some of the silliest bikes on the planet, foldable (for taking on trains), and boasting tiny wheels – all of which prompts derisive laughter from the roadside.

We have been doing this, more or less every day on the Tour, for four years; notching up a series of the most notable climbs in the history of the race, from the Tourmalet to Mont Ventoux. It is, however, not always easy cycling up a mountain on a folding bike.

One day, towards the end of the gloriously sunny 2018 Tour de France, 'not easy' became 'almost impossible'. It was Stage 17, and the race was going to a place it had never been before. Above the Pyrenean ski station of Pla d'Adet, which overlooks the pretty town of Saint-Lary-Soulan, there is a road, narrow and steep, that climbs to the Col de Portet, an exposed shoulder of mountain. It would prove to be the most important stage in the race for overall victory, coming just days from the finale in Paris.

After an early breakfast David and I rolled down into the Aure Valley from our stone-built gîte. By midday, we'd need to be in the

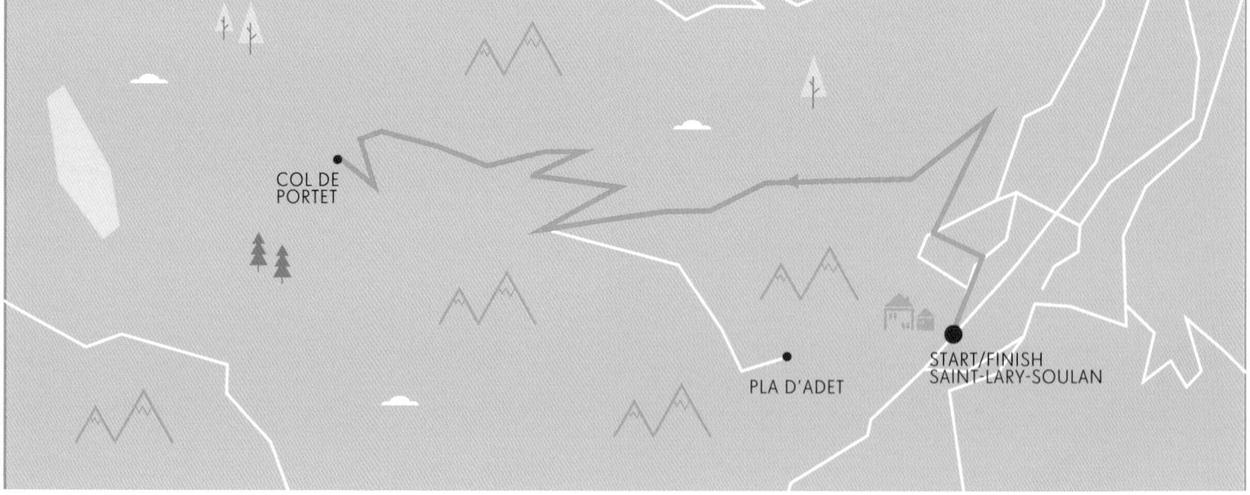

© Ned Boulting (2), Alan Gardiner / Alamy Stock Photo

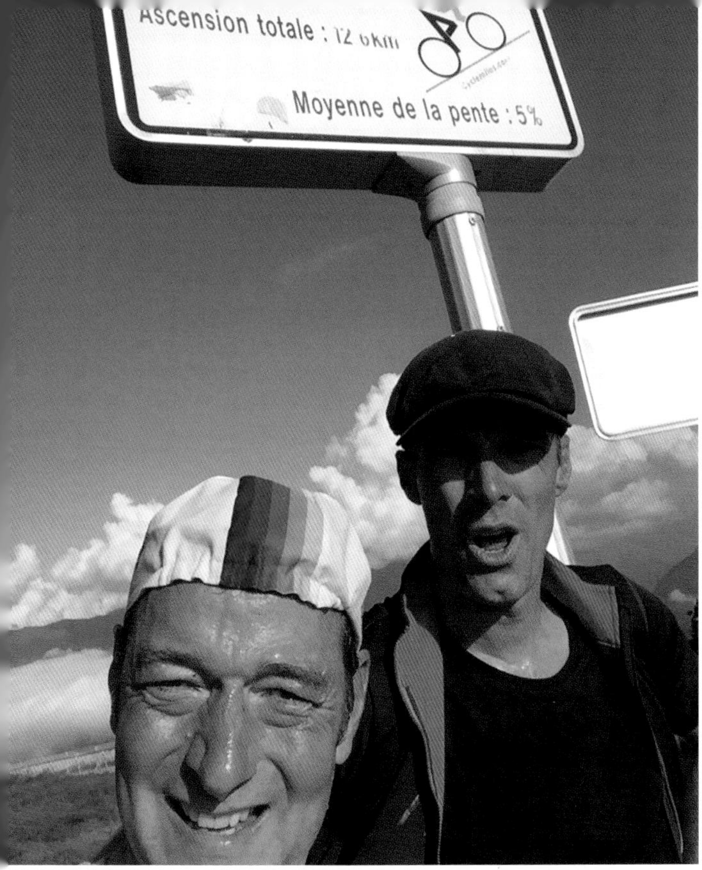
Ascension totale :
Moyenne de la pente : 5%

"The road was filling with fans opening beers. I knew this would be the hardest ascent we'd tackled. In jeans and t-shirts"

back of a truck, close to the finish line, for the day's broadcasting. We couldn't hang around. From the other side of the plain we caught a horrifying glimpse of the challenge ahead. The first few kilometres of this exceptionally hard, 10-mile (16km) climb, were among the steepest, and they were straight, sappingly, hairpinlessly-so. Already the road was filling up with fans carrying ice boxes, chalking the road, opening beers and bellowing encouragement. I knew that this would be the hardest ascent we'd ever tackled. In our jeans and t-shirts.

As we hit the climb, a rider in Team BMC red and black flashed past us. 'Nico!' I shouted. Nicolas Roche, son of the 1987 Tour de France winner Stephen, stopped; David and I spun the silly little Brompton wheels wildly to reach him.

'Are you going all the way to the top?' he asked.

We nodded, as if the folly of our enterprise had only just been made clear.

'On those?' He looked at our bikes in disgust and rode on.

'Good luck!' he shouted back down the road at us.

The first third of the climb was simply something to endure, as the road, carved out from the mountainside held a steady southwesterly path, the hustle and bustle of Saint-Lary in the grip of the monstrous Tour carnival getting increasingly distant as we climbed. This place had history. Raymond Poulidor had won on these very slopes in 1974, dropping Eddy Merckx. We were just a few cols away from the Tourmalet, the Peyresourde, the Aspin.

At the tiny hamlet of Soulan the gradient relented a little, and we stopped to form a queue at the fountain, carved out of the mossy rock and gushing cold mountain water out of an ornate spout. Without water bottles, we had to guzzle as much water as we could hold, our bloated stomachs becoming makeshift pouches.

On we laboured, all sense of amusement fading away as grim determination kicked in. We knew that the climb only really started when, in a few kilometres time, we would take a right turn off the main road and start the final ascent to the mountain pass, topping out at over 7200ft (2200m) altitude. This is big, even by Pyrenean standards; the altitude effect generally kicks in at about 6000ft (1800m).

Later that afternoon, the race would come up this climb, having already been over a series of cols on the way. The final summit finish of the Tour, it would prove to be the decisive day for Geraint Thomas' wonderful charge towards Paris and victory in 2018. The Welshman finally imposed himself on all his main rivals, and though the Colombian Nairo Quintana took the stage win, Thomas put more time into his illustrious team-mate Chris Froome, who reluctantly gave up hope of winning the Tour on the slopes of the Col de Portet.

© Eugene Kim, MARCO BERTORELLO / Getty Images

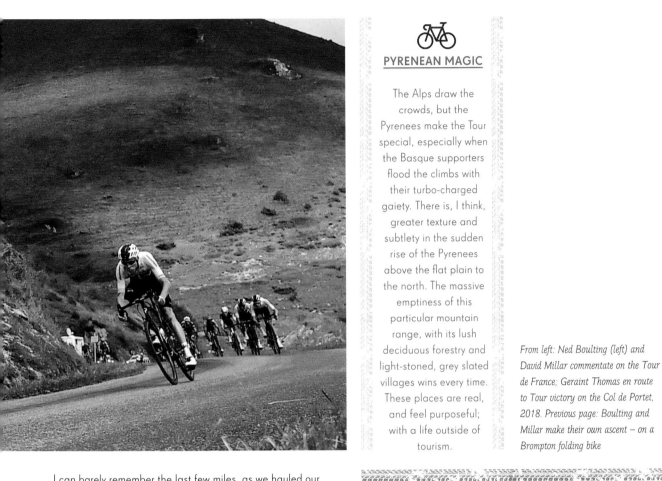

PYRENEAN MAGIC

The Alps draw the crowds, but the Pyrenees make the Tour special, especially when the Basque supporters flood the climbs with their turbo-charged gaiety. There is, I think, greater texture and subtlety in the sudden rise of the Pyrenees above the flat plain to the north. The massive emptiness of this particular mountain range, with its lush deciduous forestry and light-stoned, grey slated villages wins every time. These places are real, and feel purposeful; with a life outside of tourism.

From left: Ned Boulting (left) and David Millar commentate on the Tour de France; Geraint Thomas en route to Tour victory on the Col de Portet, 2018. Previous page: Boulting and Millar make their own ascent – on a Brompton folding bike

I can barely remember the last few miles, as we hauled our Bromptons up the side of the mountain, exposed to mist and wind, with treeless pastures flanking the route, and the smell of cow dung heavy in the air. David had dropped back to fiddle around with his new camera, because the views, when the wispy clouds lifted, were vertiginous. Eleven tightly packed switchbacks led to a finale whose presence was announced by the passage of dark tunnel. The last kilometre was brutally steep.

I do not know how long it took me to get to the top. I can only recall the huge relief, as I finally collapsed into dew-dampened grass. We had no food, no water, so we re-mounted and began the long free-wheel back to planet earth. (If the Col de Portet isn't enough, branch off 5 miles into your descent and climb to the Pla d'Adet, where Rafa Majka won in 2014 after hanging on to a TV motorbike.) An hour later, unshowered, David and I took up our microphones in the broadcast truck and commentated, with the benefit of hard-won experience, as the pros took on the very same climb. Rather faster.

It had been horrible. But wonderful, too. And when we called the race to its conclusion many hours later, I could only marvel, as I had done many times before, what Sisyphean majesty one little bike and two legs are able to conjure from the thin air of the High Pyrenees. **NB**

TOOLKIT

Start/Finish // Saint-Lary-Soulan

Distance // 21 miles (34km), 10 of which are uphill at an average gradient of 8.7%

Getting there // Bagnères-de-Luchon has the nearest train station; from there, spend a day riding over various iconic cols to get to Saint-Lary. Pau is the nearest airport.

When to ride // Before mid- to late July the upper stretch of road is in danger of being iced off. Aim for the height of summer.

What to take // Don't do as we did. Ride up with sun block, sandwiches and plenty of water. Take a warm and chill-proof jacket for the long descent.

What to ride // A Brompton folding bicycle, of course.

MORE LIKE THIS
NED'S FRENCH FAVOURITES

PORT DE BALÈS

The lesser-known Port de Balès, just above Bagnères-de-Luchon is a wondrous climb: empty, peaceful, affording quite fantastic views from the top. It often features on the Tour de France, but always as a prelude to more famous climbs. There are two ways of taking it on; either from Bourg d'Oueil, or from Mauléon-Barousse. David Millar and I rode over it in 2017 at the suggestion of our hotelier in Bourg d'Oueil who advised us that it would take, 'about an hour and a half' to get to Luchon over the top of the Bales. It was only when we got to the top of the climb, hours later, that we realised we hadn't made it clear that we would be riding folding bikes. He thought we meant by car. That day we nearly missed the start of the broadcast.

Start/Finish // Bagnères-de-Luchon
Distance // 24 miles (39km), up and down

COL DE PEYRESOURDE

The Col de Peyresourde is a beast. Mark Cavendish hates this climb more than any other on the Tour de France. His misfortune is that it is an almost annual addition to the race. In 2014, setting off from Luchon in the late afternoon towards our hotel at Saint-Lary-Soulan (some 25 miles away), Chris Boardman and I hadn't taken into account the fact that the road went straight over the top of the Peyresourde. The official climb start isn't till you have already been going uphill for 3 miles (5km) and is marked by a sign on the road that tells you there are 8 miles (13km) left, at an average of 7%. The final 2.5 miles (4km) are the greatest spectacle of all, a series of ever-tighter hairpins rising towards the summit. They unfold in front of you and appear insurmountable. In 2014, for Chris and me, they were just that. We called for a car and bailed.

Start/Finish // Bagnères-de-Luchon
Distance // 22 miles (36km), up and down

PLANCHE DES BELLES FILLES

It was in 2012 that this singular Alsatian climb was first introduced to the Tour. Chris Froome won the stage, and Bradley Wiggins took a yellow jersey he never relinquished. Since then, this 4 mile (6.5km) climb has featured a further three times, most recently in 2019, when the race organisers extended it with the addition of an extra, freakishly-steep kilometre on a gravel road. David Millar made me run up it in the morning, to celebrate my 50th birthday (a weird present). The weather in the Vosges can be tricky, but on a sunny day, there's nowhere nicer. If you can, book into the beautiful Maison d'Hôtes du Parc in Ronchamp, where, before your ride, your host Emmanuel will serve you a wonderful breakfast and point you in the direction of Le Corbusier's architectural masterpiece Notre Dame du Haut chapel.

Start/Finish // Ronchamp
Distance // 27 miles (44km)

© Tim de Waele / Getty Images, Razvan / Getty Images

From above: the Port de Balès, a 'wondrous' climb; the Col de Peyresourde, a 'beast' that defeated Boulting

THE TRANS DOLOMITI

High above the picture perfect valleys lie the dramatic Dolomites - and the remains of one of the Great War's most dramatic fronts. The result is bikepacking perfection.

I'd seen photos of the iconic, grey-blue craggy peaks of the Alpi Dolomiti that lend the range its nickname: the Monti Pallidi, or the Pale Mountains. But I never knew exactly where it was. This is not as daft as it sounds, because while there's no denying it is tucked in a nook of northeast Italy, its linguistic quirks will easily throw you off. Climb one valley and its espresso and buongiorno. Drop into another and its schnaps and guten tag. By way of further intrigue, a third language, Ladin, is also spoken.

The combination Italian and Austrian influences in the Dolomites has created a strong, independent undertone; a texture that's as important to the area as its grandest views. What better way to discover both flavours than by bike?

If you're a first-timer to the area, this week-long, 162-mile (260km) route will provide a satisfyingly broad overview of the region, circling in a clockwise direction from Bressanone (or Brixen as it's also known), all the way to Lago di Alleghe at its

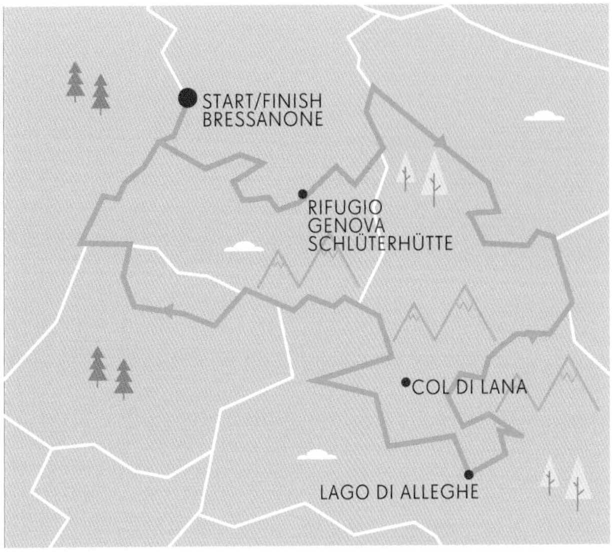

© Cass Gilbert

furthest point south. It promises one Dolomiti superlative after the next; high cols, imposing rock walls and pinnacles, and a handful of the range's 18 peaks that lie at over 9800ft (3000m) in height.

Beneath lie lush valleys that typify the alpine experience. Steepled churches and medieval castles. Apple orchards and vineyards. Ornate verandas, bedecked with potted plants, often a showcase for fine, traditional woodwork. Beer and bakeries, to sustain you over one pass after another. Pretty mountain villages and upscale Italian ski towns. And, in between, riders can happily expect swathes of thick forest, and babbling streams so clean they can scoop water straight into their bottles. The Trans Dolomiti is a bucolic slice of bikepacking perfection.

Whilst the route is mostly unpaved roads, two-track, and bike paths, the singletrack in this area is fantastic, picking its way above the treeline, over steep, rocky passes and across fast-riding, grassy knolls. Don't resist staying a night or two in a historic *rifugio* for which the area is also known. Many of these are now quite luxurious. Just bring a sleeping bag and book a bed in a dorm. It's possible to complete this loop by staying in accommodation every night – be it B&Bs or *rifugios*. (For the full experience, however, and in case of need, pack a minimal tarp and sleeping mat for discreet mountain bivouacking.)

Many *rifugios* are perched in spectacular settings and few are more atmospheric than the imposing Rifugio Genova Schlüterhütte, founded in 1898 and located at 7600ft (2306m), beneath the Col de Coltöres, the high point of a particularly brutal but rewarding climb. Tuck into a plate of garlic and parmesan pasta with fellow bikers and hikers, before retreating to your dorm room. If you're able to ignore the WiFi signal and the charging points for eBikes, it could well be a bygone era. And when the sky darkens and the clouds converge, allow yourself to be transported further into the history of the Dolomites.

"Battles took place at altitudes as high as 11,500ft, where only shepherds, climbers and herb hunters usually ventured"

During WWI, a three-year high-altitude front was established in this range between the forces of Italy and Austria-Hungary. Opposing teams of sappers attempted to mine beneath their enemy's positions, before detonating explosives. The route passes close to several sites, including Laguzoi, the Marmolada and the Col di Lana, where such military mining and detonations took place, resulting in the deaths of many troops and in some cases altering the profiles of the mountainscapes (the remnants of these mines can still be visited).

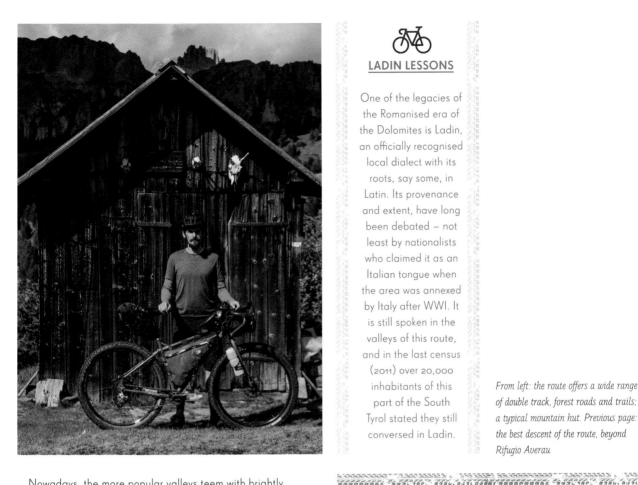

LADIN LESSONS

One of the legacies of the Romanised era of the Dolomites is Ladin, an officially recognised local dialect with its roots, say some, in Latin. Its provenance and extent, have long been debated – not least by nationalists who claimed it as an Italian tongue when the area was annexed by Italy after WWI. It is still spoken in the valleys of this route, and in the last census (2011) over 20,000 inhabitants of this part of the South Tyrol stated they still conversed in Ladin.

From left: the route offers a wide range of double track, forest roads and trails; a typical mountain hut. Previous page: the best descent of the route, beyond Rifugio Averau

Nowadays, the more popular valleys teem with brightly coloured hikers walking on trails that in some cases were made over a century ago by soldiers supplying positions high in the mountains. Battles took place at altitudes as high as 11,500ft (3500m), with soldiers forced to live year-round in places where only shepherds, wild-herb hunters, and climbers ever ventured. Clues to the 'White War', such as defensive trenches, forts, and tunnels dug deep into sheer rock, can still be seen in mountain folds. The old military roads are still there too, some of which this route follows, over the very highest ridge tops.

Back in the present, be sure to make the most of the local fare when dropping into valley towns on your journey; perhaps the hearty Tyrol favourite *gröstl*, a roast potato and lardon fry-up. Or *knödel*: *speck* (a smoked, cured ham) and dumplings, served at breakfast, lunch and dinner. There are no shortage of regional desserts to round of it all off, such as *apfelkiachl*: apple slices fried and sprinkled with sugar.

Thrilling descents of high-country trails may draw mountain bikers today, but the Dolomites is much more than white-knuckle rides: it's a magical realm characterised by its distinct geological, geopolitical and cultural past, that's unlike anywhere else in the Alps. Riding it under your own steam, slowly and thoughtfully, is surely a fitting way to appreciate it. **CG**

TOOLKIT

Start/Finish // Bressanone (also Brixen)

How to get there // Bressanone has a train station (bikes travel for a small fee).

Distance // 163 miles (262km). You'll need 5-6 days to complete it comfortably, as the terrain is ferociously steep.

What to take // The terrain is mixed, from singletrack to rock-strewn descents, to quiet bike paths. A 2in tyre or more is recommended. Bring your local gears. Even in the summer, pack a full complement of waterproofs.

When to ride // June through to the end of August is the high season, but the trails are far less busy in early September. Note the one gondola used in this route, just beyond Malga Ciapela, closes on 2 September – adjust your route accordingly.

More info // www.bikepacking.com has a full route gpx file.

© Cass Gilbert

Opposite: tackling Walna Scar Road on the Lakeland 200, one of England's most challenging bikepacks

MORE LIKE THIS
BIKEPACKING CHALLENGES

LAKELAND 200, ENGLAND

When it comes to mountain loops, the UK's Lakeland 200 is almost a match for the Dolomites – if you're lucky to enjoy it in clear weather, that is. Notching up over 20,000ft (6400m) of ascent, it's as challenging a bikepacking trip as you're likely find in England, especially when you factor in the protracted hike-a-bikes throughout. The terrain can be rocky and technical, be it up and over the fabled Black Sail Pass – home to one of the most beautifully located youth hostels in the country – or the slog up to High Street. Still, rest assured that there are tea houses and pubs offering respite and, should the sun be shining, you'll enjoy some truly dramatic views, as well as the chance to take a dip in one of the many mountain tarns. More info: A gpx file can be found at www.selfsupporteduk.net.

Start/Finish // Ambleside or Stavely are convenient

Distance // 125 miles (200km)

HIGHLAND 550, SCOTLAND

The Highland 550 is a showcase for the best mountain biking in the Scottish Highlands. Expect both technical singletrack and rugged dirt trails, along with a number of challenging hike-a-bikes. With over 52,500ft (16,000m) of climbing to its name, you'll need to be well prepared to complete this ride. Be sure your gear is well prepped too, given the typically unpredictable weather. The fastest riders can hurtle around the course in six or seven days but unless you're in a hurry (or participating in the annual self-supported time trial of the same name), you'll want to give yourself double that to enjoy it to the full. NB: the route passes over private land, some of which is used for deer stalking from from the beginning of July until February – visit deerstalkingscotland.co.uk for the implications of this. The Highland 550 begins in Tyndrum, which can be reached by train, and passes through Fort William, home to the UCI Downhill World Cup. More info: www.highlandtrail.net.

Start/Finish // Tyndrum

Distance // 550 miles (885km)

TUSHETI, GEORGIA

Arguably we're beyond Europe here, but bear with me. There's only one road in and out of mountainous Tusheti, northeast Georgia, via Abano Pass (9272ft, 2826m), the division between Europe and Asia. Consider either looping around Tusheti, tracing the ridges to the northwest of Omalo, then tackling Abano Pass again on your way out. Or, strike further west and create a larger route by hike-a-biking over Atsunta Pass (11,257ft, 3431m). You'll need a permit for the latter, given its proximity to Chechnya, but it's easy enough to procure, as the crossing is a popular summer hike amongst Poles and Ukrainians. The riding in Tusheti promises a genuinely backcountry flavour. Yet, despite its remote feel, the foot of Abano Pass is easily reached by minibus from Georgia's capital, Tbilisi. Give yourself at least a week to make the most of the area. Details can be found at www.bikepacking.com, where Tusheti forms part of the longer Caucasus Crossing.

Start/Finish // Telavi

Distance // 195 miles (314km)

© Cass Gilbert

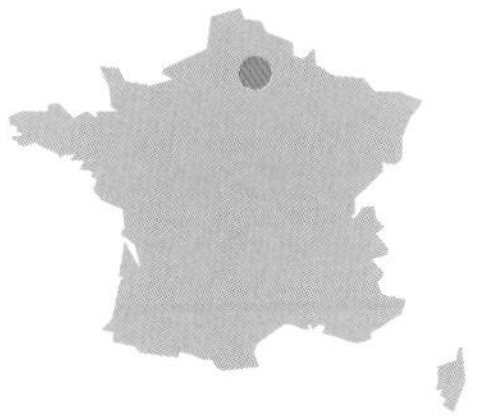

THE LESSONS OF HELL OF THE NORTH

Paris-Roubaix is that rare beast – a sportive that, instead of seducing you with picturesque countryside, asks you to confront some hard historical truths.

We're barrelling down Ave Michel Rondet towards a dark green shadow on the horizon. There's a single notch in this wall that we're aiming towards, a slot of light beneath a low, grey sky. This is the Forêt de Raismes-St-Amand-Wallers, better known as the Arenberg forest, and there's no escaping what is about to happen: the Trouée d'Arenberg.

The most terrifying 1.5 miles (2.4km) in road racing was added to the course of Paris-Roubaix, the Queen of the Spring Classics, in 1968. For several years the cobbled roads of this region of northern France had been paved over or subsumed beneath suburbs or fields. But since the first race in 1896 – when riders did indeed race north from Paris to the newly built velodrome of Roubaix – sections of cobbled roads were central to the race's identity. So the organisers turned to the 1962 road racing world champion, a man called Jean Stablinski, for help. Not only was Stablinski a champion cyclist but he had also been a miner in the coal pits of Arenberg, 50km south of Roubaix. And he knew just the place.

For our party of five, the day had started at 4am. We filled bidons and crammed as many carbohydrates into our mouths as we could before catching a coach departing Roubaix at 5am for the start of the Paris-Roubaix sportive in Busigny. The man loading the coaches grimaced as he picked up my heavy steel bike but I knew that although the course of our ride, the day before the pros' race, was 172km and took in every cobble the pros ride, it was largely flat. What 'the Hell of the North' lacks in elevation, however, it more than compensates with bone-breaking cobbled sectors, known as *pavé*. In the pro race, which covers 257km including 55km of cobbled tracks, these sectors are where moves are made, selections forced. For the amateurs they're where we realise what we've let ourselves in for.

Playing on our minds, not just that morning but for the preceding month, had been the Trouée d'Arenberg. Paris-Roubaix's cobbled sectors are graded one to five in difficulty and Arenberg is one of only three five-star sectors. Other races, notably the Tour of Flanders, feature cobbles. But while those cobbles are not quite cuddly, those of Paris-Roubaix are ogres: larger, with fearsomely hunched shoulders, unevenly laid. There's even a society, Les Amis de Paris-Roubaix, dedicated to keeping the cobbled roads sufficiently scary for cyclists. And now thousands of us were

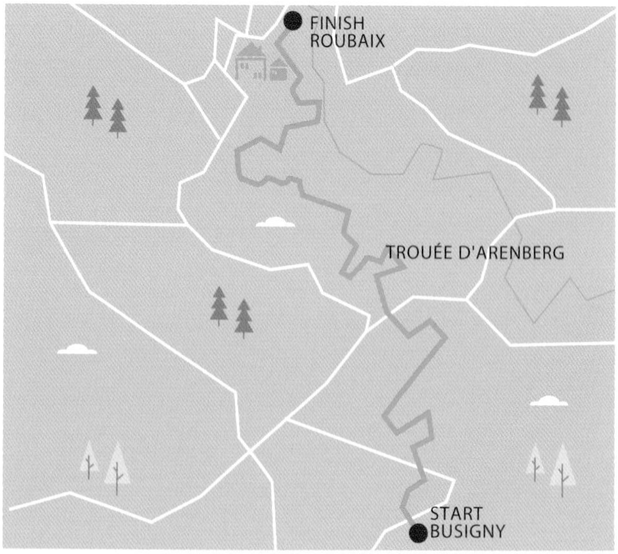

© Tim de Waele / Getty Images

POLICE

streaming past the disused coal mine heads of Arenberg towards this arrow-straight stretch of inexplicably slippery cobbles. 'Arenberg is like a descent into the coal mine,' said Stablinski. 'If you start to think of the danger you won't even go there.'

Why were we doing this? No race has played a greater part in cycling's self-mythologising than Paris-Roubaix. Monochromatic photographs of dust-streaked faces, battered bodies and the 1000-yard stare of exhausted racers fill entire books. An entrancing film of the event, *A Sunday in Hell*, charts the 1976 edition of the race. What cyclist wouldn't want to be part of its story?

Often Paris-Roubaix is framed as a battle. But lift your eyes from the cobbles, if you dare, and look around. This is a defeated landscape. It was pulverised in WWI. And since the departure of the mills and the mines of this northern-most region of Hauts-de-France, it has been on the ropes for decades. A frieze at the Hôtel de Ville illustrates the processes of weaving and dyeing of textiles that brought wealth here. But by 2014 Roubaix was the 'poorest town in France'. Unemployment remains at about 30 percent, three times the national average of France. In the most deprived neighbourhood of Roubaix, houses are being sold for €1, so long as the buyers renovate them.

There are post-industrial places like this throughout the West: the northern mining towns of the UK, Appalachia in the US. Mostly race organisers select the most scenic parts of a country to pass through. Not Paris-Roubaix. So, for all this 'noble suffering of the bike racer' (a privilege for which you pay a modest entry fee), remember that there are real battles that have been fought

"When we amateurs hit the Arenberg, all hell breaks loose. Bidons shoot from cages. Cables fly from moorings"

LA PISCINE MUSÉE

Roubaix's remarkable Art Deco swimming baths, designed by Albert Baert, opened in 1932 with the purpose of persuading the town's mill workers to wash. As Roubaix's industry dwindled so did the swimming pool, until it was resurrected as one of France's more unusual museums. Sculptures by Rodin, Picasso and Giacometti surround a shallow central pool, all illuminated through stained glass windows showing the rising and setting sun. It reopened in 2018 following a €9m renovation.

Clockwise from above: cobble sector 18 of 29 in the 2019 edition; the old pit-head at Arenberg; tyre pressure is key; 2018 winner Peter Sagan in the velodrome showers. Previous page: the feared Arenberg 'trench'

© DIRK WAEM / Getty Images, Luc Claessen / Getty Images

and lost on this land. Things may be changing. OVH, an IT infrastructure company founded 20 years ago by Octave Klaba, a Polish immigrant, is bringing 1000 jobs to the region. The former mine heads at Arenberg are the figure heads of a new digital business park and film studio.

Passing the still wheels of Arenberg's mine heads snaps riders' attention back to what is fast approaching. Eddy Merckx said of the Trouée d'Arenberg: 'This isn't where you win Paris-Roubaix but it's where you can lose it.' The professionals respond to this threat by charging straight at it at 60km/h, to be first into the trench. The very best racers, like four-time winner Tom Boonen, can make riding the *pavé* look easy, skimming over the surface of each cobble.

When we amateurs hit the Arenberg, all hell breaks loose. Bidons shoot from cages, cables fly from moorings. Because we're travelling at less than half the speed of the pros, we have to steer and pick a line as other riders judder to a halt. Somehow, we all make it through the forest unscathed. And as the cobbled sectors count down towards the lap of the velodrome in Roubaix we grow in confidence. The Carrefour de l'Arbre, the last of the most challenging five-star sectors and frequently the springboard for attacks is just 9 miles (15km) from the finish. Then we're riding through the town's streets and into the velodrome, scene of many dramatic finishes for more than 100 years.

For us, crossing the line is just as triumphant a moment; the aches and the memories linger. **RB**

TOOLKIT

Start // Busigny
Finish // Roubaix
Distance // 107 miles (172km)
Where to stay // Roubaix's hotels are a mixed bunch and are booked early for the weekend of the race. Better to try your luck with a private rental.
What to ride // The new breed of gravel bike with wider (35mm+) tyres and relaxed geometry would be ideal. Go for comfort not speed. Robust wheels give peace of mind.
What to bring // Good bottle cages (or rubber bands for securing your bidons), gloves, spare inner tubes, a pump, a windproof jacket, overshoes (wet feet are cold feet).
More info // www.parisroubaixchallenge.com; registration opens in November of the preceding year and costs €45 for the 172km distance (there are shorter options).

© ANNE-CHRISTINE POUJOULAT / Getty Images, ofrat / Getty Images

Opposite: pro cyclists rattle up the Paterberg cobbles during the 2017 Tour of Flanders

MORE LIKE THIS
SPRING CLASSICS SPORTIVES

LIÈGE-BASTON-LIÈGE

La Doyenne, the 'Old Lady', was first held in 1892. Age has not mellowed her: Liège-Bastogne-Liège is a big day in the saddle even for the pros, coming in at 160 miles (260km) or so. And the sportive, held on the day before the race in late April, offers this distance to amateurs undiluted. The route departs Liège and heads south through the French-speaking Wallonia region of southern Belgium to the town of Bastogne where it does an about-turn and meanders back to Liège via every short, energy-sapping incline the organisers can find. Legends abound, including the time in 1980 when Bernard Hinault won in a blizzard and only 21 riders finished. Around 8000 riders take on one of the three distances offered in the sportive but GPX files can also be downloaded from the organisers' website so you can follow the route (or parts of it) at your leisure. More info: www.sport.be/lblcyclo/en/.
Start/Finish // Liège, Belgium
Distance // 43-165 miles (70-266km)

TOUR OF FLANDERS

It's the most over-subscribed of the Spring Classics sportives – with 16,000 cyclists riding the event in early April – but the Tour of Flanders is popular for a reason. Every steep, cobbled climb of the Ronde van Vlaanderen has the memory of a moment attached to it, an attack from Eddy Merckx, Johan Museeuw or Tom Boonen. This is the chance to test yourself on the Oude Kwaremont and the Paterberg then swap stories over a strong beer afterwards. The steep, narrow climbs are not long; the Paterberg is just 1150ft (350m) at a gradient of 12%. But they are a challenge due to the cobbled surface, and the sportive sees many of the amateurs walking up due to the crowded lanes. Many cyclists use a GPX map file to follow the Tour of Flanders at another time of year. We think there's space for both approaches in your life. More info www.werideflanders.com.
Start/Finish // Oudenaarde (or an Antwerp start for the full-length)
Distance 46-142 miles (74-229km)

GENT-WEVELGEM

The Spring Classic race Gent-Wevelgem no longer starts in the Belgian city of Ghent, adopting from 2020 the town of Ypres, but it's lost none of its allure. For the sportive (which, slightly confusingly, starts in Wevelgem), the field is smaller than that of the Tour of Flanders so there's less congestion on the climbs. The name to fear is the Kemmelberg – a cobbled lane with a gradient of 23% that leads to the highest point in West Flanders. This is tough Flemish hill country and for one week in spring it's the centre of the cycling universe with Gent-Wevelgem, Dwars door Vlaanderen and the Tour of Flanders all taking place. This land was also fought over in WWI and since 2017 Gent-Wevelgem has featured *ploegstreets*, plugstreets of semi-paved, gravel roads to commemorate the Christmas ceasefire of 1914; you'll also pass the Menin Gate Memorial at Ypres. More info: www.gentwevelgemcyclo.be/.
Start/Finish // Wevelgem
Distance // 37-134 miles (60-215km)

© Luc Claessen / Getty Images

Boels
CANYON

THE ROCACORBA TEST

In the quiet Spanish city and emerging cycling hub of Girona, an unlikely hill climb has become a proving ground for the world's best riders.

The cycling map of the world is lumpy with classic climbs to which countless pages of purple prose have been dedicated. Mont Ventoux, Stelvio, Alpe d'Huez. Then there are the anomalies. Roads that would barely have earned a grazing cow's second glance until someone on a bike decided they had merit. Climbs like Rocacorba, a potholed cul-de-sac in Spain.

The road winds out of Banyoles, a small city outside Girona perhaps best known for its lake (it hosted the rowing events at the 1992 Barcelona Olympics), up to the summit of Puigsou. The Catalonian peak is just shy of a 1000m (3280ft) and the way up is named for the Mare de Déu de Rocacorba monastery near the summit. But the modern road only exists to serve the ungodly communications transmitters that now dominate the mountain. Much of it was only sealed with asphalt in 2006.

Professionals were already discovering Girona by then. The US Postal team made its base there in the late 1990s. Its star rider Lance Armstrong later shared a home in the city with his then-girlfriend Sheryl Crow. It was quieter than Nice, where Armstrong previously lived. 'We all knew the Spaniards were far less strict about doping,' Tyler Hamilton, Armstrong's former team-mate, wrote in his 2012 book *The Secret Race*. 'No gendarmes raiding hotel rooms, no dumpster-diving reporters...'

Today the 100 or more pros who live in Girona come for the city's medieval architecture, low-key yet entrepreneurial spirit and proximity to Barcelona's international airport. Girona is also blessed, thanks to its position between the Pyrenees and the Costa Brava, with climbs on the doorstep that regularly feature in the Vuelta a España (Tour of Spain). Rocacorba, an unassuming dead end, is not one of them. But once the tarmac arrived, it earned a reputation as a formidable testing ground for pros as they approached big races.

I take a 12-mile (20km) route from central Girona north to Banyoles, veering south briefly from the lake to the unofficial, unmarked start of the climb; a blink-and-miss-it bridge across the wooded river. From here there are 6 miles (10km) to the top. The climb's other vital stats – 7% average gradient, 2625ft (800m) vertical – do little to suggest a serious test. Moreover, the first few kilometres are gentle and, well, pretty dull. The woods obscure any views and at one point the road is more cratered than the moon.

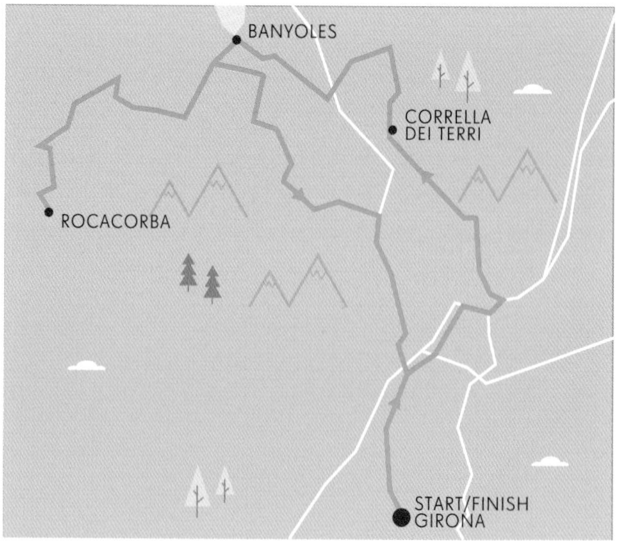

© Tristan Cardew & The Service Course

"While the average gradient is manageable, it's a head-down climb, with constant shifts that break up your rhythm"

© Gordon Bell / Gordon Bell / Shutterstock, Josep Curto / Shutterstock, Tristan Cardew & The Service Course

'Is this it?' I wonder as I pedal.

Before Strava, the popular fitness tracking app on which millions of riders record rides and compare times up notable climbs, pros would brag about Rocacorba ascents in Girona's cafes, gossip spreading thereafter, or share photos of their bike computers showing their times at the summit. A good time confirmed to a rider that he was in shape, while also serving as a warning to rivals.

Bradley Wiggins, who was based in Girona for a while, put in a time of 27 minutes 39 seconds in 2010. Ryder Hesjedal, a Canadian ex-pro and Girona man, would go all out on Rocacorba on the Friday before the Tour de France each year. He, too, has a 27-minute time. David Millar, the British ex-pro, who has lived in Girona since 2006, even founded a social cycling club inspired by the climb called Velo Club Rocacorba. He too has managed the climb in under 30 minutes.

For a while Rocacorba remained a little secret in the forest. But word quickly spread beyond the pro community as cycling magazines caught wind of an unlikely new test. By the time I got to Girona, several bike rental and tour companies, many run by pros, had popped up in the city and Rocacorba had given up its secrets. Almost 12,000 people had recorded more than 20,000 ascents on Strava – and unknowable numbers riding without devices.

The Strava leaderboard for the 'segment', as timed stretches of road are known on the app, is humbling. At the time of writing, 10 riders had times under 30 minutes, including Simon Yates, the British winner of the 2018 Vuelta, Mike Woods, a top Canadian pro, and the American Tejay van Garderen, who lives in Girona. Top spot belonged to James Knox, a young British rising talent who was filming with Millar.

Soon I get a sense of their interest in what seems like an unremarkable bit of road. While the average gradient is manageable, its constant shifts makes it hard to find a rhythm, while the tree cover means it's difficult to know where you are. It's a head-down climb, taken on purely for the sake of the climb itself. The road then ramps up considerably in the final few kilometres, with stretches of 15%. It's here that I run out of gears and adopt an ungainly grind, sweat washing sun cream into my eyes (did I mention it was 35C?).

With 4km to go, I catch a glimpse of the radio masts but they seem troublingly distant and barely appear again until they loom over me in the final stretch. There is no fanfare at the summit – only a line on the road to mark the end of the segment and, a few metres later, a heavy locked gate protecting the communications station. There is no cafe or, when I climb, anybody else at all.

The only reward – at last – is the view: a terrifying hang glider's ramp disappears off the edge of a small clearing towards the lake in the distance and the terracotta sprawl of Banyoles. I make the 10km in 52 minutes, a time I'd like to challenge the next time I visit Girona. Before that, I make the descent back to Banyoles where the peculiar new tradition of Rocacorba riding requires a beer beside the lake. **SU**

THE HINCAPIE LOOP

Don't leave Girona without taking on the 'Hincapie Loop', a stunning 63km route that was a training circuit when Lance Armstrong lived in the city with his loyal lieutenant George Hincapie. Just 2.5 miles (4km) east of the city centre, the 11km climb of Els Àngels starts before the descent to the village of Monells for an espresso on the square. The route then loops back over the climb to Santa Pellaia before a rolling return into southern Girona.

Clockwise from top left: nearby Girona is a road-riding hub; the view from the top of the climb, and a local shrine. Previous page: Rocacorba's upper reaches

TOOLKIT

Start/Finish // Girona, heading first to Banyoles, a 14-mile (23km) warm up before the ascent proper begins.
Distance // 45 miles (73km)
What to ride // Several outfits in Girona offer bike rental, guided rides and even bike sat navs with famous routes ready to follow (including Rocacorba loops). The Service Course (theservicecoursegirona.com) has a range of rare top-end bikes and a sister cafe, La Fabrica, across the river that does the best coffee in town (lafabricagirona.com).
How to get there // Girona's airport is 25 minutes away by road, Barcelona's airport is 90 minutes. Or take a train from Barcelona's main Sants rail station.
Where to stay // Girona's hotels are increasingly bike friendly, often with dedicated bike storage. For now at least, everything in the city is reasonably priced.

Opposite: rising from sea level to 7550ft, Mount Teide is the longest continuous climb in Europe

MORE LIKE THIS
PRO TRAINING CLIMBS

MOUNT TEIDE, TENERIFE

Tenerife, the largest of the Spanish Canary Islands that lie off western Morocco, is a magnet for pro training camps thanks to its mild winter weather, mountainous roads and summit hotel (sleeping at altitude is supposed to be good for your blood). Team Sky, now Ineos, have been going there every spring since 2010. But the star attraction is Teide, the volcano that dominates an island best known otherwise as a budget beach destination. The classic climb starts in the south of the island at El Médano, rising from sea level to 7550ft (2300m) in a single, barely relenting climb of 32 miles (51km) – the longest continuous climb in Europe. From the summit, roll back down to the 28.5 mile (46km) mark for a large plate of food at the low-key Parador hotel, where multiple Tour de France champions have shared rooms on their way to victory. Strava time to beat: 3hr 1m.
Start/Finish // El Médano
Distance // 32 miles (51km), there and back

COL DE LA MADONE, FRANCE

Lance Armstrong did much to put Girona on the cyclists' map, but before Rocacorba became a fitness test for the pros who flocked there, there was the Col de la Madone. It starts 20km east along the coast from Nice, another favoured destination for cyclists and another previous home of Armstrong. The American said he knew he would win a Tour if he put in a good time on the Madone in the days beforehand (this was before he admitted that drugs might also have played a part). The climb, as the pros measure it, starts inauspiciously outside an Intermarche supermarket just north of the coastal town of Menton. It then wiggles and winds prettily past the medieval village of Sainte-Agnès to the summit after 8 miles (13km) and almost 2950ft (900m) vertical. Chris Froome, who lives nearby in Monaco, has reportedly ridden it in under 30 minutes. Strava time to beat: 33m.
Start/Finish // Menton
Distance // 16 miles (26km)

MONTE SERRA, ITALY

The Italian coach Luigi Cecchini was the man behind multiple Tour de France winners during the 1990s, many of them – inevitably – assisted by more than his groundbreaking techniques. He lived near Lucca, another pro-cycling hotbed in the Tuscan hills, and would use Monte Serra as a gymnasium and laboratory in which to test his clients. The classic ascent starts in Buti, just south of Lucca and east of Pisa, and is a quick but intense 6km climb through woodland. Short enough to attack, particularly where the road flattens slightly around the hairpins, it's an effective test of true fitness for those who dare to leave everything on the road. Not that gut-busting is required; Tuscany has become such a draw for cyclists of all levels that the Monte Serra attracts thousands of riders of all shapes every weekend. Strava time to beat: 16m 31s.
Start/Finish // Buti
Distance // 7.5 miles (12km), there and back

© doleesi / Shutterstock

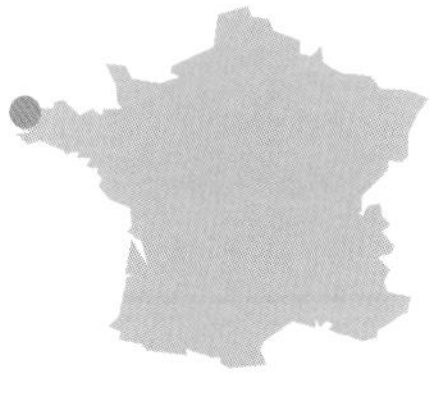

TO THE END OF THE EARTH

Farm tracks, beaches and a piglet for the winner: Tro Bro Léon is a bike race around the Finistère department of Brittany, where getting lost is part of the fun.

Strange things live at the world's end. Morgens, long-haired sirens of Breton (and Welsh) folklore, lure men to their watery graves. And the Ankou is a harbinger of death that appears across the Celtic regions (an Ankow in Cornish, yr Angau in Welsh) to collect the souls of the dead. To that list of weird and wonderful Breton phenomena you can add the Tro Bro Léon professional bike race and its sportive.

There are a few bike races that sound like an absolute blast to ride and Tro Bro Léon is one of them. It's beautiful because part of its route hugs the boulder-strewn coast of far-west Brittany. It's fashionable because the route uses as many of the *ribinou* – unsurfaced farm tracks – that organiser Jean-Paul Mellouet can piece together into a loop. A growing number of these mixed-terrain races includes Schaal Sels in Belgium, the Rutland-Melton CiCLE Classic in England, and the revitalised route of Paris-Tours.

Finally, it's unique thanks to its origins. The Tour de France was founded to promote a newspaper. The first Paris-Roubaix was

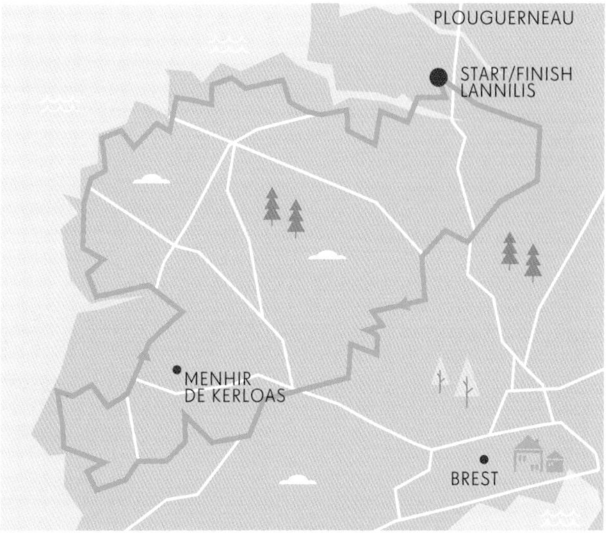

© Alex Turner

sponsored by *Le Vélo* newspaper. But Tro Bro Léon was started by Breton Jean-Paul Mellouet in 1984 in order to raise funds for Brittany's Diwan schools that teach the Breton language to local children. And to support the local farming industry, the first Breton to cross the line wins a piglet.

All these reasons put the sportive event, a ride on the route for amateurs the day before the UCI-sanctioned race, at the top of my must-ride list. And that's how I found myself wheeling my road bike off the Portsmouth-to-Caen ferry and setting off for the town of Lannilis, 15 miles (25km) north of Brest (Brest's train station is the closest to Lannilis).

On the Saturday, I make a relaxed reconnaissance of the area, following a part of the Véloroute des Abers that traces the coast from Brest via greenways for 30 miles (50km). *Abers* are inlets where rivers meet the sea and its just one word of many that reveal the close Celtic connections between Brittany and parts of Britain. With prolific 'k's and 'z's, place names could pass for Cornish villages and Brittany's flag, the Gwenn-ha-du, shares the black-and-white palette of its Kernow counterpart. The granite rock and mystic stones also remind me of Britain's West Country. Putting Stonehenge in the shade, the tallest standing stone in Europe, the 10m, Bronze-Age Menhir de Kerloas was moved, somehow, to its hilltop setting from an estuary 1.5 miles (2.5km) away. It was the focal point of a fertility cult, with half-naked newlyweds rubbing themselves against it.

"Tro Bro Léon is the coolest race out there and should be on every pro's bucket list." Dan Craven, professional bike racer

Signposted cycle routes in this corner of France lead into largely car-free byways and I follow several out to the Crêperie La Route des Phares, set on a sandy bay just outside Plouguerneau. There's a vantage point from the headland to spy the lighthouse of the Île Vierge, an essential safeguard along this treacherous coast. After a buckwheat crêpe called La Terroir (egg, smoked sausage, steamed potatoes with parsley butter, smoked chicken breast and organic cheese from Kervihan farm) and a crêpe for dessert (pear, hot chocolate and caramelised almonds) I roll slowly back to Lannilis at sunset. No half-measures for me when it comes to carb-loading.

The following day I start the sportive at the very back of 600 riders, who are sent off in staggered packs. To make up places I latch on to the wheels of a couple of very fast riders, following them out of town through Tro Bro Léon's much-photographed tunnel – a glorified, corrugated pipe between two fields. After a few miles it occurs to me that the red signs for the sportive route have ceased, leaving only the yellow race signs. Note: the full-length race is 205km (and the winner will finish in just 5hr). I'm still just hanging on to the wheel of the fast men but arrive at a good

© Alex Turner (2), Icon Sport / Getty Images

THE WISDOM OF THE BADGER

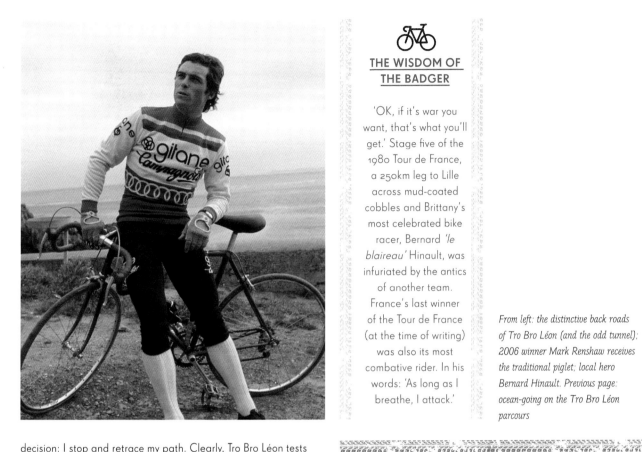

'OK, if it's war you want, that's what you'll get.' Stage five of the 1980 Tour de France, a 250km leg to Lille across mud-coated cobbles and Brittany's most celebrated bike racer, Bernard *'le blaireau'* Hinault, was infuriated by the antics of another team. France's last winner of the Tour de France (at the time of writing) was also its most combative rider. In his words: 'As long as I breathe, I attack.'

From left: the distinctive back roads of Tro Bro Léon (and the odd tunnel); 2006 winner Mark Renshaw receives the traditional piglet; local hero Bernard Hinault. Previous page: ocean-going on the Tro Bro Léon parcours

decision: I stop and retrace my path. Clearly, Tro Bro Léon tests common sense and navigation skills as much as fitness.

At a junction of *ribinou* I meet a group of riders who seem similarly lost. Luckily, there are a couple of locals present so we follow them back to the first roundabout and pick up the red markers again. Tout va bien.

The first portion of the ride proceeds without further incident, unless you count coming head to head with a herd of cows on a track and later having to repair a flat tyre beside a church. The route circles west through quiet lanes and robust granite towns. But, after we pass the phallic Menhir de Kerloas, I pick up the first siren calls of the coast: a glimpse of turquoise waves beyond a green field, a swathe of sand and a scattering of rounded boulders.

We're on the final third of the course, which hugs the coast, and the roads sweep up and down from *aber* to *aber*. It's beautiful and exhilarating and I'm feeling strong, right up to the point we turn east, still alternating between tarmac and gravel, and into the teeth of a heavy headwind. At the final refreshment stop on a road overlooking a gorgeous beach, I gather myself for the final push – the Ankou can wait for another day.

I gorged on crêpes, punctured, got lost and held up by cows, was hit square in the face by water from a Super Soaker pistol wielded by a young farm girl, battered by headwinds, and blown away by boulder-strewn beaches at the very tip of France. The standard Tro Bro Léon experience, really. **RB**

TOOLKIT

Start/Finish // Lannilis
Distance // 70 miles (112km)
When to ride // The event is in April, but the route can be ridden any time until October.
Getting there // Cycle from the closest train stations, Roscoff (31 miles, 50km) or Brest (16 miles, 25km). Or drive.
Where to stay // Get lucky with an Airbnb in the centre of Lannilis. Hotel accommodation is limited.
Where to eat // There are bakeries and supermarkets in Lannilis. For eating out, La Route des Phares (laroutedesphares.wordpress.com).
What to ride // A road bike with the widest tyres you can fit (28mm or more ideally); carry a puncture repair kit, spare tubes and pump.
More info // www.trobroleon.com, which has downloadable maps (but no GPX files); visit www.af3v.org for a map of the Véloroute des Abers around the Finistère coast.

© Gilbert UZAN / Getty Images

MORE LIKE THIS
BRILLIANT BRITTANY

NANTES TO ROSCOFF

If Tro Bro Léon has inspired you to explore more of Brittany by bicycle, a series of numbered cycle-touring routes guide you across this corner of France. They pass through towns and villages that are often linked by trains, allowing you to pedal in one direction and return by train. The Brittany section of La Vélodyssée – the name given to the French part of the enormous EuroVelo 1 route around Western Europe's coast – crosses Brittany from Nantes to the port of Roscoff (or vice versa). In Nantes, check out the Machines de l'Île – not bicycles but mammoth mechanical contraptions, such as the 12-metre tall Grand Éléphant that can carry sightseers on a tour of Nantes' island. The rest of the route to Roscoff is no anti-climax, seeing as it follows part of the Nantes-Brest canal. More info: https://en.francevelotourisme.com/cycle-route/la-velodyssee-the-atlantic-cycling-route.
Start // Nantes
Finish // Roscoff
Distance // 250 miles (400km)

BRITTANY COAST PATH

Instead of riding cross-country across Brittany on the Nantes to Roscoff route, you could cycle around the coast on the still-developing coast cycle path. With all the *abers* (inlets) this is a slow and windblown but scenic option. The path is known as Route 5 and several key sections are complete, including the Côte du Léon that you will have touched on during Tro Bro Léon, the Côte de la Mer d'Iroise out west from Plouarzel to Brest, the Bay of Audierne, the Peninsula of Quiberon and the Gulf of Morbihan. String all those together (the roads between the bike paths are quiet; or check train or bus timings at www.mobibreizh.bzh) and you could be covering more than 500km. More info: https://en.francevelotourisme.com/cycle-route/the-coastal-cycle-path-in-brittany.
Distance // up to 310 miles (500km)

LA VÉLOMARITIME

Forming part of EuroVelo 4, this signposted ride along Brittany's north coast connects Roscoff with Mont Saint-Michel via the ferry port of Saint-Malo, Europe's largest megalithic mausoleum and the pink granite of the Bay of Morlaix. The full trip is 263 miles (423km) but, as per the other cycle routes here, it is often possible to take the train between legs. If you start from Roscoff there's a reasonable chance of picking up a westerly tailwind as you shadow the GR34 Sentier des Douaniers (customs officers' path) through a maze of pink granite boulders along the coast. At Plouezoc'h, check out the Cairn de Barnenez, Europe's largest burial chamber and 2000 years older than the pyramids of Egypt. More info: https://en.francevelotourisme.com/cycling-destinations/brittany-by-bike/the-north-coast-of-brittany-by-bike.
Start // Roscoff
Finish // Mont Saint-Michel
Distance // 263 miles (423km)

© andre quinou / Shutterstock, jopelka / Getty Images

From above: Morlaix Bay, Brittany; the Nantes-Brest canal en route to Roscoff

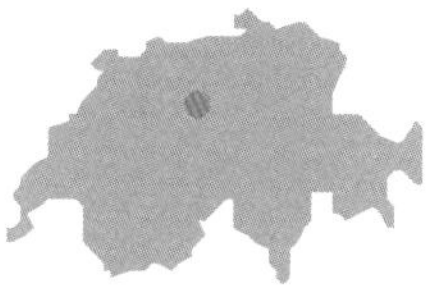

THE HOPE 1000

This brilliantly designed route through the Swiss Alps is long-distance bikepacking made easy, says champion adventure rider Lael Wilcox.

'Switzerland calling.'

Willi Felix is calling me in Tucson, Arizona, from the other side of the world. He wants to invite me to his race in Switzerland on a route he designed after decades of riding research. It's called the Hope 1000 (previously the Navad 1000) a 620-mile (1000km), self-supported mountain-bike race across Switzerland from Lake Constance to Lake Geneva with a staggering 96,218 feet (29,327m) of climbing.

'How do you fit that much climbing into such a short distance?'

'It's the Alps,' replies Willi. 'They are steep.'

Five months later, mid-May, I'm on a plane from Alaska to Zurich. I've planned to ride the entire route, for fun and in preparation for the race.

I pack light because I'll be living on my bike. Summer in Switzerland is warm and sunny for the most part, and though the route tops out at 6800 feet (2070m), most of it is much less elevated. For the race, my upper-body layering system is a long sleeved shirt, a cycling gilet and a rain jacket. I don't even pack a pair of trousers.

Willi picks me up from Zurich Airport and takes me to his home in Bettwiesen, a 30-minute drive from Zurich. I unpack and rebuild my bike, trying to stay awake to beat jet lag. A few days later, I'm out on the Hope 1000.

The route is broken into 11 segments, each a solid day's ride, and each starting and ending in a town with at least a grocery store, but typically also a hotel, restaurant, train station and possibly a bike shop. So it's a simple adventure to plan, mount and complete – and you can shorten it with ease. For instance, a great option for a week-long trip is to begin in Sursee and ride the western half of the route in the higher mountains.

I leave early morning after coffee and a croissant, riding through farm fields and along a creek. The road turns up; first it's paved, then dirt, then trail. I'm spinning my easiest gear, cranking slowly up the steep pitch (a couple of sections have to be walked). I'm alone. The view opens up. A chairlift, static, hovers above the trail. I'm surrounded by mountains with a direct line of sight to the next lake, crystal blue. This is the Switzerland of postcards and calendars, pristine and peaceful.

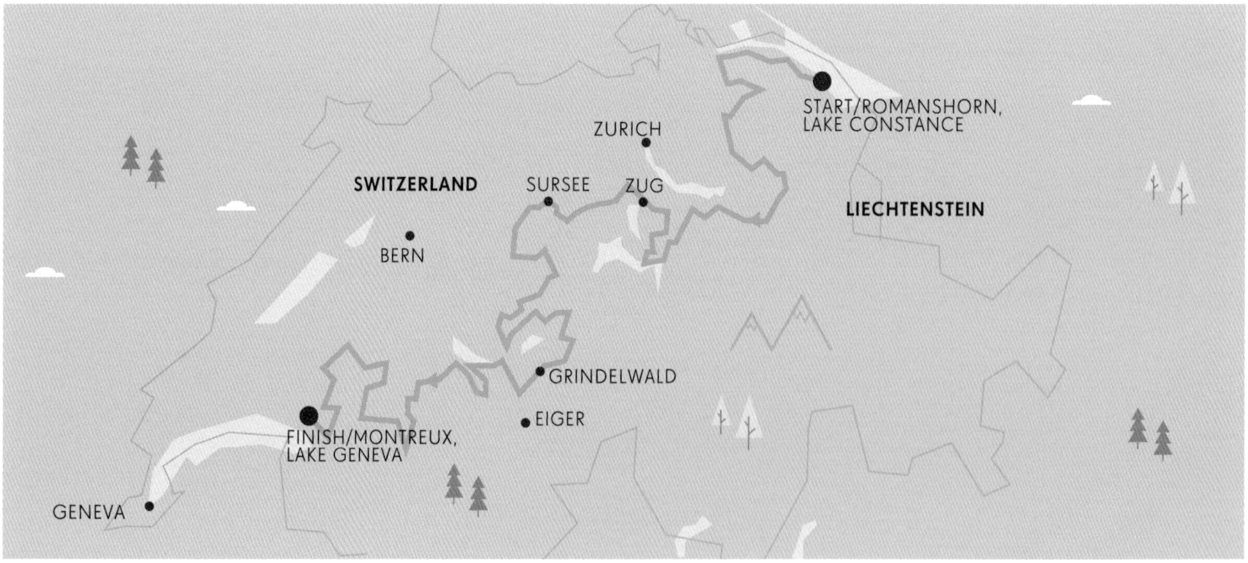

© Rugile Kaladyte

Then I descend, stopping at a spring to fill up my water bottles and a shop to buy lunch: a slice of pizza and a container of cabbage salad. The local language is German and I don't speak it, but it's easy to get by. The village stores are plentifully stocked with baked goods and yogurt drinks, sandwiches and snacks.

The day continues. If I'm not climbing, I'm descending. In the intended direction, riding west, many of the climbs are either paved or well-graded roads; Willi has ensured trails are reserved for the descents.

Past dark, I make it to a small mountain hut. It's a three-sided building, public and free for hikers and cyclists. I spook a sleeping German hiker awake. I tell him about the Hope 1000 route and that I'm riding to prepare for the race. He's hiking the Camino de Santiago de Compostela, spending the next three months walking to Spain. Your bike looks like a rocket ship, he says.

Next morning, I'm up with the sun before six. I pack my sleeping bag and mat and I'm back on my bike. The German rubs sleep out of his eyes: 'Are you already racing?' he asks.

This is how I want to spend all of my days.

In the mountains, I'm mostly alone. I encounter smiling farmers and cows, cyclists and hikers. I never go more than 9 or 10 miles (15km) between fresh water fountains or 25 miles (40km) before finding a restaurant or shop. I don't have to worry about food or

"The Hope 1000 is a masterpiece of bikepacking design. I never have to worry about where to find food or water"

THE MONTREUX JAZZ FESTIVAL

The Hope 1000 ends in the handsome city of Montreux on the shore of Lake Geneva, which for two weeks each July is home to what has become the second-biggest jazz festival in the world. The festival still has its roots in jazz, but has expanded to include every style of music with celebrated artists performing from around the world. If that blows your flute, time your ride appropriately and make sure to secure your accommodation well in advance.

From above: the Hope 1000 climbs over 98,000ft; Lael finishes with a dip in Lake Geneva. Previous page: the Hope 1000 provides picture-postcard Swiss scenery

© Rugile Kaladyte

water until I'm hungry or thirsty. It feels like an adventure without concern – which is the ultimate freedom. Most nights are clear and I sleep in fields. To avoid getting wet, I take shelter under a barn during an afternoon shower and sleep under the porch of a cabin. (There are always options for hotels and guesthouses, but I'd rather sleep out. Bivouacking on public land away from protected areas and populations is generally acceptable in Switzerland.)

The second half of the Hope 1000 route, I discover, is both better and harder than the first, with climbs up the Grosse and Kleine Schedeggs past Grindelwald, with views of the Eiger, Jungfrau and Mönch, singletrack traversing craters through Stübleni, and the final climb over the Col de Jaman to Montreux on Lake Geneva. The route ends at a statue of Freddie Mercury. After 1000km and 30,000m of climbing, Freddie is always waiting.

There are many ways to cross Switzerland, but the Hope 1000 is a mountain masterpiece. After 20 years of research, Willi published the route and organised the race to encourage more people into self-supported adventure riding. Thanks to its logistical ease, he sees it as a beginner-friendly bikepacking race.

Willi is nearly 60 and rides his own race every year. In addition, before the grand depart each June, he verifies every kilometre to make sure the Hope 1000 is both rideable and challenging. Mountain biking wasn't invented in Switzerland, but maybe it should have been. **LW**

TOOLKIT

Start // Romanshorn, Switzerland on Lake Constance
Finish // Montreux, Switzerland on Lake Geneva
Distance // 632 miles (1017km)
How to get there // Zurich Airport is half-an-hour's train ride from Romanshorn. Geneva Airport is the closest to Montreux.
When to ride // The end of May and October.
What to take // A mountain bike (hardtail or full suspension) with 2in tires, disc brakes and easy gearing.
Where to stay // The Hope 1000 is designed to pass hotels and official campgrounds.
What to eat // Croissants, sandwiches and drinkable yogurt, if you're like me.
More info // The Hope 1000 was previously the Navad 1000: full GPX track https://bikepacking.com/routes/navad-1000/. Willi Felix hosts a free race on the Hope 1000 route every June: www.hope1000.ch/.

Opposite: eating up trail on the 1000 Miles Adventure

MORE LIKE THIS
LAEL-APPROVED BIKEPACKS

THE BIKE ODYSSEY, GREECE

This mountain race, held each June, connects small, peaceful villages in Northwest Greece, via high pasture and mountain passes, verdant forest and arid Mediterranean landscapes. The route is 80% trail and 20% road, and if the gradients are occasionally demanding (you'll gain 55,000ft/16,800m over the entire route) and the surface loose, it is entirely rideable. Fresh water is abundant; camping is easy. Northern Greece is a land of feta, walnuts and honey. Away from cities, packable food and stores can be hard to source, so be sure to stock up when passing through larger towns. However, nearly every village has a cafe and place to have a meal. Race in June or tour the route between April and October. It is a particularly attractive touring destination in the spring and fall when European weather elsewhere is less friendly. More info: www.bikeodyssey.gr/en/information.html; https://bikepacking.com/routes/bike-odyssey-bikepacking-route-greece/.

Start // Smixi
Finish // Kato Tithorea
Distance // 385 miles (620km)

LA TRAVERSÉE DU MASSIF VOSGIEN, FRANCE

An official French mountain-bike route running north-south through the Vosges Mountains in eastern France, the signed Traversée du Massif Vosgien follows primarily well-graded dirt roads and trails in forested Alsace. You'll meander through many small villages and past castle ruins, with ample opportunity for lodging, camping, and sampling local cuisine and Alsatian wines along the way. The region's culture, on the border with Germany, is quite distinct and the Vosges Mountains are a quiet, natural retreat for its residents. Best ridden in the summer months (May to September), the route is 90% trail and a slice of France not often seen by visitors. The local tarte flambée, white wine and Munster cheese are not only justly celebrated, they're great fuelling options for the mountainous trail. A well-connected rail network makes this route easily accessible. More info: www.alsaceavelo.fr/itineraires/traversee-massif-des-vosges-vtt.html; https://bikepacking.com/routes/bikepacking-france-traversee-du-massif-vosgien/.

Start // Wissembourg
Finish // Thann
Distance // 252 miles (406km)

1000 MILES ADVENTURE, CZECH REPUBLIC AND SLOVAKIA

Starting in 2011, the 1000 Miles Adventure was one of the first bikepacking races in Europe. It travels through the beautiful mountains and forests of the Czech Republic and Slovakia from the German border to the Ukrainian border (the direction changes each year). And though it feels remote, you're never far from populated areas, and your next hot meal and cold beer. The route developer and race organiser, Jan Kopka, wanted to bring home his extensive experience of adventure racing around the world. Due to his efforts in part, bikepacking is popular in the Czech Republic. The race start is in July and 7 to 27 days are recommended for completion – NB, significant sections of the route are open for the race alone, so to ride its entirety, sign up for the race. More info: www.1000miles.cz.

Start // Hranice, Czech Republic
Finish // Nová Sedlica, Slovakia
Distance // 1000 miles (1610km)

© 1000miles.cz

MALLORCA'S SPRING PLAYGROUND

The largest Balearic island is a road rider's paradise, nowhere more so than on the smooth asphalt and celebrated climbs of the Serra da Tramuntana. Just check the weather forecast...

It wasn't quite meant to be like this. Scouting the road approaching Puig Major by car, the weather had certainly not been bike friendly: chilly and wet. But as we approached the tunnel beneath the highest mountain on Mallorca, a snow storm struck. We laughed. And then they closed the road off. The laughter faded.

Where was the Mallorca we had read about? The cycling playground that basks in sunshine while the rest of Europe shivers, drawing cyclists, from rank amateurs like us to elite professional squads, to its famously well-paved and traffic-light roads? That Mallorca was under an inch of snow. We retreated to our apartment in Port de Pollença, stowing the SPF 30, rummaging for gloves and overshoes.

Over the last 20 years, cycling has become big business on the largest of the Balearic islands. Now, each spring and autumn, around 200,000 cycle-tourists flock here, collectively spending around €200,000,000. Admittedly we had arrived for our three-day trip in the final days of February, a week or two before the start of Mallorca's cycling season. No minibuses ferrying expensive bikes about, few riders in Lycra lounging in cafes, the chirp of cycle computer absent on the morning air. But still, snow? It was a reminder that the Serra da Tramuntana, which dominates the

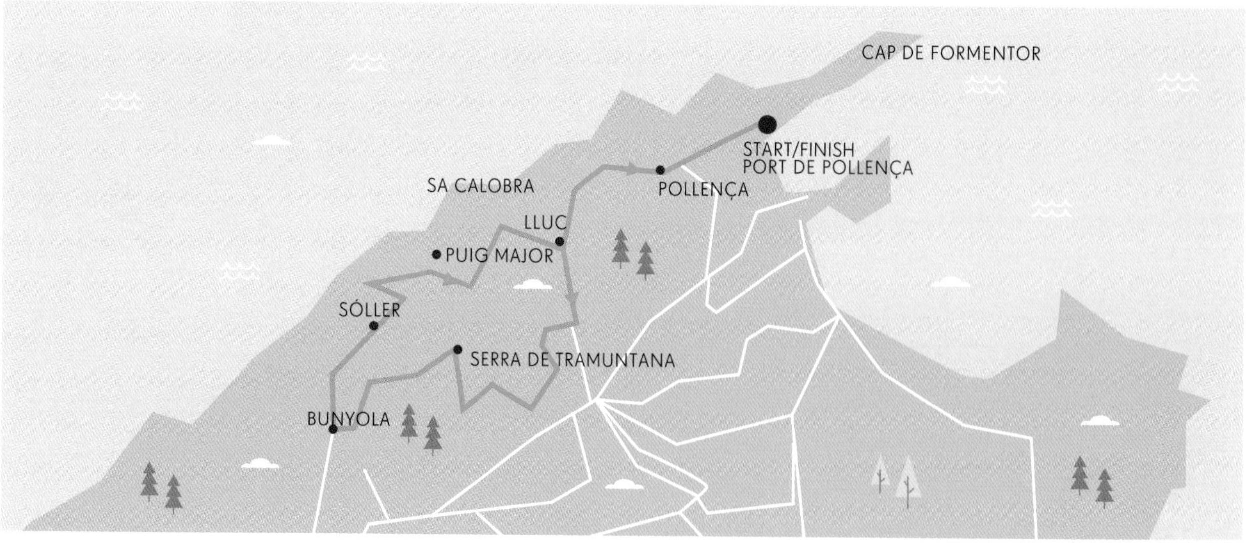

© kavop58 / Shutterstock

"We descended into Sóller, warming up with a late-morning café exprés and ensaïmada pastry under the plane trees"

northwest coastline, is home mountains that range up to 4740ft (1445m).

The next day brought better weather, so out we ventured, west and south from Port de Pollença, over the hills to Lluc – but leery enough of conditions higher up that we chose to hug the Tramuntana's south-facing slopes before turning and heading up the valley into a squall that left us soaked 10km from home. Rewarded for our timidity, it would seem.

We were determined to give a better account of ourselves the next day – and hoped that Mallorca might return the favour. The itinerary began with the road up to Lluc, then a clockwise loop via Bunyola, Sóller and Puig Major, returning via Lluc once more, a 90 mile (150km) tour of the Serra de Tramuntana. The northwest coast largely escaped the construction boom that gripped the rest of the island's coastline in the mid-20th century. Today, the Tramuntana is a Unesco-protected cultural landscape: most memorable are the slopes, riven with canyons and shored up with dry-stone olive-tree terraces, that plunge down into the Mediterranean, overlooked by the ruins of mysterious and ancient *tayalots* (watch-towers).

Day two on the bike. A weak but welcome sun was at our backs. Though big climbs and occasional steep jags lay ahead, the road from Port de Pollença to Lluc is a good leg-warmer, taking 9 miles (15km) to begin properly ascending, and even then the gradient is rarely testing. So, turning south after Lluc, it was a pleasant surprise to find that the road rapidly drops in a series of switchbacks through wood glades towards Caimari. We spun happily through the quiet foothill towns of Mancor de la Vall, Biniamar and Lloseta and the small-holdings that lie between them. Before Alaró, the route turned north between the imposing *mesa* of Puig de s'Alcadena and Puig d'Alaró, and back into the mountains proper – a steady climb that culminates in the east side of the snaking, tight hairpins of the Coll d'Honor, bosky with holm oak.

All of which served as an ouverture before the challenge at the end of the morning: the Col de Sóller. A road tunnel connects Bunyola with Sóller on the coast, but the old road up and over the pass is still in good condition. It's less forbidding than it appears, 24 hairpins easing the gradient. Nevertheless, at its foot Robin and I decide that our cheese and ham sandwiches can wait no longer. As coaches disappeared into the tunnel, we spotted the nearby, attractive-looking Jardins d'Alfàbia, but, eager to push on, we stuck to our roadside perch (later, online, I checked out the

© Mike Higgins, Magdalena Bujak / Alamy Stock Photo, kovops8 / Shutterstock

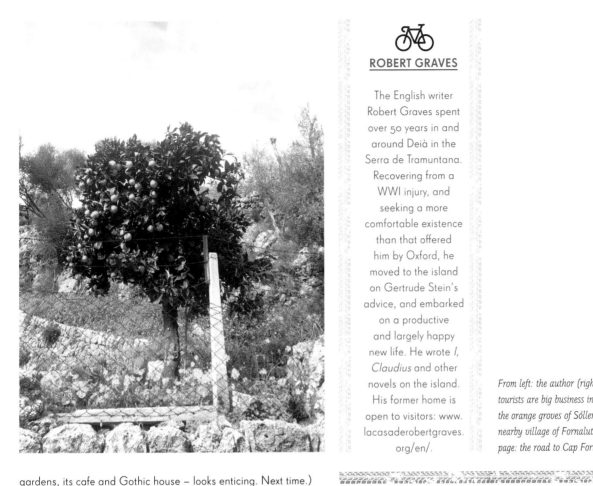

ROBERT GRAVES

The English writer Robert Graves spent over 50 years in and around Deià in the Serra de Tramuntana. Recovering from a WWI injury, and seeking a more comfortable existence than that offered him by Oxford, he moved to the island on Gertrude Stein's advice, and embarked on a productive and largely happy new life. He wrote *I, Claudius* and other novels on the island. His former home is open to visitors: www.lacasaderobertgraves.org/en/.

From left: the author (right); cycle-tourists are big business in Mallorca; the orange groves of Sóller and the nearby village of Fornalutx. Previous page: the road to Cap Formentor

gardens, its cafe and Gothic house – looks enticing. Next time.)

The 30 hairpins down to Sóller provided their own challenge: damp and shaded further by overhanging trees – don't get your braking wrong here. We soon warmed up in the busy backstreets of the prosperous town, nipping into a bar for a late-morning *café exprés* and *ensaïmada* pastry under the plane trees on Carrer de Santa Bàrbara. A map check confirmed our route: to the village Fornalutx above the town and then the Ma-10 up to Puig Major.

The town's fortune was made by the citrus fruit hanging from the trees all around us on the meandering ascent towards Fornalutx. Oh to have scrumped a Sóller orange to fortify us for the climb ahead. But no. Water, energy bars and some undignified grimacing were to be our fuel on the winding 9-mile (15km) ramp up to the road tunnel that, at 850m, punches through the massif beneath the peak and that represents the top of the climb. Thank goodness for the bowling green-smooth tarmac all the way.

The run back to Port de Pollença flatters: a 40km descent that first cowers beneath Puig Major itself and then delivers you, via contour-hugging roads and oak verges, to the coast. There we rode directly to the marina, ordered beer and toasted our legs, quivering after 93 miles (150km) and 10,500ft (3200m) of ascent. The late afternoon sun gave us its blessing. After the previous day's indignities, the Tramuntana, at last, was smiling on us. **MH**

TOOLKIT

Start / Finish // Port de Pollença
Distance // 93 miles (150km)
How to get there // Palma, in the south, has an international airport.
When to ride // March to May, September and October. Come prepared for poor weather early in the season.
Where to stay // We stayed in a private apartment. The capital Palma or Port de Pollença make ideal bases for the south and northern ends respectively of the Serra de Tramuntana. Many of the hotels cater to cycle-tourists.
Bike hire // I hired a very good quality Canyon road bike through the Palma outlet of the Rapha cyclewear brand (€20 per day; membership of the Rapha Cycling Club required, currently £70 annually). There are plenty of bike-hire businesses across the island.

© Mike Higgins

Opposite: participants in the Mallorca 312 sportive on their 194-mile (312km) tour of the island

MORE LIKE THIS
MALLORCAN CHALLENGES

MALLORCA 312

Mallorca is an island full of cycling challenges for cyclists of all abilities. If you are looking for a stiff one, head there in April for the Mallorca 312. Every year, thousands of participants from all over the world set out to circumnavigate the island during the popular sportive. Make sure you're fit, though. The 194-mile (312km) route features 10 categorised climbs – including Puig Major – and well over 16,000ft (5000m) of total elevation gain. Views over the Mediterranean offer respite, as does encouragement from fellow riders. You've got 14 hours to complete the course. If you don't feel quite up to it, there are also 140-mile (225km) and 104-mile (167km) versions.

Start/Finish // Playa de Muro
Distance // 194 miles (312km)

SA CALOBRA

On an island that can, at times, feel like a road-cycling theme park, the ride every cyclist wants to bag is Sa Calobra: a 6-mile (9.5km) ascent so tortuously picturesque it even manages to include a loop-the-loop, after a fashion, doubling back and over itself at one point. To make the ascent, riders must first descend it, taking in the fabulous sea views, to the small fishing village on the northwest coast from which it takes its name (it's also called the Coll dels Reis). Antonio Parietti, a local engineer, oversaw the road's creation in the 1920s, to encourage motor tourism. Cyclists, rather than cars, now swarm there, and it has become something of a fixture on Strava, the fitness tracking app: pit yourself against the current fastest ascent, a shade under 25 minutes (Bradley Wiggins was said to have ascended even more swiftly training for his 2012 Tour de France victory but declined to log his time).

Start // Sa Calobra
Finish // Coll dels Reis
Distance // 6 miles (9.5km)

CAP FORMENTOR

Another civil engineering gem from the mind of Antonio Parietti is the undulating road out to Cap Formentor, the mountainous cape east of Port de Pollença, where the ride proper begins. There and back is 22 miles (35km), demanding 3300ft (1000m) of climbing from you. Again, the Strava leaderboard features wincingly fast times by professional riders. But don't get drawn into that arms race unless you want the experience to pass in a hot, sweaty blur. The ride is worth taking time over. Pause at the high cliffs of the first viewpoint 2 miles (3km) in. Dip your toes in the waters of Platja de Formentor, a couple of miles further on. And of course the viewing point at the tip of the cape itself is worth lingering at. But do take another layer with you – the locals call it the Meeting Point of the Winds for a reason.

Start / Finish // Port de Pollença
Distance // 22 miles (35km)

© Mallorca 312

TORTOUR
MERIDA

THE TORINO-NICE RALLY

The bikepacking event was born of a curiosity to explore the endless trails and cols of the southern Alps in good company, writes its founder James Olsen

There are plenty of riding events on beautiful roads and trails that climb into the Alps on the Italy-France border, up famous cols and and remote, historic military paths. The Torino-Nice Rally is different. Some riders reach the Côte d'Azur days before others, but it's not a race. And though there is a route distributed among the participants, they're not necessarily expected to follow it. That's because the rally was created to offer riders the opportunity to bikepack across dramatic landscapes and enjoy the expansive views in good company.

The rally invites riders to take a meandering route through the southern Alps along roads, trails and hiking tracks. It has been running each September since 2016. At that inaugural rally, 60 or so riders gathered in Turin for the ride to Nice. In 2019 it was 170. Each year since we've gathered the participants together for dinner in a piazza the night before departure, making new friends from all over Europe and beyond. And to see the participants line up, it's evident that all are welcome: riders of varying ages making last-minute kit checks on almost every kind of bike that has lower gears and fatter tyres, with a mix of traditional panniers and modern, lightweight luggage, taking last-minute photos.

And once they're off, the start line is also likely to be the last time you'll see more than a dozen or so riders in the same place – the climbs quickly disperse the group who rolls out of Turin. It's the cols each day that determine a rider's pace, not the distance. The fastest may be in Nice within four days, in the saddle before sunrise and until after sunset each day, with few breaks. But there are many riders who will happily give the near-435 mile (700km) route eight to 10 days to complete, pausing for a lunch of cheese

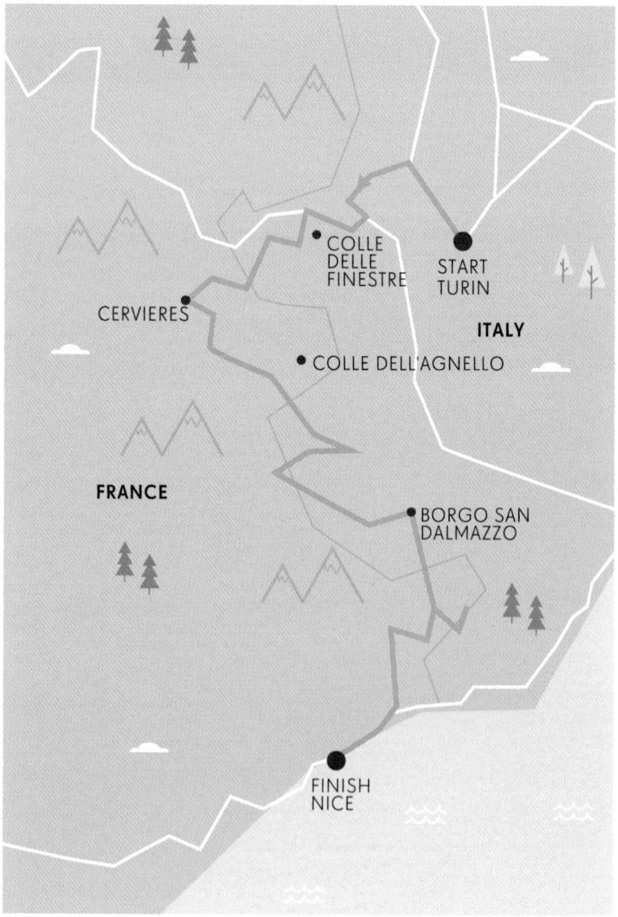

© evanoui.cc

and cured ham on a picturesque col. Some will camp, others will enjoy all the comforts of gîtes and mountain refuges along the way.

I was inspired to start exploring routes for the rally by a simpler time when a good bike would take you most places. And if the bike couldn't take you, you'd just push for a while. Those old-fashioned 'rough stuff' attitudes, combined with modern mapping technology, brought us to Turin with a few GPS route sections which would take us to Nice. Some were on roads, others were open tracks and quite a few were those 'who knows?' high paths that linked key valleys in the Alps and looked intriguing. That element of freedom is maintained in the Torino-Nice route files.

For example, early on the third day of our first exploration of the route we started up one of the high paths, unknown to us, an alternative to a familiar road climb. The contour lines on our maps suggested a walk rather than a ride and they were, as ever, correct. Soon we were carrying our bikes up a steep path at well over 2000m (6562ft), with a sense of adventure that ran out sooner than the path. Our bikes were generalists, as were we – good for a bit of most things. But the track we reached at the wide-open summit was worth the effort.

A couple of miles of singletrack led on to some fast, stony trails through small streams and wooded areas before turning into a quiet road down to the valley. It was typical of Alpine pasture access routes, that often are neither challenging enough for today's mountain bikers nor suitable for road cyclists. It was simply a great bike ride and that's what we were there for. We were in the valley in time for lunch before heading up to the ride's high point,

"Neither challenging enough for mountain bikers, nor suitable for road cyclists, the fast, stony trail was simply great riding"

SMART SHELTER FOUNDATION

The route and event management for the Torino-Nice Rally is produced by a small non-profit organisation in support of the Smart Shelter Foundation (SSF). I first met Martijn Schildkamp, the Dutch architect behind SSF, in Nepal in 2008. SSF is a charity that develops techniques to make traditional buildings earthquake-resistant – their constructions in Nepal survived the 2015 quakes. It continues to develop safer building methods in the world's poorest areas. More info: www.smartshelterfoundation.org/

Clockwise from above: a cafe stop on the rally; the former military roads of the southern Alps invite exploration; on the Colle dell'Agnello. Previous page: the Colle delle Finestre

© Adam Ferris

the Colle dell'Agnello, at 9003ft (2744m) the third-highest paved road in Europe. The rally route takes in plenty of other highlights of the southern Alps, such as the Colle delle Finestre made famous by the Giro d'Italia (see page 170), the historic trade route the Via del Sale (see page 164), and that striking high-altitude network of military roads in the Altopiano della Gardetta known as Little Peru – all worth your sweat and effort.

Which is my favourite? There's a Lost World feel to the wooded area at the end of the Via del Sale section, on the border of the Piedmont and Liguria regions, that I find calming.

Make no mistake: the Torino-Nice Rally is not easy, but it is within the grasp of any self-sufficient rider with good basic fitness and who understands the precautions and equipment necessary for riding in the high mountains. Just give yourself enough time. Logistics can be quite simple: towns in the valleys have food; water is available regularly; campsites often accommodate on-the-day booking; and there are mountain refuges which offer the perfect place to enjoy the surroundings and good food. It's those times at the refuges, restaurants and cafes, talking about the day's experiences and hopes for the next day, that keep me happily returning each year. It's also the ease with which the route is adapted to keep it feeling new.

Most importantly, the rally is about returning to those cols, trails and refuges that are some my favourite places to be on a bike. Perfect places, up high. **JO**

TOOLKIT

Start // Turin, Italy
Finish // Nice, France
Distance // 375miles to 435 miles (600km-700km), depending on route taken.
Getting there // Turin and Nice each have international airports and rail stations.
When to ride // Late June to early September; the TNR itself takes place in early September.
What to take // A reliable, lightweight bike with low gears and wide off-road tyres. Pack light, and for bad weather. Cycling shoes you can walk in. Swimwear for Nice!
What to eat // In Italy, gnocchi or polenta with ragu. In France, *civet de sanglier* (wild boar stew) or *salade des guides* (pâté, charcuterie and salad). Cycle-touring food.
More info // Route information, accommodation and restaurant tips, and GPS files are available from the Torino-Nice Rally site: https://torino-nice.weebly.com/

© evanoui.cc

Opposite Thingvellir National Park, Iceland, a short detour off Route 1

MORE LIKE THIS
BIG OFF-ROAD TOURS

LES CHEMINS DU SOLEIL, FRANCE

For other off-road routes that roll from the Alps to the Côte d'Azur, take a look at the series of mountain bike trails that come together under the name Chemins du Soleil. One is a continuous route from Geneva to Nice, another takes you from Valence to Nice via Sisteron. On these routes through the southeast corner of France you'll find some fantastic mountain-bike riding. For the trip of a lifetime, study the full route from Geneva and the foothills of the central Alps, into the Chartreuse and Vercors massifs and across the rugged Haute-Provence area to Nice. Alternatively, research a route that takes in the various Grand Randonnée (GR) paths between Geneva and Nice – none will disappoint. More info: www.vtt.alpes-haute-provence.fr/grandes-traversees-vtt/grande-traversee-vtt-les-chemins-du-soleil/

L'ALTA VIA DEI MONTI LIGURI, ITALY

A historic high-road, Italy's Alta Via dei Monti Liguri follows the coast from La Spezia in the east to Ventimiglia in the west, traversing the last sea-bounded slopes of the Maritime Alps, concluding near the French border. At 303 miles (488km) it's a demanding prospect: unpaved Napoleonic-era military roads and less travelled tracks used by the region's inhabitants to cross the hilly terrain, by turns exposed and rocky, then loamy and overhung with trees. It's possible to camp out all along the trail, though riders will need to be self-sufficient with food (alternatively there are enough small villages for you to get an excellent overview of the area's cuisine in its many osterias). Sestri Levante, Genoa, Savona and Loano along the coast are within reach of the route; if you don't fancy the entire length, it's possible to focus the sections that interest you most.

Start // La Spezia
Finish // Ventimiglia
Distance // 303 miles (488km)

RING ROAD, ICELAND

There's a reason why Iceland features on the to-do list of so many cycle tourers. Glaciers, geysers, lava fields, volcanoes, lunar landscapes and thunderous waterfalls are just a few of its geological delights, and reason enough for its nickname: the Island of Fire and Ice. The paved Route 1 – otherwise known as the Ring Road – is a popular undertaking, though head inland, following its network of highland dirt roads, to where the most remote and challenging terrain is to be found. Good waterproof clothing is de rigueur for cycling in Iceland, as inclement weather is rarely far away. Be sure to bring a sturdy tent too, as incoming fronts roll in from the Atlantic, bringing stout winds in their wake. Best undertaken in the European summer, when the days are endlessly long, and the temperatures milder.

Start/Finish // Reykjavík
Distance // 828 miles (1332km)

© Gary Latham / Lonely Planet

THE TRANSPYR

You don't need expert bikepack skills for an off-road traverse of the Spanish Pyrenees: just self-reliance, good friends and a sense of humour.

I'm lucky to have a community of female friends whom I can call on to help me live my life right to the edges. Not all of these women are seasoned bike riders but they all share essential characteristics that make them excellent adventuring companions: self-reliance, a sense of humour and the ability to problem solve. Turns out you don't need anything more to be able to complete an off-road, self-supported traverse of the Pyrenees.

I met Durita, Jenny, Rickie and Ferga on the beach at Roses on the Spanish Mediterranean coast. We all knew each other but had never before operated as a team. This would be a test. Around 550 miles (900km) of trails and 65,000ft (20,000m) of height gain separated us from Irun on the Atlantic Coast. At our disposal we each had a hardtail mountain bike to which we had strapped all our sleeping and cooking gear, a route map of the Transpyr (a seven-day mountain-bike stage race; we were just following the route, not doing the race) – and those personal qualities. Of all these assets, our senses of humour would prove the most important.

After the obligatory dip in the sea and photographs that highlighted the comical differences in the physiques of our team, we set off too late in the day to ride fully-loaded bikes comfortably under the Mediterranean sun. We had no idea where we would reach that night but we all agreed that it didn't matter. We had 14 days and everything we needed to stop and sleep wherever and whenever we liked.

We rolled slowly west and upwards away from the sea on easy, wide trail in and out of the welcome shade of the pine trees of La Garrotxa county, chatting and watching storm clouds build in the mountains. I love the freedom of wild camping, and in Spain it is

"Against the jaw-dropping background of Ordesa National Park, we experienced the most sublime few miles of singletrack"

legal and generally tolerated in unpopulated areas. But on our first night, the rain forced us to shelter under a large, all-weather community sports facility above the beautiful medieval town of Besalú. In the morning, we packed up feeling a little sheepish, but we were treated to friendly waves from local residents. A damp night is soon forgotten when morning breaks with a weak red sun and is followed by strong coffee in romantic town squares nearby. Something worth remembering at 2am when all your kit is wet.

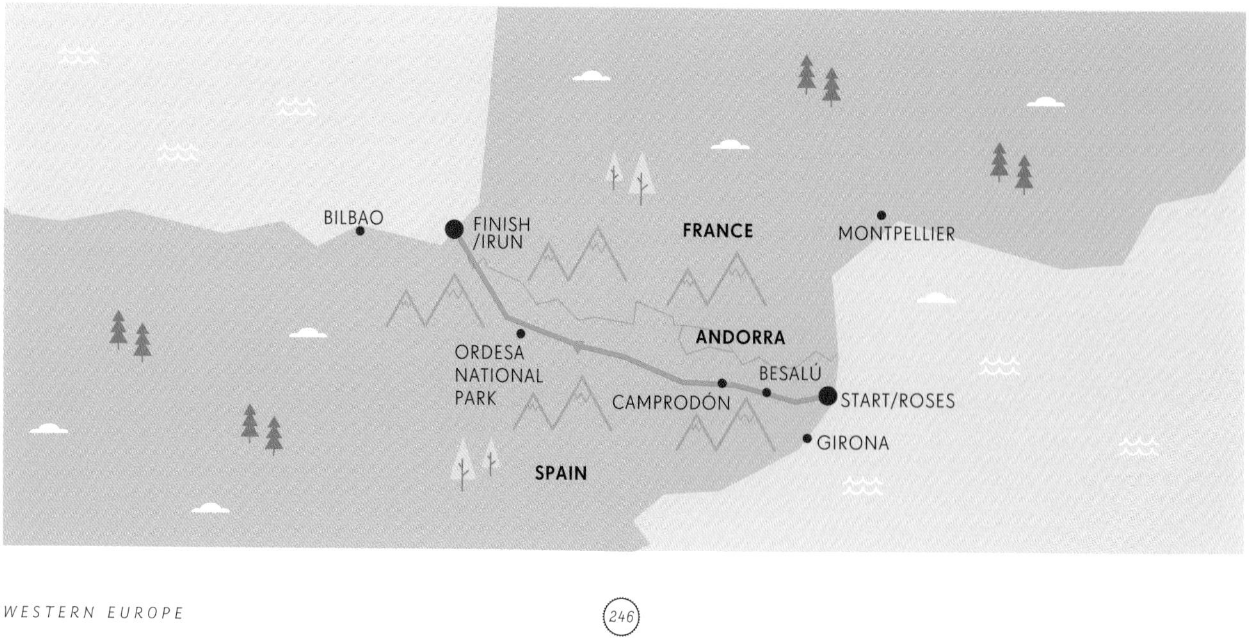

© Fotoesportbcn

008A

When we eventually prised ourselves away from Besalú it was to continue west and upwards towards Camprodón, the mountainous gateway to the Spanish Pyrenees. Here the trail kicked harshly upwards, still on dirt road but steep and loose in places; our little band settled into their separate rhythms to reach a pizza restaurant at 3280ft (1000m) that would mark the end of day two and the transition into the higher peak.

This is what is so lovely about riding in a group of self-sufficient equals. Company when you want it, unspoken acceptance when you don't, but always the comfort of others to help when challenges come along. We might have varied in fitness levels and technical riding ability, but luckily we all felt that any waiting that had to be done offered the chance to stretch or take photos. Moving as a group becomes a problem only when time is an issue.

Over the next few days asphalt, dirt road and singletrack propelled us further west with some enormous climbs and the occasional tricky descent. Each day the route conspired to take us through mountain towns where we could resupply and drink coffee before climbing high again to find camping spots on ridges that offered majestic views over to France. We enjoyed these evenings immensely. With tired limbs and sun scorched skin, we would sink into the soft earth clutching our rehydrated meals and recount stories from the day's ride while we watched the sun set.

The company was excellent, the views spectacular but for me – I come from a mountain-bike background – the riding was beginning to feel underwhelming after a week on gravel roads.

MOUNTAIN-BIKING IN AÍNSA

If you are interested at all in off-road riding then you must visit Aínsa and the Ordesa National Park. The fabulous medieval town square in Aínsa dates back to the 11th century has been declared a Historic-Artistic site. It is also the central point in a network of well-marked mountain bike trails that litter the valley and will keep you entertained for weeks. More info: https://zonazeropirineos.com/en/.

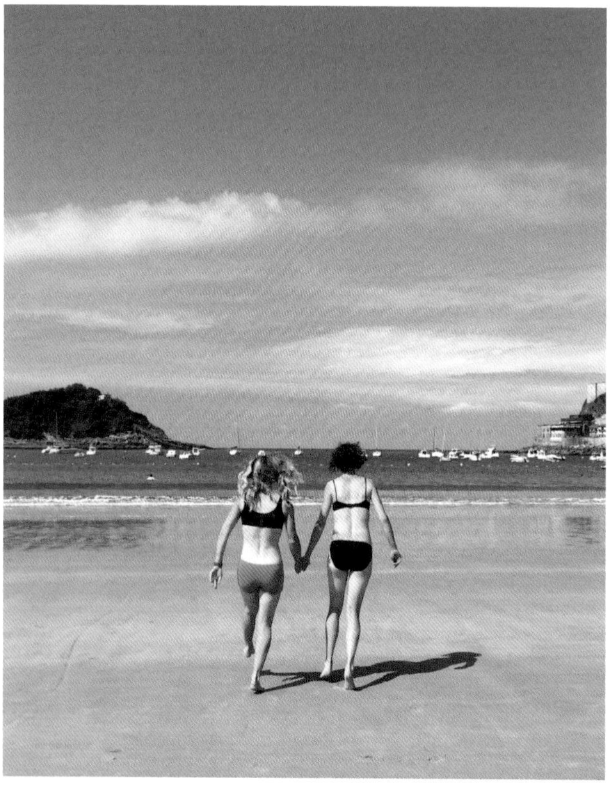

Clockwise from above: Janovas Bridge near Aínsa; Llierca Bridge near Besalú; the author and friends near Camprodón; a final dip at Irun. Previous page: Transpyr racers

Climbing out of La Collada on a spectacular, traversing gravel road towards Peña Montañesa, we paused on the high col above the famed singletrack descent into the mountain-biking mecca of Aínsa. With the jaw-dropping background of the Ordesa National Park in its autumn glory, we were about to experience the most sublime 2.5-mile (4km) stretch of unadulterated singletrack. It wasn't long before I was grinning ear to ear, flowing effortlessly downhill in a loamy paradise of young oak and old pine.

We found it hard to leave Aínsa. This time not solely because of the coffee options in its medieval town squares (although Aínsa old town does boast this luxury). Rather, we had all managed to get very sick with giardia (a parasite found in bad water). We had been careful, we thought, filtering all drinking water not sourced from a tap – but perhaps it hadn't been wise the previous night to pitch our tarp on cow poo-covered ground so we might catch the early morning sun.

We rested in Aínsa for a couple of days and then cajoled our tired bodies to limp their way towards the lush, green Basque Country. As we did so the mountains around us fell away and views

© Lee Craigie and Fergo Perry, Igor Schifris / Transpyr race

opened towards a tiny shimmer on the horizon that over time grew into the Atlantic Ocean.

Giardia or not, we managed a stagger down the beach at Irun to topple into its cleansing waters. We grinned and congratulated each other before going our separate ways. We'd come together again sometime to pull off another of these adventures. Already my mind was brimming with possibilities. **LC**

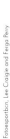

© Fotoesportbcn, Lee Craigie and Ferga Perry

TOOLKIT

Start // Roses
Finish // Irun
How to get there // There are international airports in Perpignan and Girona. Sleeper train options are available from Paris.
What to take // A mountain bike with bike-packing equipment. It would be easy to sleep indoors every night on this route, but carrying sleeping, cooking equipment and a water filter gives flexibility.
When to ride // Spring and autumn are favourite times of year in the Spanish Pyrenees; while sleeping high is pleasure in the heat of summer, water can be hard to come by.
Distance // 460 miles (740km)
More info // Try the stage race and have your food and transport taken care of for you: transpyr.com. To read more female-led adventure stories visit theadventuresyndicate.com. Bikepacking.com is a helpful resource.

Opposite: the New Forest is an ideal place to hone new bikepacking skills

MORE LIKE THIS
SIMPLE BIKEPACKING ROUTES

THE NEW FOREST, ENGLAND

One of the largest remaining tracts of unenclosed pasture land in southern England, the New Forest is 219 sq miles of heathland and ancient woodland bisected by quiet roads, double gravel tracks and copious walking trails. The gentle, accessible terrain, combined with good rail connectivity to London and a vibrant network of pubs and tea houses, makes it the perfect place to start practising self-supported bike travel. This route, put together for bikepacking.com by Cass Gilbert, begins and ends at Brockenhurst train station and makes a convoluted journey into some of the lesser-visited tracts of woodland and heathland. For the most part, it keeps to relatively wide and well-graded forest tracks, with slightly looser or rougher sections and quiet woodland doubletrack with only minimal climbing and plenty of rest stops and campsites. There is even bike hire at Brockenhurst should you prefer not to travel with your own. More info: https://bikepacking.com/routes/new-forest-gravel-taster-uk/.
Start/Finish // Brockenhurst
Distance // 62 miles (100km)

A SCOTTISH COAST TO COAST

A manageable there-and-back in the north of Scotland. Start by catching the train to Ardgay (which serves Bonar Bridge) from Inverness (or ride using Sustrans National Cycling Network and, from Dingwall, the B817 then B9176). Then ride due west to Croick on quiet tarmac. The route then turns into wide doubletrack which is rough in places but takes you deep into the hills. It's possible to make a 2-mile (3km) detour to Oykel Bridge 20 miles (32km) in if you need a break before continuing on doubletrack by loch and riversides through Strath Mulzie to reach the picturesque seaside town of Ullapool. Replenish and stay the night at The Ceilidh Place, with its award-winning fish-and-chip shop, and return the following day by the same route. More info: www.komoot.com/user/532193254039.
Start/Finish // Bonar Bridge
Distance // 72 miles (116km)

THE RHINE VALLEY, GERMANY

This undulating, heavily-forested route that winds though western Germany makes use of forest tracks, bike paths and country roads to pull together several historic castles, ruins and monasteries. The route passes through the Ahrtal region, well known for its vineyards and wineries, and the Rhine Valley (the upper middle reaches of which are a World Heritage Site). The route starts and ends at the historic Kottenforst train station which was built in 1880 and is still in use today. It also includes a ferry crossing on the Rhine towards the end. Designed by German bikepacker Lothar Linse to be ridden over three comfortable days, the route never strays far from civilisation should you prefer to sleep indoors or in campsites at night. It should be noted that wild camping is not permitted in Germany, but there are plenty of accommodation options on this route. More info: https://bikepacking.com/routes/rheintal/.
Start/Finish // Kottenforst
Distance // 165 miles (266km)

© Cass Gilbert

TEMPLE
HUNT

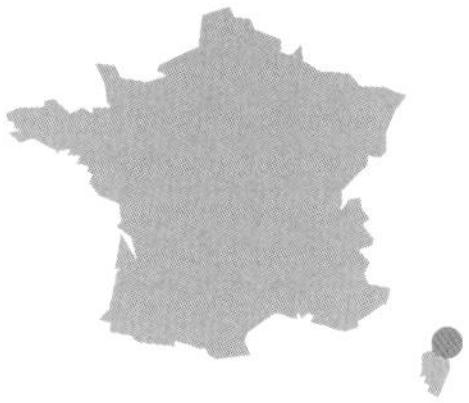

A CORSICAN CHALLENGE

A sublime cycling journey through the heart of Corsica, the Mediterranean's 'Île de Beauté', riding part of the route of the 100th Tour de France.

©Christoph Oberschneider | 500px

Corsica is a mighty lump of rock, a chain of mountains protruding proudly from the Mediterranean Sea. With 21 peaks above 2000m and over 150 cols, it is something of a nirvana for cyclists. There are glorious roads winding down through remote hamlets to turquoise coves; medieval villages untouched by the 21st century; chestnut groves, pine forests and canyons; challenging climbs and sweeping descents on well-paved tarmac with few cars; excellent local wines and sensational seafood as well as limestone hills and golden, sandy beaches, all set within a staggeringly lovely coastline. It is hard to think of another place that packs so much into such a small, beautiful space.

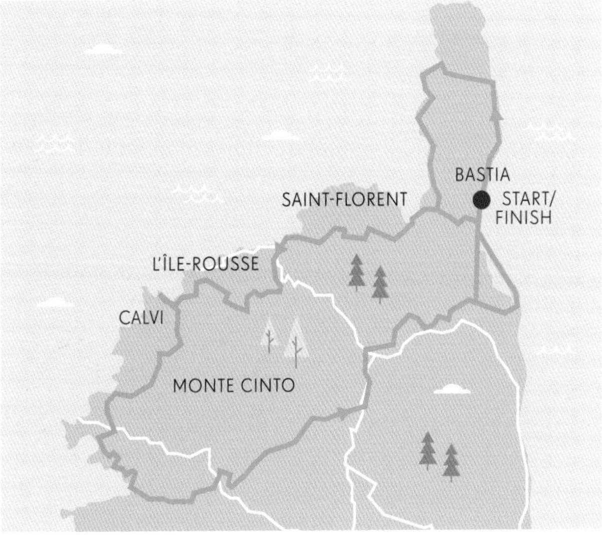

My four-day tour started and finished in Bastia, the second largest town, and took in the northern half of the island, known as 'Haute-Corse'. I concentrated on the north and west coastlines, which are more jagged, wild and wondrous.

The ride started humbly enough – on a flat cycle path between

"Breathtaking sections of road wind along the coastline, which is dotted with fishing villages and old Genoese lookout towers"

a stagnant lagoon and the sea, with the airport as a backdrop. There was no sense of the grandeur and the glory that awaited me. There was not even a hint of the beauty of Corsica – a level of pulchritude that I have seldom experienced in just a few days on a bicycle. Nor, in the cool air of the young day, was there any suggestion of the cauldron of heat I would encounter in the canyons ahead.

With memories of the airport fading, I pedalled through Bastia and north along the maquis-covered eastern coast of Cap Corse, past a series of tiny ports. Then I headed inland, up and over the spine of mountains that bisects the peninsula, past Cagnano and down to Pino. Riding south down the western side of the cape, you are never far from the sea. There are some breathtaking sections of winding road along the serrated coastline, which is dotted with tiny fishing villages and old Genoese lookout towers.

After a cold glass of Pietra, the local beer, in the Café de la Tour in Nonza, there was a sting in the tail – a 4-mile (6km) climb followed by a fast descent – to return to Bastia.

On the second day, I rode over the granite backbone of the island from east to west, via the highest tarmac col – Col de Vergio (1478m). I don't set off to ride 93 miles (150km) and climb 2750m in a day lightly. When the cycling is this good, though, when it all comes together in a day of spellbinding pedalling, I can't help but feel that every time I've ever been on a bike has been preparation for this hour, and that all my roads have led me here.

'Allez, garçon!' two old men shout, over their early morning brandies in the first village. As I started to climb towards the town of Borgo, my legs warmed, the traffic diminished and the roads narrowed.

At the first col, I passed through a notch in the rock and turned my back on the shining sea, heading inland on a beautiful balcony road that contoured the mountains. The villages – Vignale, Scolca, Campitello, Lento, Canavaggia – rolled off the tongue like an Italian football team sheet, reminding me of the island's history – it was part of the Republic of Genoa long before it was purchased by France in 1768. These sleepy villages are dominated by imposing granite churches, which, from a distance, seem to hang off the mountainsides.

After an ice cream and an espresso in Ponte Leccia, I headed southwest for the long climb. The first section is through a gorge carved into granite cliffs beside the dashing waters of the Golo River. It was like a furnace here, in the doggo hours of early afternoon.

© joningall / Getty Images, Claudio Cassaro / 4 Corners

CALANCHES DETOUR

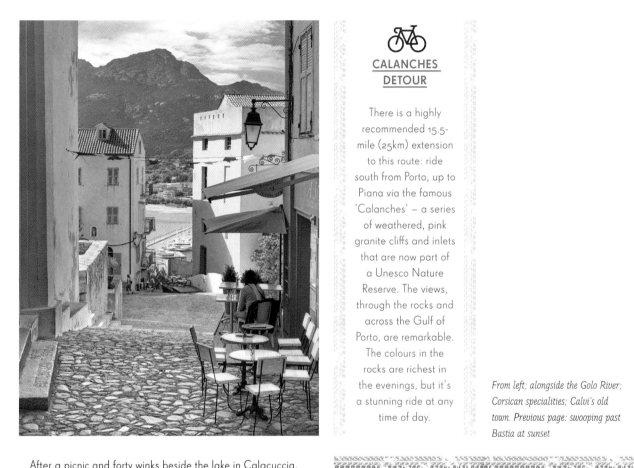

There is a highly recommended 15.5-mile (25km) extension to this route: ride south from Porto, up to Piana via the famous 'Calanches' – a series of weathered, pink granite cliffs and inlets that are now part of a Unesco Nature Reserve. The views, through the rocks and across the Gulf of Porto, are remarkable. The colours in the rocks are richest in the evenings, but it's a stunning ride at any time of day.

From left; alongside the Golo River; Corsican specialities; Calvi's old town. Previous page: swooping past Bastia at sunset

After a picnic and forty winks beside the lake in Calacuccia, I climbed again, now in the cooler air and the shade of a laricio pine forest. By the time I reached the top of the col, set beneath the great 2500m-plus peaks of Monte Cinto and Paglia Orba, the heat of the day was finally backing off.

Time stood still on the flowing, serpentine, 18.5 mile- (30km) descent through three climatic zones. It was stunning. The whole way down to Porto, there were glimpses of the Mediterranean and the path of gold on the water, leading west over the sea to the setting sun.

The next day, following the coast road north to Calvi, was easier but no less glorious. In fact, this road ranks among the most beautiful coastal roads in Europe. From Porto, I climbed up to Col de la Croix, for the first in a series of staggering views. Then it was down and up again to the Col de Palmarella, before the descent into the Fango Valley, another lovely area of undisturbed and arresting, natural scenery. The final climb of the day, up to Col de Marsolino, revealed my destination: the fashionable port of Calvi with its lofty citadel perched above the sea.

On the final day, I followed the north coast along the rocky maquis hinterland and then up into the hills again, before a long, gentle descent to the former fishing village of Saint-Florent. After a swim in the sea and lunch, I attacked the tough punch up to the ridge above Bastia, for one final eyeful of the shimmering sea. **RP**

TOOLKIT

Start/Finish // Bastia
Distance // 281 miles (452km)
Getting there // There's an airport and ferry port in Bastia. Flights to European destinations are more frequent from June to late September. Day and overnight ferries run from several destinations in mainland France and Italy year-round.
Bike hire // In Bastia, try Europe Active (http://cycling.europe-active.co.uk).
When to ride // April, May, June, September and October: in July and August it's hot and peak holiday season.
What to eat // If you're pedalling round Cap Corse and feel like lunch, try L'Auberge du Chat qui Pêche in Canari (www.aubergeduchatquipeche.com).
What to drink // Local wines (especially from the Patrimonio area).
More info // www.corsicacyclist.com.

© Jan Wlodarczyk / Alamy Stock Photo

Opposite: an unbeatable Sardinian view – but try to keep your eyes on the trail

MORE LIKE THIS
SEA-VIEW RIDES

SARDINIA

Another Mediterranean paradise for cyclists: a larger, more arid, but equally captivating version of Corsica, Sardinia, too, offers quiet roads, excellent food, mountains and endless beaches. Avoid the main roads, but you can ride almost anywhere else. Try an east-coast route from Olbia, which combines stretches of lovely coastal riding with an excursion up into Barbagia, the remote, mountainous region of central Sardinia. Here, you pass medieval towns, great lakes, rugged limestone peaks, chestnut woods, olive groves and vineyards (including Oliena, the village where Sardinia's prized Cannonau red wine is produced). The ride starts gently, beside the sea. There are then two days in the mountains, before returning to the coast for the final stretch to reach the dynamic port of Cagliari.

Start // Olbia
Finish // Cagliari
Distance // 279.5 miles (450 km)

DINGLE PENINSULA, IRELAND

Between the craggy range of mountains and rocky cliffs that plunge into the Atlantic, the Dingle Peninsula is a joy for cyclists, who can ride a demanding day-long loop that passes historic ruins, roaring coastline, and amazing beaches. The peninsula is something of an open-air museum, dotted with more than 2000 Neolithic monuments built between 4000BC and early Christian times. The village of Dunquin has many crumbling rock homes that were abandoned during the famine. You'll also pass the Gallarus Oratory, one of Ireland's most well-preserved ancient Christian churches. As you near the end of the loop, pull off for a quick stop at the 12th-century Irish Romanesque church with an ancient cemetery before returning to Dingle Town, where you'll find plenty of pubs (many of which are hardware stores by day) to toast the adventure.

Start/Finish // Dingle Town
Distance // 25 miles (40km)

THE FRENCH ATLANTIC

A trip along France's longest cycling trail, appropriately named La Vélodyssée, can be enjoyed as a day-long cruise or a multi-day epic; the full trail is about 750 miles (1200km) stretching from Brittany in the north to the Spanish border. With the Atlantic in view for most of the ride, this journey is best done at an easy pace that allows you to savour the region's pleasures – including cute seaside B&Bs, historic sea ports, and beautiful beaches. Although each of the route's 14 sections has distinctive charms, seafood lovers should make it a point to include the path from La Barre-de-Monts to Les Sables-d'Olonne, which will allow you to tuck into fresh oysters. The section between Arcachon and Léon is also stunning, as the path passes deep forests and inland lakes.

Start // Brittany
Finish // Bayonne
Distance // 750 miles (1200km)

© I just try to tell my emotions and take you around the world / Getty Images

EASTERN EUROPE

Crossing the Soca River in Slovenia (see page 278)

THE JULIAN ALPS

A tour of Slovenia's finest mountain scenery, this little-known route down the breathtaking Soca Valley should be on everyone's bucket list, says Emily Chappell.

Have you ever cycled up a hill for no reason? Or at least, for no other reason than to see what was up there? That's how I discovered Mangart Cesta (road in Slovenian). I had just abandoned a race and was plodding with exhaustion, and until I passed the turn-off for Slovenia's highest road, my intention had been to take the most direct route to the finish, where a friend was waiting to drive me home.

But curiosity got the better of me, as it often does where mountain roads are concerned – which is probably why I was never much of a racer. Why take the fast, flat route, when the fun lies elsewhere?

The first few stretches of Mangart Cesta were steep, as if the road were impatient to get me out of valley as quickly as possible, and up to the switchbacks that would haul me closer and closer to the enormous pale grey peak of Mount Mangart itself. I enjoyed the brief, dappled shade of the forests that clung to its lower slopes, knowing that there would be no escape from the sun as I got higher.

But Mangart, despite its reputation, proved to be a kinder climb than I had feared. The switchbacks, which wriggled tightly across the steep, barren slopes of the mountain, offered me alternate shade and sunlight as I went to and fro along them and, as the air cooled and the valley sank away beneath me, I began to see dozens of peaks, stretching away into the distance alongside me.

I've never found out enough about geology to be able to tell you why the Julian Alps are so beautiful. It could be the aesthetic regularity of the peaks – they are shaped as mountains should be: tall and triangular, overlapping and interlocking to create the kind of mountain range a child or a daydreamer would draw. It could be the intricately hewn beauty of their sheer grey faces which, on closer inspection, are lined with endless cracks and fissures; each one a work of art in both its largest and smallest aspect. It could be the sense of discovery I felt as I ascended among them. Mangart isn't famous like Alpe d'Huez or the Col d'Izoard. It doesn't appear on people's cycling bucket lists, and I doubt a grand tour has ever gone up there. It was easy to feel that I'd stumbled across some hitherto unknown treasure.

It could, of course, simply have been that it was a glorious day, and that, aside from a few hikers, I had the mountain to myself.

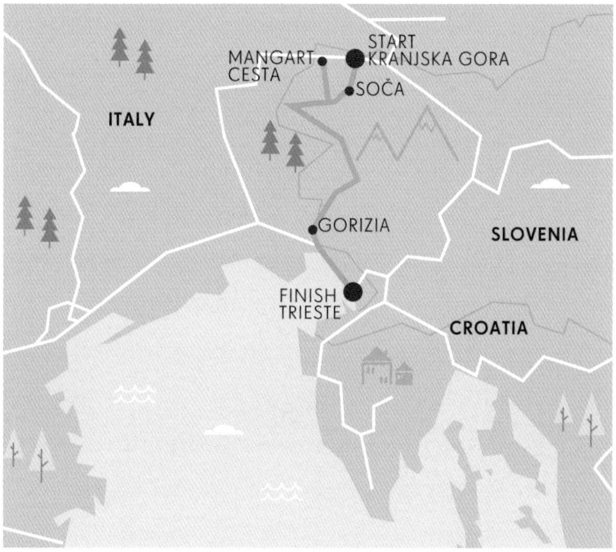

Previous page © Saro17 / Getty Images, this page © Norbert Eisele-Hein / Getty Images

I picked my way through the rocks and other debris that had accumulated on the road, jumping slightly as another handful clattered down the mountainside behind me. This was a landscape still very much in progress. The road ended at a cliff edge, overlooking a drop of a thousand metres down to the orderly fields and lakes of an Italian valley, and beneath me a lone raven drifted lazily in the sunny air.

I descended Mangart, followed the Soca River to the base of Vrsic (Slovenia's highest pass, since Mangart is a dead end), and fell into an exhausted slumber when I reached the top. The following morning, as I slid and rattled down the cobbled switchbacks, my mind hummed with the anticipation of breakfast, and with the potential of these new roads I had discovered. I had crossed Slovenia several times by bike, but never yet ridden the lofty Mangart, or the 50 switchbacks (24 up, 26 down) of Vrsic, which was built by Russian prisoners of war in 1915.

Next time I come here, I thought, *I'll start from Kranjska Gora* (the small mountain town where I was planning to eat breakfast), *and climb Vrsic from the more interesting side. I'll follow the Soca Valley west – and perhaps this time I'll stop for a swim in its sparkling turquoise river – then I'll detour north to climb Mangart again*. It's not strictly en route, but a dead-end road is never en route to anywhere, and I would never miss an opportunity to witness those views again.

And then, I mused, getting carried away as you do when designing your ideal ride, I could descend out of the mountains

"It was easy to feel I had stumbled across some unknown treasure. Aside from a few hikers, I had the mountain to myself"

THE RUSSIAN CHAPEL

The road over Vrsic Pass was built by Russian prisoners of war when the pass became strategically important in 1915, and was renamed 'Russian Road' in 2006. A slightly incongruous Russian Orthodox chapel sits partway up the northern side of the pass, to commemorate nearly 400 men who died during the road's construction, many in an avalanche in early 1916. The chapel is now considered a symbol of Russo-Slovenian unity.

Clockwise from above: Mt Mangart; crossing the Soca River; the Russian Orthodox chapel; the author's bike. Previous page: the climb up Mt Mangart

© Emily Chappell, Pavlina / Getty Images

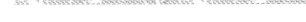

towards the coast, as I had a few years ago on my first crossing of Europe, watching the seasons change around me as I left behind the snowy pass I'd crossed, descended through autumn leaves, and finally found summer warmth again as I approached the Mediterranean.

I could revisit Nova Gorica and Gorizia – two contiguous towns that a quirk of history has bisected with an international border, otherwise they might well be one. It was easy enough to ride between the two, but you wouldn't have thought it from their different characters. Nova Gorica seemed austere, functional and post-Soviet, whereas Gorizia was a little Italianate paradise of cypress trees, red roof tiles, a labyrinthine old fort and a park where I had spent a happy morning drying my tent and reading Jan Morris's *Trieste*, in honour of the city where I planned to end that day's ride.

And Trieste would be where I ended this future ride, I thought to myself – or, at least, where I paused overnight, to drink a glass of wine on the seafront and think back to the mountain vistas I'd started the day with, and forward to whatever was to come. Perhaps a gentle roll along Slovenia's tiny but picturesque coastline, and then onto the Istrian Peninsula. Or perhaps a more rugged exploration of the Balkan interior. Or perhaps I'd just turn round and ride back up into the mountains, to see what else was up there. **EC**

TOOLKIT

Start // Kranjska Gora, Slovenia
Finish // Trieste, Italy
Distance // 137 miles (212km)
Getting there // There is an international airport in Ljubljana. The railway goes as far as Jesenice, from where it's an hour's ride, or a short taxi journey.
When to ride // Mangart Cesta and Vrsic are only accessible on skis in the winter months. The route should be fully passable between June and September.
What to take // A standard road bike but with 28mm tyres for the cobbles on Vrsic.
More info // There's a paucity of online information about cycling in Slovenia – so here's a link to a gpx file of my route: https://tinyurl.com/yyjgm6ar

© CasarsaGuru / Getty Images, Robert George Young / Getty Images

Opposite: the wild, thrilling and steep road up Bealach na Ba to Applecross

MORE LIKE THIS
RIDES WITH GREAT VIEWS

APPLECROSS PENINSULA LOOP, SCOTLAND

The Bealach na Ba is feared and celebrated alike as one of the UK's most challenging climbs, not only because of its gradient – it reaches 20% in places – but also because of the likelihood of strong winds and driving rain which can make the ascent unpleasant, and the descent downright dangerous. However, if you catch the Bealach on a good day, you'll be treated to a 360-degree panorama of the mountains and the coastline. The switchbacks, overlooking by enormous rocky crags, are reminiscent of the Alps. The scenery is as wild and remote as you'll find anywhere in the Highlands. And the coast road between Applecross and Shieldaig is equally glorious – a thin ribbon of tarmac that surges up and down through the rocks and gorse and heather, with unbroken views out to the islands of Rona and Raasay. More info: www.applecross.uk.com.

Start/Finish // Tornapress
Distance // 42 miles (67km)

AMALFI COAST, ITALY

Although it's popular with drivers, the journey from Sorrento to Amalfi is best appreciated by bike. The road soars along the coastline, swooping in and out of coves, meandering past lemon groves, and wriggling its way through picturesque towns and villages that cling precariously to the cliffs. Travel west to east for uninterrupted sea views, and make the journey in spring or autumn to avoid the worst of the tourist traffic. The island of Capri comes into sight as you round the tip of the peninsula, and you'll pass the elegant villas of Positano and Praiano en route to the bustling port of Amalfi. If you fancy extending the ride, or getting an even better view, the roads up to Nocelle and San Michele offer extra elevation and highly worthwhile detours, and if you're after a more leisurely jaunt, you're never far from an espresso.

Start // Sorrento
Finish // Amalfi
Distance // 31 miles (50km)

SH3, ALBANIA

The road between Mushqeta and Bradashesh is less than 18 miles (29km) long, but its beauty is such that you'll wish it went on forever. Gently graded switchbacks carry you up towards Gracen, out of the hustle and bustle of Tirana's suburbs, and as you exit the pine forest you'll see endless green mountaintops stretching away on both sides of you, as if you were balancing along a tightrope in the sky. The road rises and falls gently along the ridgeway, making for a joyous, swooping ride, with momentum doing most of the work – and it's usually free of cars, thanks to a bigger highway that carries most of the traffic down through the valley. The landscape opens out even more as you descend through the olive groves towards Elbasan, on some of most curvaceous switchbacks you'll find anywhere in Europe.

Start // Mushqeta
Finish // Bradashesh
Distance // 18 miles (29km)

© Annie MacDonald

INTO THE TATRA MOUNTAINS

The proving ground for generations of Polish mountaineers has plenty to test – and delight – adventurers on two wheels.

When I was 16, I went bike touring in Poland with an older cousin and some of his friends. The year was 1993, Poland had just recently emerged from decades of communism, and I had brought a fancy new Trek racing bike with me from California.

The trip was a disaster. Badly cobbled roads alternated with sandy tracks, swallowing up my skinny tires and leaving me pushing my heavily-loaded bike in clacking plastic cleats. I'll admit now that as I watched the rest of the group disappear down the road, mounted on sensible, balloon-tired city bikes, there were tears of frustration.

Decades have passed since that traumatic trip, decades that have dramatically transformed Poland and its southern neighbour, Slovakia. Somehow, though, my memories of the Polish countryside remained stuck in the early '90s. I shrugged when I saw reports on the Tour de Pologne, pitying the pros who had to deal with Polish roads. Though I regularly visit Warsaw, a straightforward train ride from my home in Berlin, I never bring a bike, despite the fact that the city has invested in a city-wide bike share programme and built 330 miles (530km) of cycle tracks in the last 15 years.

The thought of taking a road bike to the mountains never crossed my mind – until I overheard friends in Berlin enthusing about a cycling trip they'd just made to southern Poland.

That's how I found myself in front of a sharply-gabled wood cabin dating back nearly a century in Niedzica, a small town on a large lake situated in the far south of Poland. With no small amount of trepidation, I inflated my 23mm tires and hoped for the best. It took just a few turns of the crank to cross the border into Slovakia.

The route was planned to skirt the eastern edge of the Tatra Mountains, which form a natural barrier on the Polish-Slovak border. They are one of Europe's smaller mountain ranges, occupying just 300 sq miles (785 sq km). (The Alps? 115,000 sq miles.) Their highest peaks are half the height of giants such as Mont Blanc.

But size isn't everything. What they lack in square mileage and elevation they more than make up for in sheer drama. On the horizon, jagged, bare peaks playing peek-a-boo behind snowy drifts of morning cloud.

On a long, straight road headed south into Slovakia, the

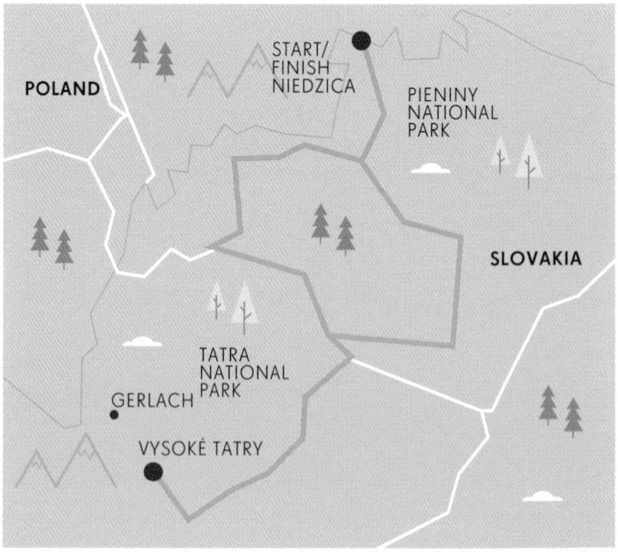

© Max Burgess

mountain range is a constant presence over my left shoulder, beckoning and threatening at the same time. Along the side of the road, entire villages seem to have turned out to harvest potatoes. Traditional log cabins, painted in bright colours, line the smooth, wide-shouldered road.

My destination is Vysoké Tatry, which translates to 'High Tatras'. It's both town and description. In the communist era, these mountains were the highest peaks available to climbers and skiers across a wide stretch of Europe. The town is Slovakia's second-most popular tourist destination; the giant hotels that squat in the shadow of the peaks host thousands of skiers in the winter. But in the shoulder season their parking lots are practically empty.

Thus far, the climbing has been moderate: mostly spectacular views, easily earned, minimal sweat. Then I turn right on to what looks like a modest paved bike trail behind a nondescript ski hotel. The road angles up and doesn't stop. For almost an hour, I struggle up grades that hover between 10 and 15 percent, blood pounding in my ears. Slovak hikers in brightly-coloured jackets wave and smile as I inch past.

Finally, I reach the top. A wooded valley narrows sharply, ending in a sheer cliff face towering above a waterfall-fed, blue-green lake. Above it all is the Gerlach, at 8700ft (2655m) the highest peak in the whole Tatra chain. It's a forbidding pyramid of snow-capped stone, off-limits to all but the most experienced mountaineers. There are a hotel and a restaurant on the lake, but I soon understand why all the hikers were bundled up: a freezing wind courses down from the cliffs above. I don't linger.

"I gaze north over a wild landscape of forested hills, rolling to the horizon. Out there somewhere is the Polish border"

HIGH STANDARDS

The Tatra can have a brutal side. Though not as tall as better-known ranges like the Alps, weather conditions there can change in an instant; storms claim the lives of unprepared hikers nearly every year. Historically the jagged range has been a sort of crucible, forging Polish climbers into some of the best in the world: In the 1980s and '90s, Poles were the first to complete winter ascents of Himalayan peaks including Everest, Annapurna and Kanchenjunga.

Clockwise from above: Czorsztyn Castle near Niedzica; over the border in Slovakia; traditional musicians; a Tatra chamois. Previous page: in the foothills of the Tatra

© Jacek Jacobi / Getty Images, Max Burgess

In Vysoké Tatry, I dive into a restaurant and warm myself with peppery goulash and *knedlíky*, thick, fluffy Slovak dumplings, washing it all down with a tall beer. Outside, children in traditional highlander garb chase each other across the grass: I've wandered into the middle of a local dance festival. I watch the high-stepping, quick-footed dancers on stage for a while, then head downhill once more.

The rest of the afternoon is mostly downhill, except for one final stinger of a hill. (OK, the goulash and beer didn't help on the climbs.) At the top, I gaze north over a wild, unspoiled landscape of forested hills, rolling to the horizon. (I'll later learn it's the Pieniny National Park, Slovakia's smallest.)

Somewhere out there is the Polish border, but for now I'm happily lost in the landscape. Over the next few days, I'll explore more of the region, returning to the Pieniny park and discovering mountain vistas and hidden river gorges all over the region. With Niedzica as a base, it's easy to weave together a multi-day trip exploring the Tatra region on both sides of the border.

But right now, with the Tatra to my back and the afternoon shadows lengthening into evening, I experience one of the most transcendent, utterly unexpected descents I've ridden in years: mile after mile of swooping, well-paved roads passing through wild forests and grassy meadows.

Somewhere along the way, I make a decision. I'll be back – and I'll be bringing a bike. **AC**

© Krzysztof Nahlik / Getty Images, Max Burgess

TOOLKIT

Start/Finish // Niedzica, Poland
Distance // 85 miles (136 km)
Getting there // Kraków is the closest airport major airport. From there it's a two-hour drive to the mountains.
Bike hire // Bike rentals are available in Kraków. Podiaventures (podia.cc) organises all-inclusive, multi-day trips to the region.
When to ride // The region is open year-round but winter is ski season, especially at higher altitudes. Go between April and October for the best chances of good weather.
Where to stay // The hotel Zespol Rekreacyjny Polana Sosny has rooms for rent and camping spots as well. There are lots of hotels in Niedzica.
More info // www.poland.travel

Opposite, clockwise from top: cafe life in Warsaw; the Vistula River; hairpins in the Bieszczady mountains

MORE LIKE THIS
POLISH ESCAPADES

BIESZCZADY MOUNTAINS

The Tatra are hardly a well-kept secret. On both sides of the Polish-Slovak border, they're popular with skiers, hikers, cyclists and climbers. To truly get off the beaten path, head even further east, to where Poland, Slovakia and Ukraine come together. Besides being nearly unpronounceable to non-Poles (biesh-CHA-dy comes close), the rolling hills here are an off-road rider's dream, with over 125 miles (200km) of mountain bike trails and even more little-used logging roads. The whole network weaves its way through the Bieszczady National Park, part of a massive biosphere reserve that straddles three countries and shelters some of the most spectacular old-growth forests in Europe. A marked trail, the East Carpathian Greenway, loops through all three nations on its way around the park.
Start/Finish // Lesko
Distance // 65 miles (105km)

VISTULA RIVER

Warsaw is Poland's bustling commercial and political capital, but Kraków and the surrounding region remain the country's cultural heart. A recently completed bike trail follows the raised banks of the Vistula River from west to east, descending gently the whole way. Along the way it passes by the Auschwitz concentration camp and Kraków's Wawel Castle, whose Renaissance architecture dates back to the early 1500s. (Local legend has it that a dragon once resided beneath the keep; look for the fire-breather as you pass below.) The trail is only partially paved, so be prepared for the occasional detour if you're on skinny tires. A worthwhile side trip from Kraków is the Wieliczka salt mine, where you'll have to leave your bike behind to descend to an underground lake 450 feet (135m) below ground. In the next few years the path will be connected to follow the river all the way north to where it flows into the Baltic Sea.
Start // Jawiszowice
Finish // Szczucin
Distance // 143 miles (230km)

CAPITAL ESCAPE

With nearly 1.7 million people, the Polish capital of Warsaw is the country's biggest and busiest city, sprawling on both sides of the Vistula River. A carefully rebuilt historic centre (most of the city was leveled during WWII) captures the city as it looked centuries ago. Hundreds of miles of bike paths weave through it all. Two of the most popular run alongside the Vistula. On the left bank, the path passes by the sights of the city centre, including the Copernicus Science Centre and the university library. For a break from the city and its bustle, cross one of the city's many bridges over to the wilder, greener right bank and stop for a beer at one of the beach bars that line the river. A newly opened footbridge makes it possible to ride on cycle paths all the way north to the small town of Modlin, where a sprawling, ruined 19th-century fortress awaits.
Start/Finish // Warsaw
Distance // 50 miles (80 km)

© Elephotos / Shutterstock, Milosz Guzowski / Alamy Stock Photo, Jean-Pierre Lescourret / Getty Images

AÏOLI
Pilsner Urquell
AÏOLI
Pilsner Urquell

ISLAND HOPPING DOWN CROATIA

Two weeks exploring the eastern shore of the Adriatic is a perfect introduction to its natural beauty, secluded beaches and quirky hospitality.

We reached Croatia in spring. Two months into a year riding east, the northwestern Croatian border was a gateway to unknown places. As we coasted along quiet roads in the north of the country, a neon pink sunset filled the sky – as pretty as it was, we were reminded that we had nowhere to stay that night.

Pausing at a cafe, Ruth found a website linking travellers with locals offering space for tents, and within moments we'd been called back. 'I'm not home but stay anyway,' Alen told us. 'Find my village and ask anyone. They all know my house. It's always open.'

This was exciting. For the next hour we raced the thickening darkness, guided by our absent host's picture-messages. Having scribbled down a Croatian translation for 'We're looking for the house of Alen', we soon found an opportunity to test it. A young, torch-wielding girl replied in English: 'I'll show you.'

Lane became track, and track became field. Then, appearing out of the darkness, a grand design of upcycled debris and

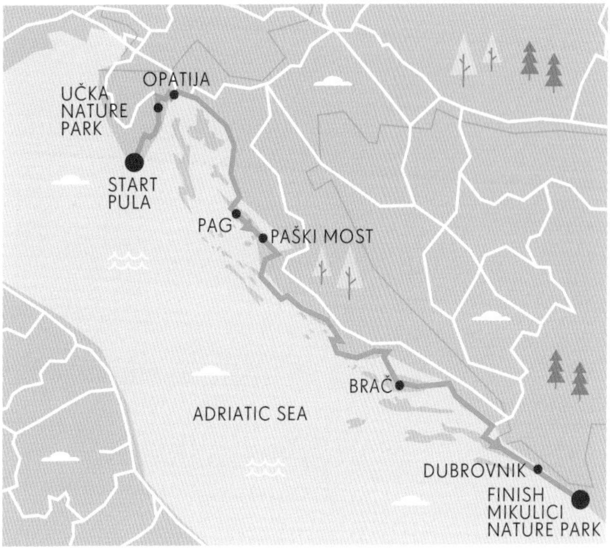

© PATSTOCK / Getty Images

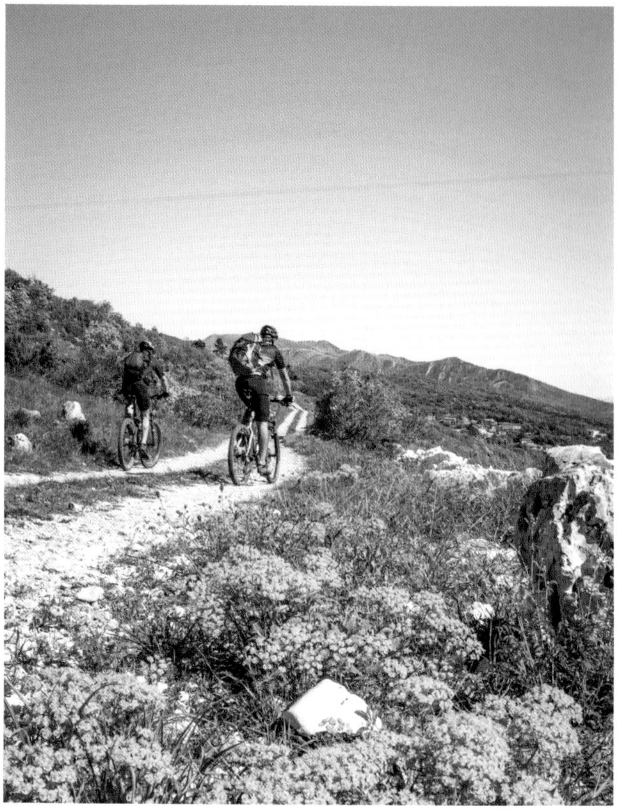

salvaged materials, perched on the side of the hill. No wonder the locals knew it; this was like something from Neverland. Alen was our Peter Pan. Rescuing us as night fell in a magical new land.

The next morning, we took in our surroundings. An act of hospitality from a man who, it turned out, we would never meet. We had a good feeling about what lay ahead.

Soon we found ourselves pushing the bikes up a loose-scree track; a 'white' road. When we reached the top we got our reward. A panoramic view of Ucka Nature Park, followed by a white-knuckle freewheel down the south side of the mountain. Hairpin after hairpin of smooth tarmac, propelled by the weight of loaded panniers, towards the Adriatic Sea which shimmered beneath us.

Halfway down we pulled over to take in the view. The scent of wild garlic and rosemary filled the air, a familiar smell in a foreign place. Our quiet contemplation was sharply interrupted by a small dog peeing on Ruth's pannier, followed by a woman screeching 'Rexxxx!' and rushing towards us.

We laughed and introduced ourselves. Tanja was dog-sitting the unruly Rex. She had lived in London for years, before settling back home in Istria. We were about to part ways when she asked if we would like to stay the weekend with her in Opatija. That evening, Tanja and her partner Marika roasted sardines for us, fresh from their local bay, served with asparagus and seasoned with salt, pepper, wild garlic and rosemary. After dinner Marika told us how to spot the asparagus along the roadside; she said it grew tall and

"We rode down hairpin after hairpin, the Adriatic Sea shimmering beneath us"

fast at this time of year, and would line much of our route south.

We adjusted our route to include the islands they recommended for cycling in spring and, via the accommodation website Warm Showers, contacted a handful of hosts dotted along the way.

Two days later, we waved goodbye to our new friends and rolled into the sunshine. We tried to call Rex over but he was busy marking his territory on a line of parked cars. With freshly formed plans, we headed down the coast towards the first island, Pag, famed for its moonlike landscape and salty cheese, before crossing back on to the mainland via Paški Most, a bridge connecting the island with Dalmatia.

Further south we caught the ferry to Brac, home to an ex-pat American Warm Showers host. Rory had paused his own world tour, having fallen in love with island life. Our bikes needed some TLC, so he introduced us to his 'adopted Dad', Dido, and after a glass of walnut liqueur, the pair led us to an incredible workshop. Dido is an accomplished sculptor and olive-oil producer, with a reputation for fixing the unfixable. We were in safe hands.

We'd happily have stayed. It's clear why Rory did. But his stories, collected over years on the road, were enough motivation for us to push on.

© Ruth Newton and Oli Townsend, Photoflorenzo / Alamy Stock Photo, Moodyblues / Shutterstock

BIKE SHELTER

'Join Warm Showers' – that is the advice we'd offer any first-time bikepackers. It's a community of cyclists-hosting-cyclists run through an app and a website. Without it we wouldn't have had half as much fun crossing Europe in winter. Warm Showers gave us access to fantastic local hospitality, knowledge, and, often, a great meal at the end of a day. More info: www.warmshowers.org

From left: Warm Showers host Marco (in white) in Mikulici; grilled sardines; trail riding in Istria; Ruth wakes up in Makarska. Previous page: the bridge to Pag island

The next few days were memorable for their routine of sun-kissed swims followed by mid-morning *börek*, a delicious flaky pastry stuffed with cheese. Our good luck continued. After camping in a secluded bay, just south of Makarska, Ruth spotted a pod of dolphins curving in and out of the waves. We rushed to a higher point and watched them move slowly up the coast, feeling a huge amount of love for a country that kept giving us such wonderful encounters. And then, as magically as they had appeared, they were gone.

We packed up in high spirits, trying to ignore the sound of barking that was getting louder by the minute. The bay was a cul-de-sac. There was only one way out. Were we about to find ourselves cornered by feral dogs?

Thankfully not. The 'pack' that raced on to the beach consisted of a fluffy white Bichon Frise, followed by two enthusiastic German nudists who, they told us, holidayed in this spot every year. We left them to enjoy their day.

Croatia is a small country with a huge heart. Everybody we met made us feel welcome. Just south of Dubrovnik, our final night was spent with a legendary Warm Showers host. A gentle giant called Marco, who has re-wilded his land and encourages travellers to stay with him as long as they wish.

Multi-lingual signs outside his home read: 'If you want to help a man, start with what you have in your hand.' A phrase that, for us, came to epitomise Croatian hospitality. **OT & RN**

TOOLKIT

Start // Pula
Finish // Mikulici Nature Park
Distance // 465 miles (750km)
Getting there and back // Both Pula and Dubrovnik have international airports.
When to ride // Spring or autumn – either side of the main tourist season.
What to take // We rode loaded touring bikes and enjoyed the camping opportunities, but there are plenty of accommodation choices (see panel); you could get by with a bike pump, repair kit, swimwear and sun-cream.
More info // www.intandemstories.com, Ucka National Park (www.pp-ucka.hr/en/), www.croatiaferries.com

© Ruth Newton and Oli Townsend

Opposite top: the Ring of Brodgar, Orkney; the Po Delta wetlands

MORE LIKE THIS
WATER-SIDE RIDES

SIX SWISS LAKES

Smooth graceful roads trace the lower slopes of the Swiss Alps, linking Lausanne in the west with Lucerne to the east. The riding is exceptional; as you might expect, Swiss bike paths are well maintained and passing cars are polite, giving plenty of room. Over the course of a handful of days you can pedal along the shores of Lac Léman, Thunersee, Brienzersee, Lungerersee, Sarnersee and end with your choice of fine dining overlooking the stunning Lac Lucerne. Between the lakes you'll pass through national parks in the Gruyère region and countless barns decorated with paintings of the cows housed within. It's worth taking the time to indulge in the region's gourmet cheese. An alpine fondue is the perfect fuel for a cycle tour and warms you up at the same time. Ask locals for the best spots; the region is full of cheesemakers and enthusiasts who are happy to share their knowledge. More info: www.schweizmobil.ch/en/cycling-in-switzerland.html.
Start // Lausanne
Finish // Lucerne
Distance // 155 miles (250 km)

NEOLITHIC ORKNEY, SCOTLAND

Off the north coast of Scotland lies the archipelago of Orkney, most romantically reached via a ferry from Thurso. As to your exact loop once on the islands, you'll be reliant on local ferry times which vary depending on the time of year: check these before making your choice of route. The roads are generally well maintained and quiet, though bear in mind it will be windy. Orkney is home to several first-rate Neolithic sites, such as the Ring of Brodgar and the extraordinarily well-preserved shoreline settlement Skara Brae. On Hoy, to the south, you can spot any number of birds from eagles to curlews, visit the famous rock stack the Old Man, and perhaps even brave the Scottish waters (the seals will gawp). You are free to camp anywhere, within reason, just be sure to take your best sleeping bag because it gets chilly at night. More info // www.northlinkferries.co.uk/orkney-blog/orkney-cycle-routes/.
Start/Finish // Stromness

THE PO DELTA, ITALY

Where the River Po flows into the Adriatic Sea you'll discover a network of waterways leading to Venice. Light ferries (or friendly fishermen, if you arrive out of season) run between islands, connecting strands of EuroVelo 8. Part of a sublime nature reserve, the area is home to hundreds of bird species. Most memorable were the flamingos standing proud at sunset, reflections glistening in the silver lagoons. We would recommend starting at Cremona or Piacenza; beautiful cities located further west along the Po. This is a gentle ride on established cycle routes, with plenty of old towns and cities dotted along the way, providing ample opportunity for espresso and cannoli pit-stops. When you arrive at Venice, we suggest finding accommodation outside the old city and enjoying it on foot – Venice wasn't exactly built with touring bikes in mind. More info: http://en.eurovelo.com/ev8/from-turin-to-venice.
Start // Cremona
Finish // Venice
Distance // 242 miles (390km)

© Justin Foulkes / Lonely Planet, Ruth Newton and Oli Townsend

THE TRANS DINARICA TRAIL

New World adventure meets Old World culture on this still-expanding mountain-bike trail through the entire Western Balkans, says Alex Crevar.

On the fourth day cycling the Croatian stages of the cross-border Trans Dinarica mountain bike trail, we started the climb straight up from the sea. Our goal was the Velebit Mountains, a string of peaks lining the coast and a highlight on this three-country route, which we followed from Slovenia in the north and would continue along as we pedaled south and east to Bosnia and Hercegovina. When we reached the ridgeline, the reward for climbing 6000 feet (1830m) in under 25 miles (40km) of elevation gain suddenly became clear. An archipelago, backlit and purple, spread out across the northern Adriatic as the sun tumbled over the western horizon. The islands seemed to be guiding us along the path, and region, we would discover in the coming days.

'There are very few spots on earth where you can ride around peaks that hang over the sea – *and* get happily lost in villages,' said Edo Vricic, one of Trans Dinarica's developers, as we stood watching the sun set over the coast and ridge leading south. Vricic, the co-owner of Croatia-based tourism operator VMD Adventure Travel, told me the route's conception, in 2016, was motivated by a desire to provide better access to the Western Balkans for mountain bikers and adventure travellers.

'You can go to cities anywhere,' Vricic continued. 'Some are great, but they are just cities. Trans Dinarica is special because it puts travellers in the middle of culture that hasn't changed for centuries. And no matter which stage you ride in any of the countries, you feel like you are on the edge of the world.'

Launched in 2017, the Trans Dinarica connects three countries as it follows the Dinaric Alps, which dominate the western half of the Balkan Peninsula and includes several sub-ranges. The trail

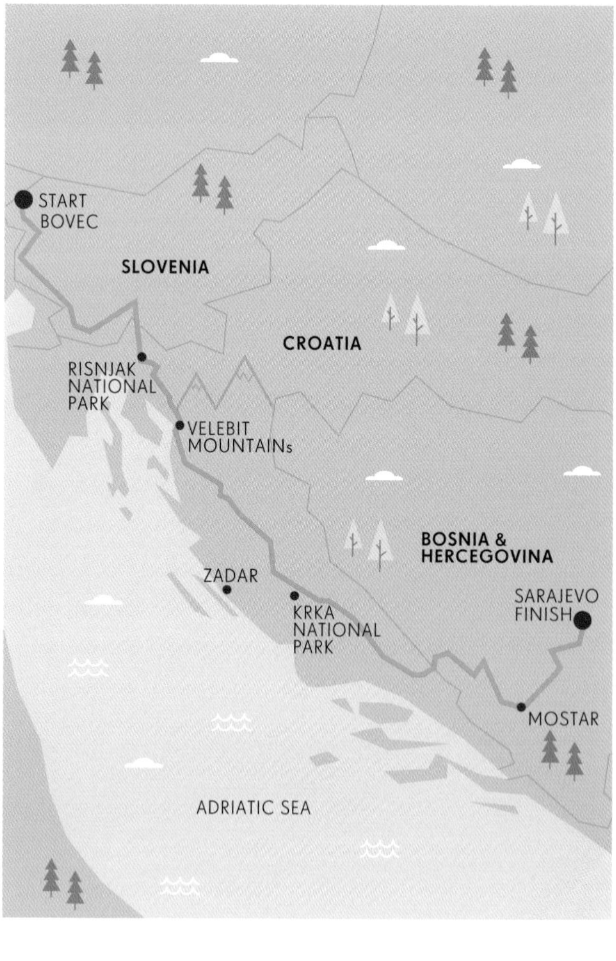

© Uroš Švigelj

starts in Slovenia's Soca Valley, on the southwest edge of Triglav National Park and near the country's highest peak, Mount Triglav (9396ft, 2864m).

The route rolls south through the foothills of the Julian Alps along the Italian border until it dips into Croatia and passes through the remote forests of Risnjak National Park. There, it twists and turns through the Velebit Massif and hugs the Adriatic, with its more than 1000 islands, before drifting inland at the Zrmanja River, near the city of Zadar. After passing above the waterfalls of Krka National Park, the path wiggles around Mount Dinara, for which the Dinaric Alps are named, before making its way to the border with Bosnia & Hercegovina.

Across the border, riders have the choice of either booking a private transfer (see More info in the Toolkit) or riding 37 miles (60km) on local roads to Bosnia & Hercegovina's Blidinje Lake. From there, the route continues again to the town of Mostar, famous for its rebuilt, Ottoman-era bridge and now a Unesco World Heritage Site. The trail then works its way north toward Sarajevo. Just south of the capital city, the path winds through villages, which welcome riders in homestays and local pensions, and the peaks that hosted the skiing events during the 1984 Winter Olympic Games.

The original idea behind the Trans Dinarica was to act as a sister path to the Via Dinarica hiking trail, which traverses all of the Western Balkans region and includes Slovenia, Croatia, Bosnia & Hercegovina, Montenegro, Albania, Kosovo, Serbia, and North Macedonia. Like the Via Dinarica, the hope is to create a more authentic and responsible way to go deeper into the region. And, like its more established trekking relative, this mountain biking corridor is ambitious in nearly every sense.

"The Trans Dinarica puts riders in the middle of cultures that haven't changed for centuries. It's special"

For the developers, the Trans Dinarica represents the stitching together of new and ancient paths – some used for centuries by traders, soldiers, and shepherds. The ambition is to go beyond the present three, cross-border members and eventually connect and incorporate all the Western Balkans countries. For the local residents of this rugged swathe of land, tucked into the south-eastern corner of Europe and oft-overlooked as an adventure destination, the route and ambition represent the promise of sustainable, village-to-village tourism. For travellers, the Trans Dinarica is a chance to test New World, adrenaline-pumping skills on a journey through Old World cultures and to do so surrounded

© Piotr Krzeslak / Shutterstock, Uroš Švigelj

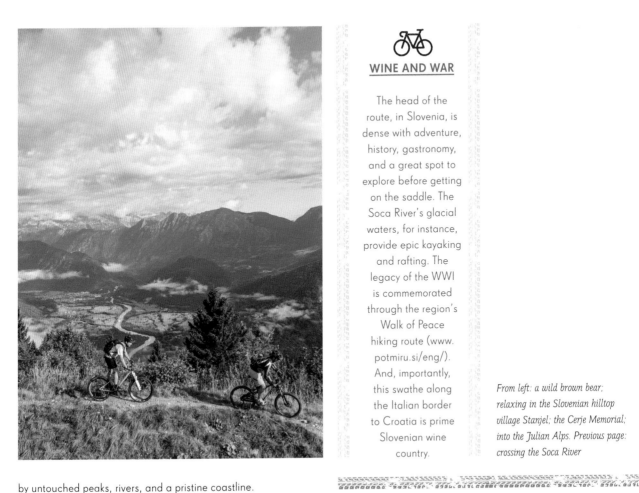

WINE AND WAR

The head of the route, in Slovenia, is dense with adventure, history, gastronomy, and a great spot to explore before getting on the saddle. The Soca River's glacial waters, for instance, provide epic kayaking and rafting. The legacy of the WWI is commemorated through the region's Walk of Peace hiking route (www.potmiru.si/eng/). And, importantly, this swathe along the Italian border to Croatia is prime Slovenian wine country.

From left: a wild brown bear; relaxing in the Slovenian hilltop village Stanjel; the Cerje Memorial; into the Julian Alps. Previous page: crossing the Soca River

by untouched peaks, rivers, and a pristine coastline.

Nearly any cyclist will find the right level of adventure along the Trans Dinarica, as our group discovered on different sections of the route using a mixture of gravel and mountain bikes. The routes in all three countries offer a combination of surfaces – asphalt, gravel, dirt roads, and singletrack – and provide alternative trails to accommodate skill levels. The most technical riding is in Slovenia, where the mountain biking culture is older, and the trails and infrastructure more developed.

In each country, riders can expect B&Bs, lodges, farms, and locally-run hotels at a stage's end. They will also discover lost-in-time villages, tucked into hillsides across the region, where locals serve wine and homemade schnapps and provide the backdrop for one of the most authentic adrenaline corridors in Europe.

'I never worry about whether mountain bikers will have a good time on this route,' says Jan Klavora, a partner at Visit GoodPlace, a company that leads adventure tours out of Ljubljana, Slovenia. Klavora is also one of Trans Dinarica's founders and developers. 'Not only is there diverse terrain and riding conditions, but much of the region has been virtually untouched by industry. Instead there are mountains, high passes, rivers, glacial lakes, and villagers waiting for adventurous visitors. The Western Balkans feels like a secret, eco playground.' **ACr**

TOOLKIT

Start // Bovec, Slovenia
Finish // Sarajevo, Bosnia & Hercegovina
Distance // 758 miles (1220km)
Getting there // There are international airports in Ljubljana, Zagreb, and Sarajevo. There are regular buses from Ljubljana to the head of the trail, Bovec, about 81 miles (130km) away.
Bike hire // In Slovenia, Ljubljana-based Visit GoodPlace (www.visit-goodplace.com). In Zagreb, Croatia, VMD Adventure Travel (vmd.hr/eng). In Sarajevo, Bosnia & Hercegovina, Green Visions (greenvisions.ba/en).
When to ride // In the shoulder months: late May and June; September and October.
More info // www.transdinarica.com

© Uroš Švigelj

Opposite: Ushguli village in the Greater Caucasus Mountains

MORE LIKE THIS
MOUNTAIN VILLAGE RIDES

SVANETI TRAIL, GEORGIA

Over the course of four days, this remote mountain-biking route combines great riding, village life and the grandeur of one of the planet's up-and-coming authentic tourism stars, Georgia. Set in the Greater Caucasus Mountains, in the country's northwest section, the trail rolls across a combination of surfaces, including dirt roads, hard-packed gravel and some asphalt. Cyclists should keep their cameras ready for a preponderance of panoramas after big climbs – particularly the one that tackles nearly 4600ft (1400m) of elevation gain and ends in one of Europe's highest continuously inhabited settlements, Ushguli. In the evenings, adventurers can choose to camp or stay in guesthouses and small hotels. The advantage of sleeping under a roof? The chance to visit and eat with locals, who grow their own food and make honey.
Start // Tsageri
Finish // Mestia
Distance // 143 miles (230km)

TRANS SLOVENIA

This mountain-biking route is a rush of adrenaline, a test of skills, and a chance to enjoy genuine village culture tucked into hollows and behind ridges. Extending along Slovenia's northern border with Austria and ending near the tri-border point between Slovenia, Austria and Italy, it is also a perfect way to discover what is, arguably, one of the most underrated cycling countries in Europe. The trail, which is a microcosm of the breadth of possibilities in peak-strewn Slovenia, stretches over three sub-ranges within the Alps. From east to west riders pedal through the Julian Alps, the Karawanks and Kamnik-Savinja Alps, while rolling over single-track, asphalt, and gravel trails. The seven-day path offers big climbs and descents into valleys. A major highlight includes a stage-ending stay on the shores of Lake Bled.
Start // Maribor
Finish // Kranjska Gora
Distance // 209 miles (336km)

ALPE ADRIA RADWEG

The seven-day expedition from Salzburg, Austria, to Grado, on the Italian coast between Venice and Trieste, is a chance to experience cycle touring at its most classic. Connecting the Alps to the Adriatic Sea, as the name implies, the route gives riders the best of both worlds: snow-topped peaks with a relaxed, Mediterranean pace. Averaging around 31 miles (50km) per day – while rolling past highlights that include churches, museums, and waterfalls – the path makes stops in Bischofshofen, Bad Gastein, Spittal an der Drau, Villach, Venzone and Udine. A host of tourism operators service the culture and adventure corridor to supply everything from bike rental to luggage transfer. Lodging through this typically Central European outing includes, as you might guess, cosy pensions and spas.
Start // Salzburg, Austria
Finish // Grado, Italy
Distance // 235 miles (378km)

© Maya Karkalicheva / Getty Images

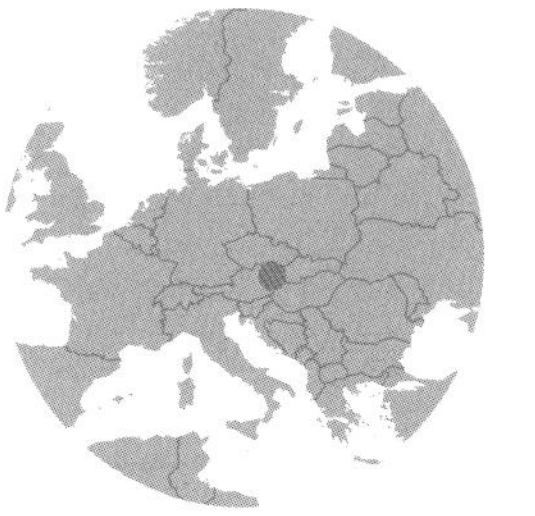

EUROVELO 6'S EASTERN HEART

EV6 rolls from the Atlantic to the Black Sea – but it's in the riches of south-eastern Europe that it truly find its way.

Daylight broke as I pedalled east on the trans-continental EuroVelo 6 cycling route along Serbia's stretch of the Danube. Across the river, Romania still slept. With the dawn, the silhouette of the 14th-century Golubac Fortress appeared, glowing in the distance. Moments later, its round towers and crenellated ramparts loomed above me, atop a rock outcropping, and then disappeared as the road entered a tunnel beneath the citadel's stone walls. When I reached the other side, the Danube had suddenly changed. Its rolling banks were replaced by a string of narrow, steep gorges, known as the Iron Gates. For the next 60 miles (100km), limestone cliffs – hundreds of feet high and representatives of the Southern Carpathian Mountains to the north and the Balkan Mountains to the south – squeezed the mighty waterway.

Cycling through the Iron Gates, I couldn't help but think the eastern end of the EuroVelo 6 (EV6) – extending from southern Hungary into Croatia, Serbia, Bulgaria, and Romania – was as dramatic as any of the stages I'd ridden while crossing the continent. The EV6 spans more than 2860 miles (4600km) in total and starts on the Atlantic Coast. The trail connects 10 countries: France, Switzerland, Germany, Austria, Slovakia, Hungary, Croatia, Serbia, Bulgaria, and Romania. Every section had its

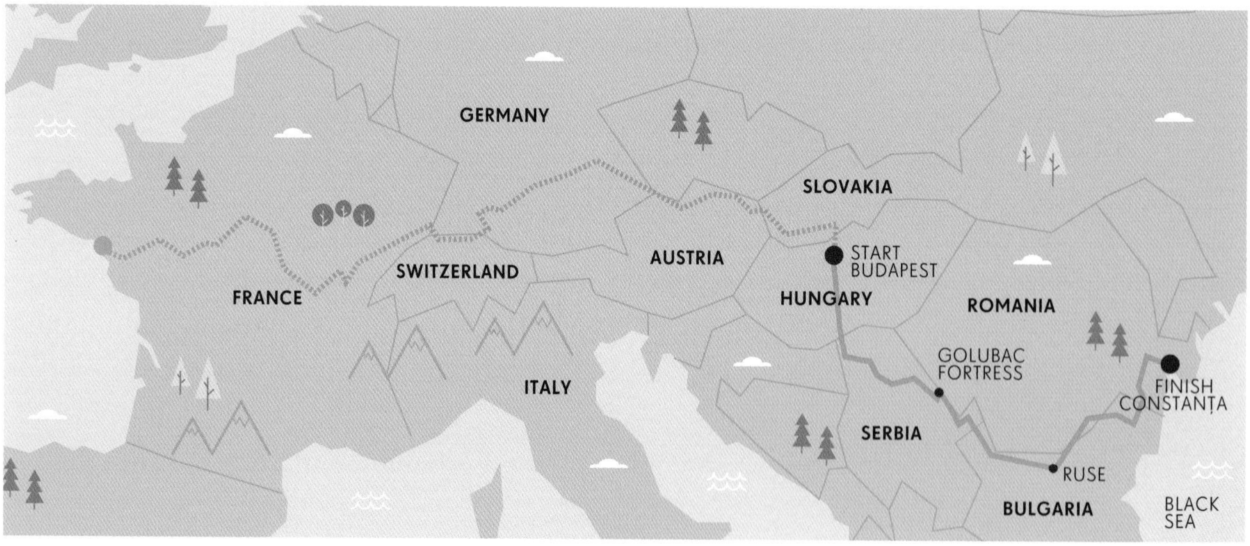

© PavleMarjanovic / Shutterstock

highlights. As I discovered, however, no section is more overlooked or more deserving of two-wheeled, human-speed inspection than the 1100 miles (1770km) snaking along the Danube, running south from Budapest, Hungary, then east to the Black Sea.

When I first contemplated an end-to-end EV6 ride, the idea seemed unhinged. Would I be able to handle a continent of logistics? Would I rise to the physical and mental challenge of being in the saddle all day, every day? By the time I arrived in Budapest, the EuroVelo 6's philosophical and ideological junction between its western and eastern European identities, my body was a machine. More than three weeks and 1800 miles (2900km) of biking east had honed me.

I was, though, more keenly aware than ever that the EV6 plays no favourites. The trail's only tacit promise had been to guide me across Europe and along its most famous rivers, flanked by France's Atlantic-bound Loire and the Danube, which runs to the Black Sea. Coming to a mental, emotional, and spiritual communion with that process was still my responsibility. I reached that communion as I followed the Danube into the Balkan Peninsula from the Hungarian capital.

The timing was perfect, but no accident. I was warned the eastern end of the EuroVelo 6 was still raw. I was told navigating the Balkan stages and the landscape forged by empires and political complexity – Roman, Byzantine, Ottoman, Austro-Hungarian, Yugoslav, Soviet – necessitated map-reading proficiency, a multitude of apps, and patience for infrastructure that was, largely, still 'under development'.

All of this was true. However, what the stretch between Budapest and the Black Sea lacked in the way of a constant turn-by-turn signage, bistros and boutiques – as was the case on the western EV6's stages – it made up for with inexpensive accommodation, generosity from the locals I met, animated directions and the obvious connection between slowing down and true self-sufficiency.

What I found was a release from the trappings of tourism. I cycled on a combination of surfaces – roads, bike paths, and hard-packed trails on levees – past communities surrounded by fruit tree orchards, farms and terraced expanses of grape vines from Croatia into Serbia and then to Bulgaria and Romania. The result? I became less concerned about getting lost, and more determined to be found.

Leaving Budapest, the route headed south through Hungary to eastern Croatia's vineyard-heavy Slavonia region with stops in Osijek, Vukovar, and Ilok. The EV6 then pedaled into Serbia to Novi Sad, capital Belgrade and then cycling nirvana engulfed by the Iron Gates. In Bulgaria, the trail markers became less frequent as the stares from locals grew and the route became a black ribbon flowing through undulating sunflower fields. The layovers included the riverside towns of Vidin, Oryahovo and Svishtov, before arriving in Ruse, Bulgaria's largest Danubian city famed for Neo-Baroque architecture. The tour ended on Romania's coast

SLAVONIAN WINE

Croatia's Slavonia region – bordered by Hungary, Bosnia & Hercegovina, and Serbia – produces some of southeastern Europe's best wine. Part of the fertile Pannonian Plain, and surrounded by the Sava, Drava and Danube Rivers, the area is most famous for white varieties such as Graševina and Traminac, but also produces excellent reds like Cabernet Sauvignon and Zweigelt. Before leaving the country, stop for a wine tasting in the town of Ilok at the Ilocki Podrumi, or Ilok Cellars (www.ilocki-podrumi.hr/).

Clockwise from above: Belgrade; the Iron Gates Gorge; the Danube Cycle Path. Previous page: Golubac fortress

© Florian Augustin / Shutterstock

in Constanta, where the Black Sea extends beyond the horizon. Standing on the beach, journey complete, I wondered if I was ever riding at all.

'In recent years, the interest to travel all the way to the Black Sea has increased,' says Vladan Kreckovic, Serbia's National Coordinator for EuroVelo Routes. The EV6 is one of 16 routes within the EuroVelo network (five cross the Balkans), which touches every corner of the continent and forms something like Europe's bicycle highway system. 'Tourists realise there is a whole undiscovered area after Budapest. We are working on cycling services here – but we definitely already have the nature, an incredible amount of culture and food, and real people, who are proud to welcome guests and show off their countries.'

For nearly two weeks I pedaled in a daily, seven-hour state of meditation. I swooshed past cathedrals, fishing shacks, communist-era river resorts, and the hulking remains of long-shuttered factories. For days at a time, I saw no other cyclists. Cycling here, though, created less a sense of 'Here be dragons' and more the experience of unfettered exploration and pure discovery. At least once a day, while riding along the Danube's banks, through villages floating like islands in yellow oceans of sunflowers that extended out of sight, I said out loud and to myself: 'This is freedom.' **ACr**

© ezdan / Shutterstock, imageBROKER / Alamy Stock Photo

TOOLKIT

Start // Budapest, Hungary
Finish // Constanta, Romania
Distance // 1107 miles (1782km)
Getting there // Fly or catch a train to Budapest, to start the eastern sections of the EV6. At route's end, take the train from Constanta to Bucharest for regular flights (that allow bicycles) or trains throughout Europe.
What to take // A mountain or gravel bike is best because of mixed surfaces. Use panniers or bikepacks to take the minimum possible. Suggestion: two cycling outfits, rain gear, set of post-ride clothing, optional tent and cooking gear.
When to ride // Before or after tourism-season traffic and before or after the heat of summer: late May to June and September to late October.
More info // https://en.eurovelo.com/

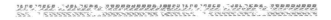

Clockwise from top: Vienna; remains of the Iron Curtain in the Czech Republic; Bézier's old bridge and cathedral

MORE LIKE THIS
EUROPEAN ODYSSEYS

EUROVELO 8: MEDITERRANEAN ROUTE

An epic coastal ride, the EV8 gets intimate with some of the continent's most famous and revered shorelines and continues through 11 countries while rolling by 23 Unesco sites. A cyclist could be forgiven if she swore off other long-distance tours after this itinerary, which includes Spain, France, Monaco, Italy, Slovenia, Croatia, Bosnia & Hercegovina, Montenegro, Albania, Greece, Cyprus. Along the way, travellers will pedal and sightsee along the Atlantic Ocean, the Mediterranean Sea (also passing its smaller Alboran, Balearic, Ionian, and Aegean seas), and the Adriatic, which hugs the Balkan Peninsula's northern half with more than 1000 islands. The last stages require a ferry from Athens to Cyprus – a final curtain call before completing this tour.
Start // Cádiz, Spain
Finish // Cyprus
Distance // 4700 miles (7560km)

EUROVELO 9: BALTIC-ADRIATIC

The EuroVelo 9 (EV9) is among the shortest of the EuroVelo network's 16 routes. (The trails are listed up to EV19 because of the more numerous, odd-numbered, north-south paths.) Still, there is something special about its sea-to-sea symmetry. Starting on the shore of the Baltic Sea, the tour heads due south across the heart of Central and Eastern Europe. The EV9 connects six countries: Poland, Czech Republic, Austria, Slovenia, Italy, and Croatia. The brevity of this path, and the fact that it passes through several cultural hubs – Vienna, Ljubljana and Trieste to name three – also makes it a particularly good choice to start ticking off one's pursuit of EuroVelo itineraries. The trail ends on the Adriatic Sea, at the tip of Croatia's Istria Peninsula, famed for wine, olive oil and truffles.
Start // Gdansk, Poland
Finish // Pula, Croatia
Distance // 1274 miles (2050km)

EUROVELO 13: IRON CURTAIN TRAIL

For cyclists with more time on their hands – and confidence in their legs – the EuroVelo 13 (EV13) is the longest of EuroVelo's routes. The path is big in every way. The trail passes 14 Unesco sites, pedals along three seas, and crosses the borders of 20 countries, nearly half of the entire number of nations, 42, connected by the overall network. The EV13 encompasses extremes, with a northern starting point in the Arctic Circle in Norway, and a terminus on the coast of the Black Sea in Tsarevo, Bulgaria, just above the Turkish border. Finally, even the itinerary's theme is big, with a ride down the corridor that once divided political ideologies and separated Cold War-era Europe.
Start // Kirkenes, Norway
Finish // Tsarevo, Bulgaria
Distance // 6462 miles (10,400km)

© V_eronicka / Shutterstock, 7Horses / Shutterstock, Richard Semik / Shutterstock / Shutterstock

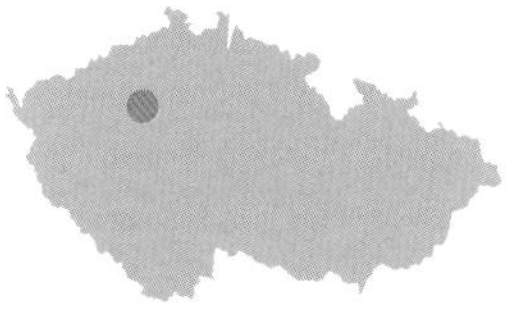

THE RIDE OF A THOUSAND YEARS

Escape the bustle of Prague with a loop that absorbs the ups and downs of the city's appealing hinterland and its seething, bloody history.

Prague is not a place known for being bike-friendly. Cobblestones, rumbling trams and narrow lanes make the centuries-old city an unlikely place to ride. And in recent years, the city has become clotted with stag parties and package tour groups, making the narrow streets even less navigable for the two-wheeled set.

Yet things are changing, quietly. Outside the Czech capital's crowded centre, cycling is on the increase, supported by a growing network of bike lanes. And the popularity of central Prague means the hilly, thickly forested area around the city is largely ignored by the hordes elbowing their way on to the iconic Charles Bridge. One hot late-summer day, I struck out to see what the countryside around Prague offered.

A lot, it turns out. On a hilly, 75-mile (120km) loop that began and ended in Prague, I pedaled through 1000 years of Czech history, from the earliest days of Bohemian royalty to the relentless turmoil of the 20th century. Along the way, there were medieval monasteries, castles perched atop craggy cliffs, swooping descents and, of course, time to stop for coffee and cake.

My ride started and finished in the Vyšehrad neighbourhood south of central Prague. From there, a freshly-paved bike path threads its way between recently restored Art Deco apartment buildings and the blue-green Vltava River. After a few miles, I crossed to the opposite riverbank and began to climb along a twisting road shaded by trees. As I rounded a bend, a fox darted into the middle of the road and paused to size me up, a cunning character out of Central European folklore contemplating how prepared I was for the ride ahead.

At the top of that first short ascent, I emerged from the forest to a view of Prague's skyline. The vista spread from one edge of the horizon to the other, and spanned centuries – to the west, hillsides were lined with long ranks of communist-era apartment blocks punctuated by one of the largest stadiums in the world, a 1920s-era behemoth with room for 250,000 spectators. To the east, I could just pick out Prague's Castle Hill, where the first royal residences of Bohemia were built in the 10th century.

With every turn of the pedals, I felt myself leaving the expected further behind.

Noticing a cluster of cars parked on the side of the road, I pull over and find myself peering into a chasm 330ft (100m) deep and

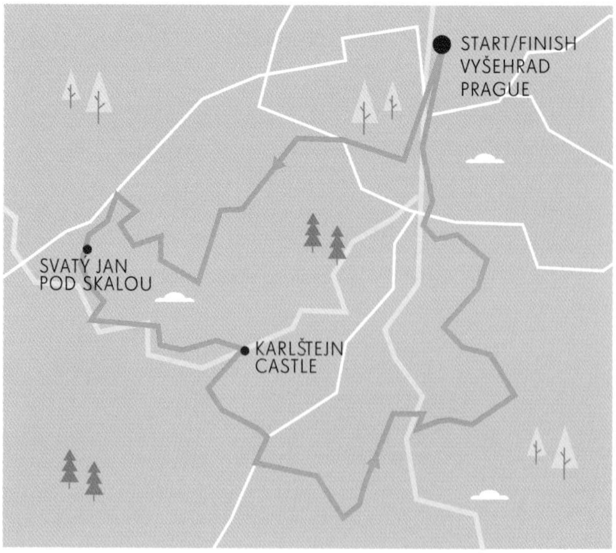

© BIKO Adventures

over a half-mile long. It's an abandoned, partly flooded stone quarry incongruously named 'Velka Amerika' (Great America) perhaps because it reminded locals of the Grand Canyon. Not much further, there was Svatý Jan pod Skalou, a medieval monastery built against tall limestone cliffs with a clear, fast-moving stream running past.

After a few hours, I found myself riding along the meandering Berounka River, keeping pace with kayakers bobbing along in its placid waters. Limestone cliffs soon rose up to my left. Suddenly a broad gap in rocks drew my eye up, and up – to Karlštejn Castle, the ride's mid-point. Karlštejn's medieval mass perches with unlikely grace atop a rock promontory, with a single stone tower commanding a view of the river below.

You wouldn't know it to ride through the quiet countryside today, but the forests and valleys of Bohemia once seethed with violence. Built in 1348 to safeguard the crown jewels of the Bohemian kings, Karlštejn became important in the religious wars that raged for decades across these forested hills.

Between 1419 and 1434, a dizzying collection of splinter Christian sects battled for control of Bohemia. On its craggy hill, Karlštejn Castle was never conquered. But attackers still tried: after one failed assault in 1422, the frustrated attackers resorted to early germ warfare, catapulting dead bodies and wagons full of cow dung over the castle walls.

"Suddenly a gap in rocks drew my eye to the medieval Karlstejn Castle, on a craggy promontory – it was never conquered"

THE NATIONAL DRINK

When it comes to beer, the Czech Republic doesn't mess around: beer consumption is the highest in the world, at over 140 litres per person per year. Most towns had their own breweries until the communist era, when production was largely centralised. Today, the number of breweries is on the rise again – it's nearly quadrupled since 2008, and there are now 450 producing traditional and craft styles across the country. *Na zdravi!*

Clockwise from above: riding along the Vltava River; Prague's Charles Bridge; Karlstejn Castle (and on previous page); the national drink

© Matt Munro / Lonely Planet, walencienne / Getty Images

Six centuries later, that mess has been cleaned up. But I couldn't verify that: for all its picturesque beauty, Karlštejn itself isn't yet geared towards pedal-powered visitors. The steep road from the touristy town below to the mighty front gates is closed to cyclists, and there's nowhere to safely store bikes during the hour-long guided tours of the royal chapel and treasure vaults.

Not far down the road, I braked to take in yet another monument to conflicts gone by. A squat, round bunker, painted in garish red, orange and green camouflage, is part of a line of nearly 1000 fortifications built in the 1930s to protect Prague against invasion by the Nazis. Unlike the castle that towers above it, of course, it never saw a shot fired in anger – Nazi Germany swallowed up Prague, and the rest of Czechoslovakia, without firing a shot in 1939.

Bohemia isn't all fairy-tale castles, breweries and sleepy villages. The Czech countryside is home to plenty of heavy industry, and the area around Prague is no exception. Abundant train crossings, ageing cement plants and stonecutting facilities are as much a part of the landscape as Karlštejn and Svaty Jan.

Riding through one small town, I spotted a cafe stocked with a selection of tempting pastries. The slices of traditional apple cake looked so good I ordered two – just enough fuel to carry me the last few miles back to the spires and alleys of Prague, where a tall glass of beer was a perfect reward for a hard day of hills in Bohemia. **AC**

TOOLKIT

Start/Finish // Prague

Distance // 75 miles (120km)

Getting there // Prague is a popular tourism destination, well connected by plane or train to the rest of Europe.

Bike hire // Biko Adventures (www.bikoadventures.com) rents road bikes and mountain bikes. For this ride, road bikes are best; there are also off-road trails. The company also offers guided tours.

When to ride // April to October.

Where to stay // Prague offers a wide range of options, from budget hostels and vacation rentals to high-end hotels. Consider staying outside the city centre for better bargains.

What to eat // Czech food tends towards meat-and-dumplings. Save the heavy meal and Pilsner for Prague, but stop at a cafe (like Cafe Davle in Davle, just before crossing the Vltava again) for ice cream, coffee or cake.

© BIKO Adventures, Xantana / Getty Images

Opposite, top: a spin through the vines of southern Moravia; Pravcicka Brana sandstone gate, Bohemia

MORE LIKE THIS
CZECH ADVENTURES

PRAGUE-DRESDEN

The ride from Prague to Dresden in southern Germany links two of the region's most beautiful cities along a mostly flat, well-paved cycling route that parallels the Vltava and Elbe rivers. The trail is well signed and paved, and mostly flat. Along the way there are Renaissance-era castles and medieval Czech villages. There's also the Terezín concentration camp, an 18th-century fortress where over 150,000 Jews were interned during WWII (30,000 died). Along the border, the route crosses 'Saxon Switzerland', a dramatic landscape of sandstone cliffs and thick forests, before leaving the Czech Republic to take a detour up the hill to Pravcicka Brana, one of the region's most recognisable landmarks. Museum lovers should plan extra time to spend in Dresden, whose offerings range from the Zwinger's collections of Old Masters and porcelain to the offbeat Hygiene Museum and German Military History Museum.
Start // Prague, Czech Republic
Finish // Dresden, Germany
Distance // 139 miles (224 km)

BOHEMIAN BORDER

The mountainous region along the German-Czech border is popular with gravel riders, who revel in its unpaved roads, steep climbs and thick forests. The best riding is in and around a national park area that straddles the border between the two countries: in Germany it's called the Saxon Switzerland National Park; in the Czech Republic the Bohemian Switzerland National Park. The resort town of Bad Schandau is a great place to start, but the region can also be easily reached by train from Prague or Dresden. For a commanding view, plan a climb to the top of Jested, the area's highest mountain – its trippy TV tower contains a hotel and restaurant to replenish your energy levels before the descent. Roads in the park are typically car-free but can be rough, so mountain, cyclocross or gravel bikes are recommended.
Start/Finish // Bad Schandau, Germany
Distance // 50 to 90 miles (80 to 150km)

MORAVIAN WINE COUNTRY

Though pilsner (named for the town of Plzeň) has made the Czech Republic synonymous with beer, its southern region, known as Moravia, has been a wine-lover's paradise since the third century, when homesick Roman legionaries tried planting grapes in the limestone hills north of Vienna. These days, cycle tourists can ride from vineyard to vineyard through the Moravian Hills, sampling the region's award-winning whites – Moravian pinot blanc and Rieslings are particularly prized. Parts of the route follow the Czech Greenways, a network of cycle paths connecting Prague and Vienna. Along the way it passes by Unesco World Heritage Sites such as Telc, a spectacularly preserved Renaissance town situated in the midst of dense forests, and Olomouc, once the Moravian capital. It's not all wine – the town of Ceske Budejovice is the home of Budweiser, where brewery tours are available.
Start // Mikulov, Czech Republic
Finish // Cesky Krumlov, Czech Republic
Distance // 350 miles (560 km)

© Petr Pohudka / Shutterstock, Ondrej Prosicky / Shutterstock

TO DURMITOR AND BACK

A tour of Croatia, Bosnia & Hercegovina and Montenegro reveals a timeless, rustic way of life worlds away from the tourist delights of Dubrovnik.

On the late September day I set off on this loop from the Adriatic Sea into the heart of the Balkans, there were almost perfect touring conditions: clear skies and sunshine for three-and-half days, with temperatures ranging from 25°C on the plains in the middle of the day, to around 5°C in the mountains at dusk. On the last afternoon, a storm came off the sea and I got soaked.

While there are numerous hotels around the honey-coloured, historic Old Town in Dubrovnik, the options are more limited in rural Bosnia & Hercegovina (BiH). I arranged accommodation in advance, staying in the house of a history professor in Mostar, at a family-run river-rafting lodge on the Tara River and in a small motel in Nikšic. The food is simple peasant fare and inexpensive (at least away from the Adriatic). A highlight was the 'set' breakfast in a roadside cafe in Montenegro: two pork chops, green salad, flatbreads, fruit juice, double espresso and a large glass of homemade brandy.

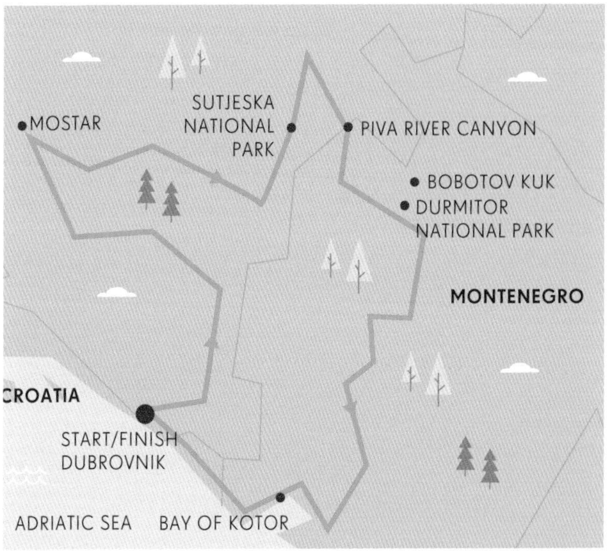

© Domingo Leiva / 500 px

"I rode past donkeys, conical hayricks in fields, goat-herders ambling on verges. There were almost no cars at all"

Of course, I hadn't come to the Balkans for fine dining. Rather, I had come for big landscapes, clean rivers, wild forests, exotic plants and empty roads. Cycling out of Dubrovnik and along the main coastal highway from Croatia to Montenegro was hectic, but as soon as I turned my back to the sea and crossed the border into BiH, the traffic tailed off. Some 25 miles (40km) after that, heading west towards Mostar, there were almost no cars at all. I rode past conical hayricks in fields, donkeys, goat-herders ambling along verges to the sound of bells, and tractors chugging out of the woods with trailers full of coppiced oak and hornbeam, for winter firewood. Occasionally I felt like I'd vaulted back in time, to the beginning of the 20th century and into the plot of some Balkan version of *Cider With Rosie*.

Any sense of pastoral reverie is, however, periodically punctured by reminders of the complex, ethnically-rooted civil war that ripped through the former Yugoslavia in the early 1990s. I pedalled past numerous, small graveyards and many deserted farm buildings pock-marked with bullet holes. As I have friends who worked as journalists and served as soldiers in BiH during the war, the road signs to Srebrenica, which I passed at dusk on day two, stirred dark memories. An estimated 100,000 people were killed during the conflict. In BiH, a further two million – about half the population – were displaced.

The UK Government foreign travel advice for BiH still carries a warning about landmines and other unexploded ordnance, particularly away from tarmac roads in rural areas. The vast majority of mines have, of course, been cleared. In fact, the war has largely been forgotten – many of the English-speaking staff you meet in bars and hotels are too young to even remember it. There is no evidence of the bombing Dubrovnik suffered in 1991. In Mostar, I walked across the famous Stari Most, the elegant, hump-backed 'Old Bridge' first built by the Ottomans in the 16th century and blown up by Croat soldiers in 1993. When I visited Mostar shortly after the war in 1998, the bridge was still in pieces, at the bottom of the Neretva River. It has since been immaculately re-built, as a symbol of national repair. Today, locals leap off it plunging 25m into the river, for the entertainment of tourists.

I travelled light, carrying tools and clothes in bikepacking panniers. I navigated easily enough, using a combination of digital and paper maps: there aren't many roads, so it's hard to go wrong. I rode a gravel-style bike with a steel frame, disc brakes and large road tyres. In the event, the road surfaces were good and I didn't have a single puncture.

Leaving Mostar, I climbed 3300 feet (1000m) over 9 miles (15km) out of the Neretva Valley, past the crumbling, medieval

© utamaria / Getty Images, James Perrott, Alina_Stock / Shutterstock

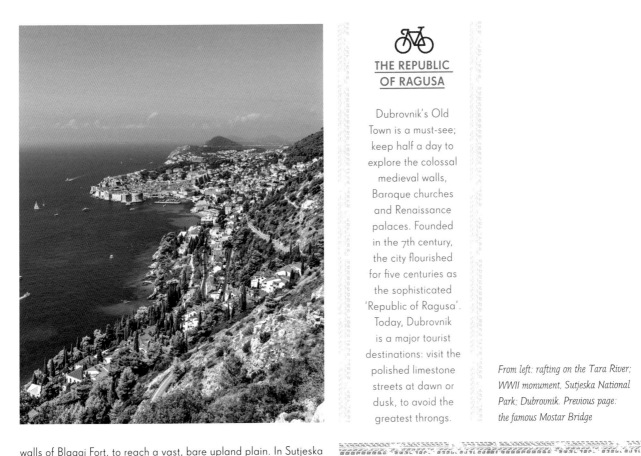

THE REPUBLIC OF RAGUSA

Dubrovnik's Old Town is a must-see; keep half a day to explore the colossal medieval walls, Baroque churches and Renaissance palaces. Founded in the 7th century, the city flourished for five centuries as the sophisticated 'Republic of Ragusa'. Today, Dubrovnik is a major tourist destinations: visit the polished limestone streets at dawn or dusk, to avoid the greatest throngs.

From left: rafting on the Tara River; WWII monument, Sutjeska National Park; Dubrovnik. Previous page: the famous Mostar Bridge

walls of Blagaj Fort, to reach a vast, bare upland plain. In Sutjeska National Park, a natural pearl of BiH where locals recorded a famous victory over the Nazis during WWII, I flew down through a beautiful, deep canyon, beside the Sutjeska River, riding through pools of dazzling sunlight, beneath hillsides covered in ancient forests of beech and pine. Following the Tara River just after dawn, I rode between high limestone walls, in and out of plumes of mist.

Nothing, however, prepared me for the mountain road up and over Durmitor National Park, Montenegro's wondrous Unesco World Heritage Site. From the Piva River Canyon, I climbed through limestone tunnels, past oak forests populated by wild cats, bears and wolves, and crossed alpine meadows surrounding the karst massif. The road finally reaches a shallow bowl encircled by savagely contorted, parallel slabs of limestone protruding from the earth at 90 degrees. Above that, across a rising plateau of karst ridges and tectonic fissures was Bobotov Kuk (8278 feet, 2523m), one of the highest mountains in Montenegro. Beyond, there were yet more staggering views across glacial lakes to rows of mountain peaks, deep river gorges and pine forests.

On the last day, I followed quiet backroads through central, southern Montenegro, chasing the clock and the impending storm. On the thrilling descent to the Bay of Kotor – another amazing road with 25 hairpin bends – the clouds began to thicken. Curtains of rain then swept in off the sea as I thrashed my way back to the bright lights and the big city of Dubrovnik. **RP**

TOOLKIT

Start/Finish // Dubrovnik
Distance // 397 miles (635km), with a hefty total vertical ascent of some 28,000ft (8650m).
Getting there // The easiest airport is Dubrovnik, 9 miles (15km) from the city centre.
When to ride // May, early June, late September and early October. July and August can be very hot.
Where to stay // I booked accommodation before setting off: in rural BiH, accommodation options are limited. Stay at Blue River Tara in Scepan Polje (Plužine), Montenegro: https://bluerivertara.me; if you have a spare day, book a rafting trip on the Tara River.
Bike hire // There are several bike hire companies in Croatia. Try Meridien Ten (http://www.meridienten.com/category/rentals/5) or Biking Croatia (https://www.bikingcroatia.com/bike-rental).

© Leonid Andronov / Shutterstock

Opposite: the Carpathian range, Romania, has long been a mountain-biking destination

MORE LIKE THIS
LESSER-KNOWN MOUNTAIN RANGES

PINDUS MOUNTAINS, GREECE

Extending from southern Albania across northern Greece, as far as the northern Peloponnese, the Pindus range is known colloquially as the 'spine of Greece'. Like the Balkans, riding here feels wild and remote. You need to be completely self-sufficient. There are deep canyons, rounded massifs (the highest point is 8651ft, 2637m) and great forests of black pine and beech which are home to bears. The development of skiing, and to a lesser extent mountain biking, has brought some tourists to the region, but you are unlikely to meet anyone else on a road bike. The villages of shepherds and farmers are connected by a lattice of small roads. A few villages have tavernas and guest houses. Beware the dogs that protect the livestock. The road surfaces are okay and the views, particularly in spring when the wild flowers are out and the distant mountains are sugar-capped with snow, are staggeringly lovely. More info: www.visitgreece.gr/en/nature/mountains.

Start // Kastoria
Finish // Patras
Distance: 300 miles (480km)

TRANSYLVANIA, ROMANIA

The Carpathian and Apuseni mountain ranges have been luring adventurous mountain bikers to Romania for years. Touring cyclists are slowly following. This is an amazing place to ride, at its best from the beginning of June to the end of October. There are great forests of beech and oak, castles (including, most famously, Count Dracula's fictional castle), hilltop citadels, stunning fortified churches and glacial lakes. The Transfagarasan Highway, which includes a monster climb over the Carpathian Mountains, is on the route (the Highway is open 1 July to 30 October, which is pretty much the window for cycling in Transylvania). The complex history of the region is reflected in the medieval cities that you can drop down to when you've had enough of the mountain roads and the villages and the rich contemporary culture. Traditional Romanian food tends to be hearty, homemade and filling – perfect, then, for hungry cyclists. More info: http://romaniatourism.com/transylvania.html.

Start/Finish // Sibiu
Distance: 385 miles (620km)

GENEVA TO STRASBOURG

The Jura and Vosges mountain ranges are often overlooked by road cyclists seeking higher cols and deeper thrills further south and east in the Alps. This route traverses the length of both ranges, connecting the cities of Geneva and Strasbourg. Though the mountains are not high, this is a lumpy ride with few flat sections except for the Belfort Gap. The Jura Mountains form part of the boundary between the drainage basins of the Rhine to the east and the Rhône to the west, so there is a sense of being in the middle of this great continent. You will pedal in and out of Switzerland, France and Germany, past crumbling castles and through vast woods on very good road surfaces. The quiet villages and medieval towns have retained much of their distinct cultural identity, while the cuisine across the region is very good.

Start // Geneva, Switzerland
Finish // Strasbourg, France
Distance // 286 miles (460km)

© Photography 4 You / Shutterstock

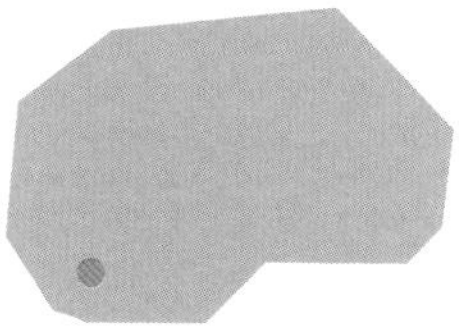

TUNING UP IN MACEDONIA

Bike, spare tubes, waterproofs, mini-synthesisers and Bluetooth speakers – check. If you're riding across North Macedonia for its music, come prepared.

North Macedonia doesn't often appear on cycle-touring bucket lists. As we pedalled through the national parks and mountains of this often forgotten state of Eastern Europe we struggled to see why. On our two-day ride around the magnificent, remote lakes, mountains and national parks of the country's southeast, we came to realise that Macedonia is a jewel in the Balkan crown for riders – and music makers. I should explain: Adam and I, Tim, were in Macedonia as part of a 14-month ride from England to Japan, with the mission to write an album of music with the people we met and the sounds we heard.

Our sonic adventure began in Struga, a small but popular tourist town in the southeast, that sits on Lake Ohrid (one of Europe's deepest). As we left, we passed what we took to be a promising omen: a graffiti-ed David Bowie. Hugging the shoreline, a flat, quiet road connects Struga to nearby Ohrid. There, among the medieval churches and traditional red-tiled roofed houses of the Old Town, we tucked into coffee and a local staple, *börek* – a delicious filo pastry filled with spinach, cheese or minced meat.

The easy introduction to our two-day tour continued as we pedaled south, passing through a handful of smaller, quieter lakeside towns, where locals made the most of the small, sandy beaches to cool off in the lake. To the east, though, was the path ahead, a more formidable prospect: the flat of the lake's coastal path slowly but surely gives way to the inclines of Galicica National Park and the mountains that loom to the east.

A 10-mile (16km) climb switches back and forth into the mountains of the park, the only relief being the occasional roadblock of cattle and the gentle cacophony of their cowbells. And the view: on the pass we paused to reflect on that fact that we had climbed a vertical kilometre – and to take in Lake Ohrid to the west, Lake Prespa to the east, snow-capped mountains in the distance and lush woodland everywhere else. It was the perfect place to take a breather, break out the *börek*, brew up a coffee – and make some music! Our synths were small enough to run from chargeable batteries so we sat in the grass and broadcast our creations via Bluetooth speakers across the lakes of Macedonia.

On the descent towards Lake Prespa the bustle of Lake Ohrid gave way to abandoned holiday resorts (definitely worth snooping around) and quaint villages, with opportunities to interact with

© Eric Beallet

friendly locals who were more than happy to entertain, feed and accommodate us. Be sure to keep your eyes peeled for a restaurant called Klarite just before you arrive in the town of Sirhan. Mario, its guitar-toting proprietor, offered us a hearty meal and a barn to sleep in. Which was lucky as we were winging it during this stage of our adventure.

A morning of coffee, guitars, synthesisers and a little moonshine put some wind in our sails. On his guitar, Mario demonstrated the characteristic sound of Macedonian traditional music – alternating Ionian and Dorian mode throughout his composition, if you're interested. With that musical insight ringing in our ears, we said goodbye to our maestro and headed towards Bitola. Through lush forests we span, along quiet, navigable lanes, smooth tarmac occasionally giving way to cobbles, and sign upon sign warning of bears, wolves and boars (alas, we saw none). En route to Bitola, we admired the quaint Orthodox churches hewn into rocky outcroppings that surround the lake. (There were also plenty of opportunities for detours into the Pelister National Park and up into the Baba Mountains for hiking or trail riding.)

And when the heavens open, you'll get to practise your Macedonian in whichever cafe offers you shelter: *zdravo* (hello), *blagodaram* (thank you) and, of course, *börek*. And practice a lot – out here little English was spoken.

"We were in Macedonia en route to Japan, with the aim to create an album with the people and sounds we encountered"

A COUNTRY WITHIN

High up in the hills north of Lake Ohrid is the village of Vevcani, which, following the break-up of Yugoslavia in the '90s, declared independence, after a fashion – the community has its own 'passports' and currency. The village is a cultural hub for the area and is nationally famous for its springs, which are certainly worth a visit if you've the time. It's said that if you drink enough Vevcani wine, you can become an honorary citizen.

Clockwise from above: Galicica National Park; traditional musician; music-making; an omen in Struga

© Total Bike Forever

That evening we rolled into Bitola, North Macedonia's second-largest city after the capital, Skopje. In this busy city there were plenty of English speakers – and more music. We were taken in by an electronic musician who showed us the highlights of the city, such as Magnolia Square, the main pedestrian drag, and Širok Sokak Street with its Neoclassical architecture and the ancient bazaar. He was also able to get us a gig in one of the city's coolest bars, Radost. The bar is situated in one of the more modernised areas in the city, which blends into the Ottoman and Baroque styles that surround it.

There are plenty of options for accommodation with guesthouses, hostels and hotels across the city that range from basic to swanky – though we also recommend trying Warm Showers, not just for the quality of the accommodation. On our trip to Japan, we invariably found its hosts to be the quickest and friendliest way to get to know a city.

We spent that night in Bitola being introduced to musicians, artists and poets. For us the musicians were particularly intriguing; from people making electronic ambient music in a similar style to our host's through to traditional musicians playing instruments such as the *kaval*, a kind of Macedonian wood flute. With a thunderstorm raging over the nearby Baba Mountains, we toasted to our new friends with a Skopsko beer and reflected on a cracking few days in North Macedonia and the strings we had added to our musical bow. **TS & AF**

TOOLKIT

Start // Struga
Finish // Bitola
Distance // 84 miles (135km)
Getting there // Ohrid has an international airport. Trains from Serbia and Greece (bikes to be booked in advance).
When to ride // June to August is hot (25-30C). Autumn and spring are cooler but expect rain.
What to eat and drink // Macedonian cuisine has Mediterranean and Middle Eastern influences and the country is rightly proud of its wine: try a bottle of Vranec.
Where to stay // Warm Showers (warmshowers.org) is worth researching for local hosts. Wild camping is reportedly not a problem, but ask for permission if in doubt.
What to listen to // Our London to Tokyo playlist: https://tinyurl.com/y5wcmegw
More info // www.exploringmacedonia.com; totalbikeforever.com for our album and documentary.

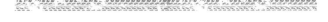

© Agrofruti / Alamy Stock Photo; pawopa3336 / Getty Images; Total Bike Forever

Opposite: sunrise at the Meadows in the Mountains festival, Bulgaria

MORE LIKE THIS
THE BEAT GOES ON

BULGARIAN BEATS

While the ride in and out is pretty flat, the forested peaks of Rhodope Mountains in between are anything but. All that climbing is worth it, though. Incredible lakes, lush pine forests, ancient bridges and quaint settlements are around every corner – not to mention the occasional abandoned village to explore. If you're planning a mid-summer trip, the Rhodope Mountains host the celebrated annual Meadows in the Mountains music festival each June in idyllic surroundings, working closely with the residents of the local community. Expect Bulgarian bands and DJs and experimental music, and mind-bending views of the mountains at sunrise (the site is at an altitude of 850m). Not there in June? Be sure to track down local village choirs to hear Bulgaria's world famous choral folk stylings. More info: www.meadowsinthemountains.com

Start // Svilengrad
Finish // Plovdiv
Distance // 185 miles (300km)

A BORDER SONG

If you've a few days to spare in July, you'll pack in a wide range of music on this trip from northeast Italy into Slovenia. First, enjoy the Roman ruins at Aquileia and a meal in the town at the excellent Pizza e Sapori Soles. Next take in Trieste's annual international jazz festival (throughout July) before heading north, over the border, towards the wild western tip of the Dinaric Alps. Stay off the H4 highway by tracking the easy-to-follow side roads then take the 207 towards Godovic before heading down from the mountains into Logatec and picking up a cycle path directly into Ljubljana. There are brilliant wild camping options throughout, and, of course, tunes: Slovenian traditional music has elements of polka and oom-pah which you'll hear in towns and villages. Once in Ljubljana check out Metelkova, an old military barracks transformed into an autonomous culture centre featuring the city's best clubs and bars.

Start // Aquileia, Italy
Finish // Ljubljana, Slovenia
Distance // 60 miles (100km)

AN ITALIAN SYMPHONY

This route through Lombardy and Veneto takes in ancient cities but also uncovers the region's growing alternative culture. Milan has a thriving electronic music scene that's even been taken up by the techno buskers in the Piazza del Duomo. Check out the music store Serendeepity (https://www.serendeepity.net) if you've room in your panniers for a couple of records and make the most of the world-class summertime open-air clubs along the city's ancient canals. From Milan, head north to Bergamo and its hilltop Roman architecture then follow a cycle route east via Lake Iseo to arrive in Brescia. Aim for mid-July to enjoy MusicalZOO festival and the city's thriving coffee culture. For Lake Garda head east, picking up the Brescia Salò bike path. Cruise the serene, cycle-friendly highways around the lake, keeping an ear out for events in its year-round programme of classical music concerts. From Garda it's only a short hop to Verona.

Start // Milan
Finish // Verona
Distance // 155 miles (250 kms)

© Meadows in the Mountains

TURKEY, HERE I COME

Emily Chappell, the first woman home in the 2016 edition of the Transcontinental Race, explains how to survive – and even have fun – on a self-supported dash across Europe.

I didn't want the Transcontinental to end, which is a strange thing to say about a race that lasted for almost two weeks and during which I covered just short of 2480 miles (4000km), riding from the cobbled farm tracks of Belgium to the windswept coastline of Turkey.

I rarely got more than four hours' sleep (many racers slept even less), and after a few days' struggle my body seemed to submit to this torturous new regime. By the time I entered the Alps, the exhaustion and reluctance with which I'd battled through the quiet French countryside, wondering how I'd keep this up when I already felt desperate to stop, had evaporated. My feet ceased to throb, my stiff back felt nimble again, and on the morning of the fourth day I found myself pelting along the road that led to Grindelwald, the quiet grey expanse of Thunsee to my right, and a series of cliffs and steep Alpine meadows to my left, as the mountains rose straight up from the water. Four hours' sleep in a hostel bed in Fribourg, and a breakfast of coffee and cake in Thun had done their work, and I pedalled furiously, enjoying the inexplicable feeling of strength in my legs, and belting out power ballads at the top of my voice.

I suspect the Swiss commuter had been slipstreaming me for quite some time before I heard his freewheel and glanced round to

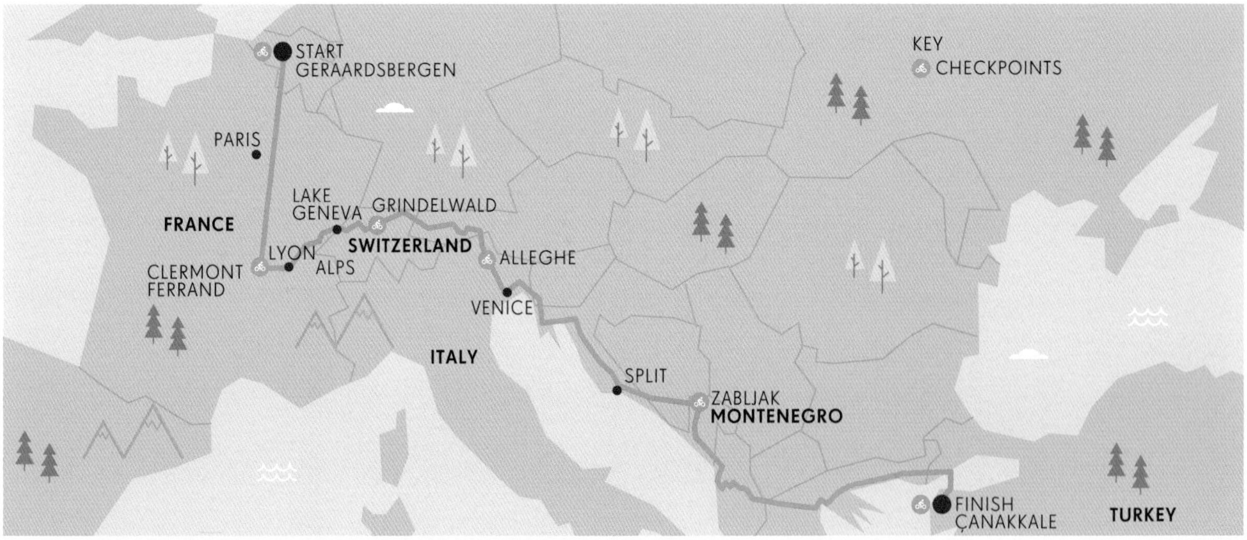

© Kristian Pletten

PEdAL ED
Rapha

find that I wasn't alone. I abruptly stopped singing, he overtook me with a wave, and I continued at a more sedate pace, remembering the mountain passes I had to climb later that day. The road tilted upwards and I was in the Alps.

The Transcontinental encouraged self-sufficiency, dictating that racers visit four checkpoints scattered unevenly across Europe, but generally leaving the rest up to us (the checkpoint locations change each year). However, as well as nestling the checkpoints in hard-to-reach locations among Europe's mountain ranges, the organiser had decreed that racers must approach (or depart) each by a set route – invariably one that included some of the region's choicest gradients.

So after being stamped in at Checkpoint Two, I left Grindelwald by a winding singletrack road, closed to all traffic but the yellow post buses, whose distinctive three-note horn heralded their appearance around the hairpins as I climbed higher and higher. The fresh young grass, not long emerged from the winter snows, sparkled with tiny flowers, and placid brown cows serenaded me with their bells. Up above me, the dark grey rocks of the Eiger and her brethren mingled with the clouds that had begun to sweep in.

Grosse Scheidegg was the first of four passes that day. At the top of Grimsel Pass I found two fellow racers in a cafe, and we chattered ebulliently at each other as we wolfed down soup, coffee and pasta, our taste buds ignited by our hunger, if not the quality of the food, and our consciences untroubled by the €35 price tag.

"Fiona Kolbinger won the 2019 Transcontinental – men and women will compete equally in long-distance cycling"

The clouds were hanging low over Furka Pass, so I didn't hang about, and down in Andermatt I wistfully watched other racers pull up outside hotels. It was still light and felt too early to stop. Several hours, and one more pass later, I got out my bivvy bag, lay down in a pile of mouldering leaves, and sank into blissful oblivion.

Two days – and countless mountains – later I crossed the flat plain of northern Italy under a pink sunrise, and by bedtime was high up on the great karst shelf that overlooks the Croatian coast, following gravel tracks through the sunbaked Mediterranean landscape very different from the Alpine meadow where I'd woken up. I managed to rent a room in a tiny village just before it got dark, and felt smugly vindicated when I was woken in the night by thunder and pouring rain.

And then it was into the Balkans – long one of my favourite regions to cycle through. I rolled happily through the lush green

© Kristian Pletten

From left: Emily Chappell in Montenegro; a brevet card; Fiona Kolbinger, winner of the 2019 Transcontinental Race. Previous page: map check

GOING THE DISTANCE

The Transcontinental has been held annually since 2013. I was the first woman to finish the Transcontinental in 2016, arriving in Çanakkale after 13 days, 10 hours and 28 minutes. In 2019, Fiona Kolbinger became the first (and probably not the last) woman to win the race overall, happily fulfilling my prediction that long-distance cycling is one of the arenas where women and men will compete on equal terms.

fields of the Croatian interior, worlds away from the busy tourist traffic of the coast road. And I crept into Montenegro via an unpaved mountain road, crossing the border unseen and unknown, delighted by the thought that no one (save the legions of invisible spectators watching me on the online tracker) knew where I was.

I slept badly that night, woken by rain hammering on my bivvy bag. And as I breakfasted on stale bread and chocolate spread outside a closed cafe in Pluzine, social media showed me images of the racers ahead of me cowering and shivering at Checkpoint Four, having been caught in a storm on the Durmitor massif.

But the weather was kinder to me. The day brightened as I climbed the quiet road up out of the Piva river gorge, and the clouds were whipped away from the grey mountainsides like a magician's tablecloth. I hadn't known this mountain range even existed until planning my route through it two weeks previously, and now I was awestruck by its beauty. Grey-white rocks thrust their way out of the dense grass, and towered all around me in strange geometrical formations. Here and there dramatic ripples and whorls showed where the mountains had been wrung out by forces so much bigger and slower than my puny pedalling.

I could have stopped and stared – and I wanted to. But they were waiting for me at the checkpoint, and I still had over 600 miles (1000km) to ride to Turkey. So I kept going. **EC**

TOOLKIT

Start // In 2016, Geraardsbergen, Belgium
Finish // In 2016, Çanakkale, Turkey
Distance // In 2016, 2480 miles (4000km)
Getting there and back // Should you wish to recreate an edition of the race (or parts of it), previous checkpoints are listed in the Records section of transcontinental.cc.
When to ride // The race takes place in August.
What to eat // A typical race strategy is to raid supermarkets every few hours, load the bike with food, and consume it while riding.
What to take // The bare minimum: basic tools, a lightweight sleeping system, and a waterproof. A dynamo hub means you can charge electronics on the go.
What to ride // Steel-framed bikes fare best.
More info // www.transcontinental.cc/

© James Robertson, Damien Meyer / Getty Images

Opposite: the TransAtlanticWay race – here at Slea Head, Dingle – is thought to be even tougher than the Transcontinental

MORE LIKE THIS
SELF-SUPPORTED EVENTS

NORTH CAPE-TARIFA, NORWAY TO SPAIN

Using as much of Europe as it possibly can, North Cape-Tarifa starts at the continent's most northerly point and finishes over 4580 miles (7370km) away, at its most southerly. Riders must be prepared – and carry kit – for huge climactic variations, and as finishing times typically approach a month, wear and tear on both bike and body are significant. The route leaves the Arctic Circle via Finland, passes through the Baltic states, Poland and the Czech Republic, before crossing the Alps to Nice, taking in cols such as the Iseran and the Galibier. Racers then skirt the Mediterranean, cross the Pyrenees via Andorra, and head south via Pico de Veleta, Europe's highest road. Unlike the Transcontinental, North Cape-Tarifa cannot be squeezed into a two-week holiday from work, meaning that it typically has far fewer entrants. More info: northcape-tarifa.com.

Start // Nordkapp, Norway
Finish // Tarifa, Spain
Distance // 4580 miles (7370km)

TRANSATLANTICWAY, IRELAND

Racers who approach this relatively short challenge as a rehearsal for the Transcontinental are quickly dismayed to discover that it's even harder. Its 1550-mile (2500km) route (the winner typically takes around a week) takes riders around every fold and frill of Ireland's rugged West Coast, and over some of its most daunting climbs. (There is a competition within the race, for the rider with the shortest cumulative time on the race's five hardest climbs.) Headwinds and torrential rain are to be expected, and riders also face the psychological difficulty of a route that constantly folds back on itself, following every bay and peninsula, making southward progress frustratingly slow. But these hardships are amply compensated by Ireland's spectacular scenery, including Malin Head, Achill Island's magnificent cliffs, and the picturesque Ring of Kerry. More info: transatlanticway.com.

Start // Dublin
Finish // Cork
Distance // 1550 miles (2500km)

THE FRENCH DIVIDE

Founded by a veteran of the Transcontinental, this 1370-mile (2200km) race follows France's most beautiful gravel roads and MTB trails, and traces a diagonal from the Belgian border to the Basque Country in the south, via the cobbled roads of the Ardennes, the vineyards of Champagne country, the Massif Central and the Pyrenees. In a nation most famous for road cycling, the French Divide offers an opportunity to go behind the scenes, taking riders through many of France's most remote rural areas, and showcasing the nation's rich agricultural heritage. The route flirts with the pilgrimage trail to Santiago de Compostela towards the end, and the organisers haven't been able to resist working in an ascent of the Col du Tourmalet. The race is described as 'a road trip at the limit between cyclo-cross and the mountain bike', giving riders yet another difficult decision to make as they plan their attack. More info: frenchdivide.com.

Start // Bray-Dunes
Finish // Mendionde
Distance // 1370 miles (2200km)

© Rick Marshall

INDEX

G

H

I

J

L

M

Epic Bike Rides of Europe

Managing Director, Publishing Piers Pickard
Associate Publisher Robin Barton
Commissioning Editor Mike Higgins
Art Director Daniel Di Paolo
Designer Ben Brannan
Picture Research Ceri James
Print Production Nigel Longuet

August 2020
Published by Lonely Planet Global Limited
CRN 554153
www.lonelyplanet.com
10 9 8 7 6 5 4 3 2 1
Printed in Malaysia
ISBN 978 1788 68942 7
© Lonely Planet 2020
© photographers as indicated 2020

Although the authors and Lonely Planet have taken all reasonable care in preparing this book, we make no warranty about the accuracy or completeness of its content and, to the maximum extent permitted, disclaim all liability from its use. All rights reserved. No part of this publication may be reproduced, stored in a retrieval system or transmitted in any form by any means, electronic, mechanical, photocopying, recording or otherwise except brief extracts for the purpose of review, without the written permission of the publisher. Lonely Planet and the Lonely Planet logo are trademarks of Lonely Planet and are registered in the US patent and Trademark Office and in other countries.

Lonely Planet Offices

Australia
The Malt Store, Level 3,
551 Swanston St, Carlton,
Victoria 3053
T: 03 8379 8000

Ireland
Digital Depot,
Roe Lane (off Thomas St),
Digital Hub, Dublin 8, D08 TCV4

USA
Suite 208, 155 Filbert Street,
Oakland, CA 94607
T: 510 250 6400

Europe
240 Blackfriars Rd,
London SE1 8NW
T: 020 3771 5100

STAY IN TOUCH lonelyplanet.com/contact

Authors Andrew Bain (AB) is the author of Lonely Planet's A Year of Adventures. Alex Crevar (ACr) contributes to such publications as The New York Times, National Geographic Travel, and Lonely Planet (www.alexcrevar.com). Andrew Curry (AC) is a journalist who lives in Berlin. As Total Bike Forever, Tim Stephens and Adam Faulkner (TS & AF) cycled from London to Tokyo, making music with the people they met; album released in 2020. Cass Gilbert (CG) is a writer, photographer and contributor to www.bikepacking.com; his website is www.whileoutriding.com. Clover Stroud (CS) is a journalist and author. Daniel Cole is a Berlin-based writer, editor and music journalist. Diane Daniel (DD) is a writer based in the Netherlands and Florida specialising in travel, culture and sustainability. Emily Chappell (EC) is a writer, cycle explorer, founder of The Adventure Syndicate and author of Where There's A Will: Hope, Grief and Endurance in a Cycle Race Across a Continent. Ernesto Pastor (EP) lives in Teruel, eastern Spain, surrounded by maps. Felicity Cloake (FC) is the award-winning food writer. She cycled around France for her book One More Croissant for the Road. Hannah Reynolds (HR) is a writer and former fitness editor of Cycling Weekly. Helen Pidd (HP) is the Guardian's North of England editor and the author of Bicycle – The Complete Guide to Everyday Cycling. Jack Thurston (JT) presents The Bike Show podcast and is the author of the Lost Lanes series of guidebooks. James Olsen (JO) has worked in cycle design for 20 years. Jasper Winn (JW) writes and photographs journeys by bicycle, on foot, with horses and in kayaks (www.theslowadventure.com). Joseph Delves (JD) is a writer and editor from London. Keir Plaice (KP) has raced his bike all over the world. He writes about cycling, culture, and travel. Kerry Christiani (KC) is a Lonely Planet writer. Lael Wilcox (LW) is an ultra-endurance adventure rider (Instagram: @laelwilcox). Lee Craigie (LC) was British Mountain Bike Champion in 2013. She rides and races long-distance, self-supported routes. Max Leonard (ML) is the author of books including Higher Calling and Bunker Research, and creative director of Isola Press. Mike Higgins (MH) is a writer and editor who lives in Crystal Palace, south London (www.mikehiggins.org). Ned Boulting (NB) is ITV's Tour de France commentator and the author of several books. Oli Townsend and Ruth Newton (OT & RN) cycled from Bristol to Bangkok in 2018 (www.intandemstories.com). Robin Barton (RB) has ridden mountain and road bikes on five continents. Rob Penn (RP) is a journalist, TV presenter and author of the bestselling It's All About the Bike: the Pursuit of Happiness on Two Wheels. He is a director of cycle-holiday specialists Bikecation (www.bikecation.co.uk). Stefan Amato (SA) is founder of bikepacking tour operator Pannier. Simon Usborne is a London-based writer and a contributor to publications including The Guardian and the Financial Times. Tom Hall (TH) is VP, Experience of Lonely Planet. **Cover and illustration** by Ross Murray (www.rossmurray).

FSC www.fsc.org MIX Paper from responsible sources FSC™ C021741

Paper in this book is certified against the Forest Stewardship Council™ standards. FSC™ promotes environmentally responsible, socially beneficial and economically viable management of the world's forests.